How did the Japanese achieve their unrivalled position in world banking? This book provides the first full account in English of the banking industry in Japan for the century following the opening of the country to the outside world in 1859. Professor Tamaki begins by considering the period of experimentation during the Meiji Restoration which resulted in the adoption of the Gold Standard in 1891. He then offers a detailed examination of the highly profitable years up to the end of the First World War and of the subsequent crisis which was hastened by the earthquake that devastated Tokyo and Yokohama in 1923 and sealed by the financial collapse of 1927. New light is thrown on the extraordinary role played by the banking industry during the period of military expansionism which culminated with defeat in the Second World War. The book ends with an assessment of the post-war financial system which developed out of the Macarthur directives and the subsequent American 'democratisation' programme.

Japanese Banking

Studies in Monetary and Financial History

Editors: Michael Bordo and Forrest Capie

Japanese Banking

A History, 1859–1959

NORIO TAMAKI

Keio University, Tokyo

CAMBRIDGE
UNIVERSITY PRESS

Published by the Press Syndicate of the University of Cambridge
The Pitt Building, Trumpington Street, Cambridge CB2 1RP
40 West 20th Street, New York, NY 10011-4211, USA
10 Stamford Road, Oakleigh, Melbourne 3166, Australia

First published 1995

Printed in Great Britain at the University Press, Cambridge

A catalogue record for this book is available from the British Library

Library of Congress cataloguing in publication data applied for

ISBN 0 521 49676 4 hardback

For
S. G. Checkland
in warm recollection,
and
E. O. A. Checkland
with affectionate thanks

Contents

Preface

Eleven of the top twenty international banks in the world in 1992 were Japanese, and yet on 1 July 1859, when the treaty port of Yokohama was finally opened to the importunate westerners, Japan had no companies which could undertake modern banking business. The present book will chart the course by which the Japanese transformed their early proto-banking into a modern banking system which would compete with, and ultimately outclass, that of other nations.

It should be noted that nineteenth-century Japanese treaty ports, which Japan in her weakness was forced to concede, were, however, never bridge-heads from which foreigners could penetrate into Japan, but rather enclaves into which the foreigners were penned. Foreign banks, originally British, represented in Yokohama and at other treaty ports from the 1860s, were doing business on the periphery of a country which was for all intents and purposes barred against them. Within Japan proper various banking experiments were undertaken as the new Meiji government, from 1868, struggled to create a new system of currency by repressing the debased coins of the old Tokugawa regime as well as by replacing the paper currency (*hansatsu*) of nearly two hundred and fifty clan governments. The resultant inflation caused much suffering and hardship as, for nearly a quarter of a century, the Japanese plunged from one ill-conceived banking experiment to another. It was Shigenobu Okuma, who had himself never experienced the sophisticated banking system of a western country, who presided over the financial muddle which existed in Japan at that time.

Nevertheless was it Okuma who began to see a way out for Japan? Japan had lost her gold reserves in spectacular fashion following the opening of the treaty ports when foreign merchants took the opportunities of depriving Japan of her undervalued gold. Following this disaster Japan was always starved of gold and silver coinage, that is, specie. In 1880 Okuma determinedly established the Yokohama Specie Bank, which eventually, regardless of Okuma's initial intention, would not only undertake banking business for the Japanese government and those Japanese merchants embarking upon overseas trades, but would also attempt to attract to Japan specie hoarded elsewhere. As its name implied the Yokohama Specie Bank was founded to do ordinary banking business but also to amass specie whenever possible to ship back to Japan.

It is as well to remember that Japanese actions, in relation to banking and much else, were and are done by Japanese on Japanese terms. This necessarily excludes non-Japanese and so appears to be secret. Such reticence has proved very valuable to Japan and has been a feature of much of Japanese banking: remember, no Japanese banking history has hitherto been available in English. *Ginko*, the Japanese equivalent of the English bank, has been ambiguous to the westerner.

But Japanese exclusiveness did not in any way outlaw the borrowing of banking methods and ideas believed useful from the West. Indeed, the Japanese were 'shopping around' over most of the Meiji period searching for banking ideas from abroad which might fit their needs. In the early Meiji years the imperial mint was set up in Osaka using machinery imported from Britain via Hong Kong. Later in the 1870s Hirobumi Ito returned from the United States enthusiastic about National Banks, originally intended to aid State economic recovery after the Civil War. National banks were set up and the over-issue of notes by them triggered dangerous inflation. The Regulations of the Bank of Japan (1882) were based on those of the National Bank of Belgium, the most recent, and therefore relevant, national bank charter in Europe. The English banking system was much admired: young Japanese bankers were sent to study it, hoping to discover how to organise a sophisticated banking system without discovering profitable initiatives.

But in general the British were too *laissez-faire* for the Japanese, who increasingly looked to the newly united Germany for their inspiration. The Germans, coming late to industrialisation, had rejected economic liberalism in favour of state intervention. This encouraged the emerging German economy to compete against Britain. It was also relevant to Japan. In the case of German banking the rise of designated banks to fund industrial development found an echo in Japan where the Industrial Bank of Japan was set up in 1902 to fund, among other concerns, state projects and new Japanese colonies in Manchuria and Korea. Notwithstanding the usefulness of some banking models from overseas for Japan, its banking system, built up painstakingly after various setbacks, was unique to Japan.

In the political power struggle in Japan in 1880–1, Okuma was ousted and Masayoshi Matsukata, the strong man of Japanese banking, became Finance Minister. Matsukata remained the dominant figure for twenty years until 1900. He transformed the hopes and expectations of Japanese banking, driving out inflation by a series of severe and painful measures through which he built up a banking system unique to the Japanese. It had in a sense no model to follow, because no other western, nor eastern, country had experienced the problems which the Japanese encountered in the middle of the nineteenth century. Following the successful Sino-Japanese War of 1894–5, and using the large Chinese indemnity, Matsukata brought Japan on to the gold standard in 1897.

Japan thus arrived in 1897, on equal terms, on the international money market in which the Japanese had to compete and co-operate with the westerners. Although the Russo-Japanese War of 1904–5 strained her resources to the limit, the boom years of 1915–18, during the First World War when Japan was an ally of Britain, France, Italy and America, gave tremendous stimulus to her burgeoning economy. It was the post-war slump of the 1920s which brought economic hardship and encouraged those who saw Japan's future as a military power. Japan, an economically poor country, had a rapidly growing population: it was not surprising that the idea of expanding into resource-rich Manchuria should prove so attractive. The financial collapse of the Bank of Taiwan and many other banks in 1927 deepened the sense of crisis, and, following the Wall Street Collapse of October 1929, plunged over 2.5 million men into unemployment.

The military men, especially those serving in Manchuria and northern China, were increasingly difficult to control. They marched steadily to war from 1931 when, having engineered various incidents against the Chinese, they were fighting in Manchuria and northern China. Certainly from 1937, if not before, Japanese banking and businesses were inexorably being placed on a war footing. Although many of the more internationally minded Japanese appreciated that Japan could not win in a struggle against the United States, adherence to the military option remained strong.

The war began on 8 December 1941 (Japan time) with the attack on Pearl Harbor, and ended, following the dropping of atomic bombs on Hiroshima and Nagasaki, in August 1945. The 'saturation' bombing of Japanese cities left hunger and dislocation. The Supreme Commander, General Douglas MacArthur, and his government demanded the disbandment of the Japanese *zaibatsu*, the powerful financial institutions which had, as loyal Japanese, supported the military regime. However, American intervention was easily dealt with, especially as Communism soon replaced Japan as the American public enemy. The Japanese economy could before long resume its growth. In the course of the recovery Japanese banking soon arrived in a position to support Japan and her economy.

Japanese banking is well documented in the sense that much material is available in Japanese. On the macro level, the Ministry of Finance and the Bank of Japan have prepared, compiled and published a series of statistics, documents and official histories since 1873 and 1882 respectively, on which the present book has drawn heavily. Unless otherwise mentioned, all figures discussed in the text are in appendices taken from the Bank of Japan statistics either on their own or based on those prepared by the Ministry of Finance. On the micro, or individual bank, level, there are numerous, and indeed innumerable, volumes of firm histories. Some of them are useful and helpful in interpreting and understanding Japanese banking from the other side and fill gaps left either by the Finance Ministry or by the Bank of Japan. The financial support which I have received from Keio University, the Japan Foundation, the Ministry of Education and the Nomura Foundation for Social Science, has been much appreciated. Keio has also generously released me from teaching duties by granting sabbatical leave during 1992–3.

During the preparation and writing of the present work many debts have been incurred. Chuhei Sugiyama has been an encouragement throughout and kindly invited me to take part in his venture on the history of Japanese economic thought, my contribution to which has been incorporated in the present book though in a very different form. Kazui Tashiro has provided me with her expertise on pre-modern Japanese financial technique which is essential in understanding the workings of *ryogae*. Akira Hayami has given access to opportunities of presenting papers on Japanese banking at the Reading conference on multinational banking and at the World Congress of the International Economic History Association held in Milan, 1994. Shizuya Nishimura kindly commented upon my works on multinational aspects of Japanese banking and has efficiently co-operated with me in organising a session in the Milan Congress. Shigeru Tamura induced me to write a chapter in his edited book, which encouraged me to review the whole history of Japanese banking from 1859 up to 1945. Shunsaku Nishikawa, in addition to his friendly scholarship, allowed me, in his capacity of Director of Fukuzawa Memorial Center for Modern Japanese Studies at Keio, to travel in search of banking materials in the south-west of Japan. I am grateful to all for their generosity and encouragement. The staff of Keio Library have been excellent, never failing to respond to my endless requests, and I am especially indebted to Masayoshi Higashida and Toshiko Hirota for their expertise.

From the West have come stimulation, encouragement, criticism and assistance. My gratitude is owed to Maxwell Gaskin, Geoffrey Jones, Frank King, David Merrett, Leslie Pressnell, Barry Supple, J. W. Taylor and Mira Wilkins and to Forrest Capie for his encouragement throughout, as one of the general editors of the series. I am also grateful to Charles Munn, through whom the present book has been included in the Cambridge series. It has been a privilege for me to make full use of the visiting fellowship at Clare Hall, Cambridge, between October 1992 and May 1993. I am grateful to President Anthony and Mrs Belle Low for their unfailing hospitality, and to J. A. Garrod, the bursar, and their efficient secretariat and the staff for their helpfulness and friendship. Near Clare Hall the Backs along the River Cam are dominated by the tower of the Cambridge University Library which proved to be one of the best in the world both in terms of the Japanese collection and the staff. I am grateful to them all.

The present work of the hundred-year history of Japanese banking has its genesis in the discussions with Professor and Mrs S. G. Checkland in the autumn of 1984 when they were staying with us as visiting professors to the Faculty of Business and Commerce at Keio University, Tokyo. The discussions, taking place in between the Checkland lecture series, an unprecedented event at Keio, attended by many young Japanese scholars and post-graduate students, had something in common with the supervision of research students in the University of Glasgow where Professor Checkland remained in the chair of economic history from 1957 to 1982. I was one of the last students of this demanding but excellent supervisor. After Professor Checkland's death in 1986, Mrs Checkland became my adviser. The writing of the present book started while Mrs Checkland was in Keio in the autumn of 1990 working on her own project on Japan's Red Cross. It is, therefore, to Professor and Mrs Checkland that my greatest debt is due, and as such the present book is dedicated to them.

Then, last but not least, is my wife Setsuko, who throughout has typed the drafts and in addition has acted as research assistant working in Keio Library and elsewhere. She has been joined by our son Taku at Tokyo, Boston and Cambridge, pleasantly enriching the family environment in which writing could thrive.

Genealogy of leading Japanese banks, 1859–1959

Table 1 *Banks of ryogae (merchant banker) origin*

Date	Place	Name	Purpose	1946–8 American intervention, and after
1876	Tokyo	*Mitsui*	Originally Edo (now Tokyo) *ryogae* much used by Shogunate government, keen to modernise to finance various industries, notably silk and rice	*Mitsui* (see Table 2) had amalgamated with *Daiichi* in 1943 as *Imperial*, but was forced to separate from Daiichi in 1948 and prohibited to use the *zaibatsu* name remaining Imperial, renamed Mitsui 1954, amalgamated with *Taiyo Kobe* 1990, renamed *Sakura* 1992, still operating
1879	Tokyo	*Yasuda*	Small *ryogae* in Edo, modernised to do extensive banking	Forced into independence, prohibited to use the *zaibatsu* name, designated as *Fuji* 1948, still operating
1895	Osaka	*Sumitomo*	Originally *ryogae* in Osaka, modernised to finance various industries, notably copper mining	Forced into independence, prohibited to use the *zaibatsu* name, renamed *Osaka* 1948, restored *Sumitomo* 1952, still operating
1927	Osaka	*Nomura*	Osaka *ryogae*, long remained as private financier, modernised to do banking for various industries including gasworks in Osaka	Forced into independence, prohibited to use the *zaibatsu* name, renamed *Daiwa* 1948, still operating

Banks of ryogae and national bank origin

Date	Place	Name	Purpose	1946–8 American intervention, and after
1933	Osaka	*Sanwa*	Amalgamation of three banks to supply funds to regional industries	Unaffected by American intervention, still operating
1941	Nagoya	*Tokai*	Amalgamation of three banks to supply funds to regional industries	Unaffected by American intervention, still operating

Bank founded by samurai

Date	Place	Name	Purpose	1946–8 American intervention, and after
1895	Tokyo	*Mitsubishi*	Founded by Yataro Iwasaki	Forced into independence, prohibited to use the *zaibatsu* name, renamed *Chiyoda* 1948, restored *Mitsubishi* 1953, still operating

Table 2 *The national bank movement*

Date	Place	Name	Purpose	1946–8 American intervention, and after
1873	Tokyo	*Daiichi*	Organised by the government initiative with ex-*ryogae* as big shareholders, designated the First National Bank of Tokyo to finance modern industries	Amalgamated in 1943 with, and separated in 1948 from *Mitsui* (see *Mitsui* in Table 1), amalgamated with Hypothec to become *Daiichi Kangyo* in 1971 (see Japan Hypothec Bank in Table 3)
1877	Tokyo	Fifteen (*Jyugo*)	Founded by a group of new nobilities to utilise their bonds for railway building, financed rigorously the government during the *Satsuma* Rebellion 1877, closed temporarily in the 1927 banking crisis, finally absorbed by *Mitsui* in 1944	

Ordinary (commercial) bank – national bank origin

Date	Place	Name	Purpose	1946–8 American intervention, and after
1936	Kobe	*Kobe*	Amalgamation of seven banks to finance regional economy	Amalgamated with *Taiyo* 1973 and with *Mitsui* 1990, renamed *Sakura* 1992, still operating (see Mitsui in Table 1)

Bank which emerged from savings banks

Date	Place	Name	Purpose	1946–8 American intervention, and after
1945	Tokyo	Japan Savings (*Chochiku*)	Amalgamation of nine savings banks to strengthen their resources	Renamed *Kyowa* 1948, amalgamated with *Saitama* to become *Asahi* 1992, still operating

Table 3 *Special Banks, or government-sponsored 'development' banks*

Date	Place	Name	Purpose	1946–8 American intervention, and after
1880	Yokohama	Yokohama Specie Bank	To do Japanese government business abroad, and to attract specie to Japan, immense importance to Japanese development, but became tool of Japanese military, overseas, handling imperialist business	Closed by Americans 1946, became much smaller Bank of Tokyo which is still operating
1882	Tokyo	Bank of Japan	Japanese Central Bank which controlled all Japanese banking developments, closely linked to Yokohama Specie Bank, opened regional offices in all major economic centres in Japan	Still operating
1897	Tokyo	Japan Hypothec (*Kangyo*) Bank	To finance industrial and agricultural development	Converted into ordinary bank and amalgamated with *Daiichi* to become *Daiichi Kangyo* 1971
1900	Sapporo (*Hokkaido*)	Hokkaido Development (*Takushoku*) Bank	To finance development of all kinds in Japan's under-developed Hokkaido	Converted into ordinary bank, still operating
1902	Tokyo	Industrial (*Kogyo*) Bank of Japan	To finance industrial development, also acted overseas to collect specie	Once reconsidered its aims, still operating

Abbreviations

BM	*Bankers' Magazine*
BOJ	Bank of Japan, or *Nichigin*
MF	Ministry of Finance
Nichigin	*Nihon Ginko*, or Bank of Japan
SCAP	Supreme Commander of the Allied Powers
Shokin	*Yokohama Shokin Ginko*, or Yokohama Specie Bank
¥	yen
YSB	Yokohama Specie Bank

Japanese names are presented in western style with given name followed by family name.

Main regions and principal cities in Japan

Part I

A bankrupt Shogunate, 1859–1868 (sixth year of Ansei to first year of Meiji)

Historical background, 1859–1868

The opening of Japan to the western powers in 1859, after a 230-year seclusion, was to prove fatal to the Tokugawa Shogunate regime. Shogunal concessions, agreeing to open Japanese ports to foreigners, aroused, especially among the influential feudal lords and their *samurai* subjects, bitter passions which were embodied in the slogan 'Revere the Emperor, expel the barbarian'. This extremist slogan and movement, however, did not survive even the first half of the 1860s when two of the strongest domains, Satsuma and Choshu, reversed their anti-foreign stance. These two enlightened domains, situated in the far south-west of Japan where western things and influences entered Japan via Nagasaki, recognised the brutal reality, following the western powers' bombardment of Kagoshima, the capital of Satsuma, and Shomonseki in Chosu territory, that 'expel the barbarian' policies were absurd. The union of the two domains, armed with some rudimentary western science, technology and, above all, modern weapons, gathered forces at an astonishing speed to lead the attack on the Shogunate from the autumn of 1867 to the spring of 1868. As the young *samurai* of Satsuma and Chosu and their allies had to shoulder all the burdens, including those of financial management, in a new administration (the Meiji government), an enormous amount of hitherto pent-up energy of young ex-*samurai* was released. For the time being, of necessity, the young oligarchs had no option but to rely heavily on the old merchant bankers.

1   Japanese merchant bankers: *ryogae*, 1859–1868

Prior to the arrival of the demanding foreigners on Japanese soil on 1 July 1859 there was a quasi-banking system operating in Japan. The *bakufu* government had earlier authorised certain merchants, *ryogae*, to trade in Edo (Tokyo) and Osaka. With the reluctant acceptance by the *bakufu* of treaty ports at Yokohama, Nagasaki, and Hakodate, at which foreigners had the right to reside and trade, the government licensed a handful of *ryogae* to operate in Yokohama and Nagasaki. Japanese and foreigners using silver Mexican dollars (which were the universal currency in the East at this time) made their financial arrangements on a day-to-day *ad hoc* basis, paying partly in cash and partly by barter. The fact that, before 1859, Nagasaki was the only port open to the Chinese and Dutch enabled various sorts of financial arrangements to develop there which provided valuable experience for the many young *samurai* who were to become powerful leaders in the new Japan after 1868.

The fundamental fact underlying the Japanese economic system prior to the upheaval consequent on the arrival of the foreigners was that taxes were paid in rice, in kind. Until 1873, when the system was abandoned, rice was the real currency. The commercial houses which had developed in Edo and Osaka, from which were to evolve the great present-day financial institutions of Japan, were essentially rice-handling agencies which had in the course of their business as collectors of rice taxes developed quasi-banking functions. It should also be remembered that in Japanese society at this time the merchant was socially of humble rank, classed only marginally higher than the peasant.

The standard coin available in Japan was the *ryo*. Within Japan there were coins and *han* or domains paper money in circulation; many of the coins were debased and much of the paper devalued. The *han* issued paper money, *hansatsu*, which circulated locally. The *bakufu* issued coins. There was little understanding of the inflationary danger of issuing more paper than was required and the least knowledge of Gresham's Law by which 'bad money drives out good'.

The pre-banking scene in the Edo era, that is, prior to the advent of western merchants in Yokohama in 1859, was dominated by *ryogae* who were primarily merchants but who also offered a variety of banking services to approved customers. They could well, therefore, be called merchant bankers[1] in western terminology. The most important and influential *ryogae* were those based in the two great cities, Osaka and Edo, which were the commercial and consumer centres of Japan. Osaka's growth had been encouraged by its proximity (made easier by water transport) to Kyoto (the capital) where the Emperor lived in seclusion but in the company of a large and expensive court. Edo, now Tokyo, the eastern capital, was the power base of the Tokugawa Shogunate and as such had steadily grown both in importance and population.

There were two types of *ryogae*, the *hon ryogae* and *zeni ryogae*. The former were large merchants dealing in gold and silver coins while the latter were those lesser men who operated only with copper coins. During the last decade of the Shogunate regime more than 1,300 *ryogae* were trading in Osaka. They were led by *junin ryogae*, a council of the ten most opulent houses, who disciplined the whole merchant community in Osaka. *Hon ryogae*, headed by *junin ryogae*, supplied funds to the Shogunate government and to the domains and acted as agents for sales of goods, chiefly rice, in Osaka. Two celebrated houses in Osaka were Konoike and Sumitomo, both of which became important in banking in modern Japan and the latter of which also had a shop in Edo. In Edo some 750 *ryogae* houses were operating, the most notable of which was the house of Mitsui which had offices in Osaka and Kyoto and agents all over Japan, including Nagasaki. It should be noted that Mitsui also succeeded in making the transition to modern banking speedily. Those notable houses of *ryogae* in Edo and Osaka were commissioned by the Shogun's government, *bakufu*, to sustain the Shogunate system, most significantly by the making of direct loans to the *bakufu* and domains and the exchange of old coins for new at the time of recoinage. In the loans business, *ryogae* houses in Osaka were much more heavily involved than their colleages in Edo. Some of the *ryogae* houses, notably Mitsui, regarded such lending as very risky and they believed that many merchants failed because of such loans.[2] When a further issue of new coinage was necessary, the *bakufu* specially appointed the prestigious *ryogae* houses, including Mitsui in Edo and Konoike and Sumitomo in Osaka. Mitsui was also privileged to handle the *bakufu*'s money in Edo, Kyoto and Osaka.[3] What is important in terms of present-day Japanese banking is to examine the role of the *ryogae* as antecedents of bankers today and to investigate that part of their business which was done on genuine banking principles.

The resources which the *ryogae* had at their command consisted of their own money and that entrusted to them by others. *Ryogae* operated with caution and circumspection. Even if father and son were operating independently, they would not disclose any details of their monetary transactions to each other. Whether or not a *ryogae* could increase his capital depended upon his willingness to pay interest on money deposited and his skill in negotiating an interest rate favourable to him as lender and yet satisfactory to his client as borrower. Japan had a very long history of paying interest on deposits, a practice which originated earlier in the business of the *doso* during the mid-fifteenth century.[4] It is, therefore, not surprising that interest payable on deposit became a very common practice during the Edo period. Of course enterprising *ryogae* offered rates of interest according to the length of time and the amount of deposits. By the mid-nineteenth century, towards the end of the Shogunate period, customers were offered two types of accounts, current and deposit.[5]

Innovation in deposit-taking at the very end of the Shogunate regime resulted in the establishment of two important proto-banking concepts. Deposit interest was directly related to the availability of interest previously levied on borrowers. Profit from such business came from the difference between deposit and lending interest rates and was in modern terminology the 'banking margin'. The idea was explicitly put forward by Zenjiro Yasuda, an important *zeni ryogae* merchant during the last decade of the Shogunate regime, who wrote:

We lend at the lowest at 5 sen and take money in at the highest at 1 sen 6 rin. Then you can earn 3 sen 4 rin if you loan out conservatively at 5 sen. If you like to be more aggressive, you can give at 8 sen 3 rin money which you have taken in at 1 sen 6 rin.[6]

Another important banking concept, based on a long experience of deposit management, was the deposit reserve ratio. *Ryogae*, proto-bankers in Japan, were well aware of how much deposit money could be set aside for withdrawals by depositors. An ex-*ryogae*, questioned in 1900 by a committee organised by the Osaka Chamber of Commerce, explained that:

We kept in our safe as much sum of deposits as possible. The sum was not less than one-fourth of the total deposits.[7]

On the basis of the two concepts the *ryogae* devised many methods, which enabled them to operate useful and profitable businesses.

In this type of banking two sorts of instruments were vital, the *ryogae*'s note and the depositor's order. The note was issued by the *ryogae* as a receipt for money deposited. It was the *ryogae*'s promise to return the sum deposited either on demand or with notice. The depositor had the right to issue an order signed by himself for any sum up to that of his deposits, and this was in fact a cheque in modern banking terminology. Both instruments were transferable as means of payment among merchants known to each other. Throughout the Edo era, the order was much preferred to the note mainly because it could carry any sum up to the amount of deposits, or even beyond, as will be discussed shortly. This wide circulation of the order had another advantage, because each time it changed hands the order was usually endorsed by the former bearer. Therefore in case of difficulty or insolvency, the liability could be traced through each endorser.

Ryogae usually allowed their customers to negotiate an overdraft. As another ex-*ryogae* explained:

When the issuer's account does not have sufficient funds, an order issued against this account will be stamped but will not be honoured. It is not the case that the *ryogae* has agreed to allow the issuer to overdraw his account. This overdrawn amount is called an unpaid balance.[8]

The overdrawn order was of course transferable too. As a result the order inevitably came into the possession of other *ryogae* with whom the original issuer was not necessarily in direct contact. In this case the transaction had to be concluded through exchanges between the two houses. The transfer of the overdrawn order effected three kinds of transactions. It was, firstly, a loan as the issuer was allowed to overdraw his account; secondly, a payment from a merchant to another; and, finally, the clearing of bills among *ryogae* as the order was eventually returned to the house of *ryogae* against whom it was initially issued.

The order and overdrawing were thus of vital importance for banker–customer relationships. Inter-*ryogae* relationships were also based upon these two facilities, for those of smaller resources, the 'sons', were usually dependent upon larger *ryogae*, the 'fathers', and this came to be called the father–son *ryogae*. This hierarchical relationship involved every house for no one could remain independent in such a system. It was a remarkably sophisticated financial world, as was explained:

A small *ryogae* X, having resources of only 10,000 *ryo* but having [over]drawn his account with his fellow *ryogae*, will have to issue another order against his friend *ryogae* Y. If Y has not sufficient sum to meet X's order, he then will have to overdraw his account with fellow Z, who, if having not enough, will in turn overdraw his account on fellow W. This overdrawing connection eventually reaches the father *ryogae* who settles transactions daily and prevents any inconveniences from arising. In one extreme case, a *ryogae*, with a basic resource of 10,000 *ryo*, issued overdrawn orders of 60,000 to 70,000 *ryo*.[9]

In this case, Y was the 'father' *ryogae* and X the 'son'. The ultimate 'father' was the house coming at the top of this line. This relationship can easily be seen in modern banking, as present-day interbank lending operates on a similar basis. In reality the ultimate heads were the *junin ryogae* in Osaka and three houses of *hon ryogae* in Edo. The groups of 'fathers', the last resort for the 'sons', effectively played a role in central banking, probably without any pecuniary charges, as they guaranteed the payments and cleared the balances among themselves.

The roots of modern Japanese banking lie in *ryogae* business which had already embraced the concept of the deposit reserve ratio, allowing full use of surplus money. The surplus was utilised by being supplied to customers and fellow *ryogae* through allowing them to issue orders. Deposits in one *ryogae*, without really being transferred, formed another sum in another *ryogae*'s account. This was in fact credit creation, the core characteristic of modern banking. Both overdrafts and fictitious orders were typical examples of credit creation. Thus in business terms the parallels between *ryogae* and modern banking are not hard to find.

The link between *ryogae* and modern Japanese banking is very strong. Of the six great Japanese banking houses during the second quarter of the twentieth century, Mitsui, Yasuda, Sumitomo and Sanwa can claim direct descent. Konoike was one of the most celebrated *junin ryogae* in Osaka, establishing the Konoike Bank in 1897 and later merging with two other banks in 1933 to form Sanwa Bank. Sumitomo, or Izumi, an Osaka house which had, also in Shogunate times, opened an office in Edo, founded Sumitomo Bank in 1895. The house of Mitsui in Edo was, as early as 1871, calling itself Mitsui Gumi Bank and by 1876 had emerged as Mitsui Bank. Daiichi Bank, now Daiichi Kangyo, was a joint venture of Mitsui and other *ryogae* houses while being strongly supported by the Meiji government. Only Mitsubishi was an entirely new foundation, although the founder, Yataro Iwasaki, had learnt *ryogae* business as a clan businessman in Nagasaki[10] and it also absorbed some of the *ryogae* tradition from four banks with which it merged in the 1930s.

It should be noted that although the common people did not use the money merchants they had other financial facilities for their modern needs. Through the *mujin* or *tanomoshiko*, or in western terminology 'mutual loan association', the common people in the pre-modern period could obtain financial services. The *mujin* had its origins as early as the thirteenth century and lingered on well into the twentieth century when it adapted itself to the modern banking system. As we will see in due course, the *mujin* became an indispensable part of the Japanese banking system by the second quarter of the twentieth century.[11]

It was fortunate that the system of banking instituted by the *ryogae* merchants was available over the turbulent years of the Restoration. After 1868 Meiji officials attempted to find a way forward for Japanese banking. After several false starts and much experimentation, some of it disastrous, the Bank of Japan was founded in 1882, on which the modern Japanese banking system grew. But the ideas and principles upon which *ryogae* had relied were neither invalidated nor denied. Such was the situation in Japan as far as the banking system was concerned. It would, therefore, not be at all easy for the forthcoming western bankers to deprive *ryogae* of their long-standing customers.

2 A bankrupt regime, 1859–1866

On 3 August 1858, a day before the proclamation of the successor to Iyesada, Shogun XIII, who was dying, a small, lightly armed British squadron under the command of James Bruce, Earl of Elgin and Kincardine, left Nagasaki for Edo.[1] A Dutch consul resident in Deshima in Nagasaki had informed the Japanese that the British had bombarded South China Canton[2] and were on their way to confront Japan, but it must be doubted that the *bakufu*, struggling for a way out of a grave political crisis, understood the implications of this information. What the Dutch consul really wished to convey was the fact that although the Americans had been the pioneers forcing their way into Japan, it was the British whom the Japanese had most to fear at that time. Even Lord Elgin, a modest man, would have been astonished and piqued to know that the *bakufu* government did not know who he was, or that he represented the then most powerful nation. The Japanese recognised that they had to negotiate to comply with his demands, that is all.[3]

On 12 August 1858, Lord Elgin on board the *Furious*, 'from which the main-deck guns had been removed',[4] penetrated deep into Edo bay, casting anchor off Shinagawa which was a mere four miles away from the seat of power at Edo castle. He was accompanied only by the *Retribution* and the *Lee*, together with a steam yacht – a gift for the Japanese Emperor. Elgin was supremely confident in himself and in the nation he represented and, without hesitation, he sailed north to the Bay of Tokyo. The American Townsend Harris had been forced to sign the treaty of 1858, of which he was so proud, on a spot off Koshiba, twenty-six miles south of Shinagawa. In 1853 the American squadron, led by Commodore M. C. Perry, had anchored off Uraga further round the Miura peninsula. Nevertheless Elgin's position was not recognised in Japan. The *bakufu* government only knew that the foreigners were hammering at their gates, that they did not have the guns to scatter them, and that they had no option but to comply. The Japanese made five treaties 'of amity and commerce' in the space of ten weeks.

The British party stayed in Edo between 12 and 26 August 1858, when Lord Elgin signed the British treaty. He then left. Was Elgin the only western signatory to a treaty with Japan to worry over the consequence of his actions?[5] On the Japanese side, by signing these foreign treaties, the government had signed its own death warrant. There was to be nearly a decade of confusion and upheaval out of which was to come the new Japan. The same day that Elgin cast anchor off Shinagawa, the *bakufu* began the search for the next Shogun. The list included two names from the three Houses, members of the Tokugawa family,[6] that is, Iyemochi Tokugawa and Yoshinobu Hitotsubashi.[7] The former won. It was Naosuke Ii who led the government in the crucial process of selecting the Shogun and of course in concluding the treaties with the westerners. All his policies aroused furious opposition in Edo. In Kyoto, the Emperor, isolated and ignorant of the reality of the threat from the West, angrily rejected all talk of foreign treaties. From mid-October 1858, a few days after the conclusion of the treaty with the French, the *bakufu* embarked upon a large-scale suppression of their opponents, later to be named after the Japanese era title, the Ansei purge. The purge continued throughout the year of 1859, and the *bakufu* arrested more than a hundred activists, of whom ten were executed. It was against this terrible background that the *bakufu* opened the three treaty ports of Nagasaki, Yokohama[8] and Hakodate to the westerners in July 1859.

In March 1860, a band of masterless *samurai*, mainly consisting of those who had deserted Mito domain and were infuriated by recent events, assassinated the regent minister, Naosuke Ii. The main stream in the administration which had believed that the *bakufu* could still survive recognised, with the death of Ii, that a fundamental change in their policies was essential. Searching around for compromise, the idea emerged of drawing the Shogunate closer to the court, an idea sometimes expressed by scholars in Japan. Fortunately for the *bakufu*, the idea had potential as the new Shogun – Iyemochi – was, at the age of fourteen, unmarried and pliable. The negotiations, which were ultimately successful, started immediately and continued for eighteen months. At the end of 1861 Emperor Komei, father of future Emperor Meiji, agreed to send his sister Princess Kazu to Edo to marry the Shogun. The wedding ceremony, a brief celebration in March 1862, did nothing to quell the disturbances and upheavals elsewhere in Japan.

Not unexpectedly the opening of treaty ports provoked trouble between xenophobic *samurai* and the westerners. In September 1862, a British merchant in a party on an afternoon excursion outside Yokohama, deliberately crossed the Satsuma procession and was killed by Satsuma warriors. There were two other British wounded. In the ensuing confrontation Satsuma refused to apologise, punish the murderers, or pay an indemnity. This resulted in the British bombardment of Kagoshima, Satsuma's capital, in August 1863. A year afterwards, in September 1864, officers in the Choshu domain – the most determinedly anti-foreigners clan – deliberately attacked western ships passing through the straits of Shimonoseki which Choshu controlled. A united squadron of British, French, Dutch, and American ships immediately countered and destroyed the Choshu batteries at Shimonoseki. The two incidents convinced the young leaders of the two strong domains that they must change course and they both embarked upon a programme of learning from the West and introducing the western sciences, technologies and weapons.[9] A year and a half later, in March 1866, Satsuma and Choshu reached a secret agreement by which they would unite to counter the *bakufu*. A unified power representing both Shogun and Emperor could not prevail against the combined strengths of Satsuma and Choshu. The death of the young Shogun Iyemochi in Osaka in the course of a military expedition against Choshu marked the effective end of the Shogunate in August 1866. Iyemochi was succeeded by Yoshinobu, former contender and the last Shogun.

3 *Ryogae* struggling for survival, 1859–1868

Under the terms of the treaties of friendship, concluded between 1853 and 1856, the *bakufu* officials were required to handle foreign exchange business. The treaties engaged them to supply food, water, coal and other necessities to the western ships for which hard cash – Mexican dollars – should be the payment. The exchange rate was to be negotiated between the *bakufu* and the western representatives, and the business of supplying the necessities was to be done only under the strict supervision of the *bakufu*. The opening of three ports totally changed the situation. Trade was strictly confined to the three treaty ports from which the export of silk and tea started immediately. The most astonishing result was the outflow of gold from Japan. The *bakufu* financial experts did not understand that gold in Japan was, in relation to the rest of the world, too cheap.

In June 1859, a month before the opening of the ports, the parity of exchange between gold and silver was 1:6.44,[1] gold being markedly undervalued compared with the internationally prevalent parity of 1:15. Despite this alarming situation, the *bakufu* financial authorities failed to respond and there was serious disagreement between the financial and foreign ministers.[2] Western diplomats, including the British consul-general Rutherford Alcock, were alarmed and urged the *bakufu* officials to change the coinage.[3] A large-scale recoinage was eventually carried out in the spring of 1860. In the mean time between 100,000 and 150,000 *ryo* of gold was drained overseas through the faulty exchange and this sum did not include gold lost through other channels.[4] It is abundantly clear that the *bakufu* authorities were unaware of the operation of Gresham's Law, first enunciated in England during the reign of Elizabeth I and later termed by Henry Dunning MacLeod in 1858, that 'bad money drives out good'. In this case the gold disappeared – into the pockets of the foreigners – while the debased coins continued to circulate.

Article III in the treaties of 1858 stipulated that the *bakufu* would open Kanagawa as an outport of Edo to the westerners,[5] but they deliberately ignored it. The *bakufu* officials thought Kanagawa unsuitable for the port as

13

it was situated right on Tokaido, a main road out of Edo along which count-
less processions of *daimyo*, chiefs of clans, escorted by hundreds of *samurai*
wielding their two swords passed. The *bakufu* preferred Yokohama, which
meant 'a wide strand', over two miles south-west of Kanagawa. The *bakufu*
planned to isolate Yokohama which was designed to be another 'Deshima',
the small artificial island where the Dutch had been incarcerated for years
in Nagasaki harbour. For development of the three ports 200,000 *ryo* had
been designated; half of this sum was invested in the building of another
'Deshima', as Yokohama was intended to be.

The *bakufu* ordered some one hundred houses of Japanese merchants
from Edo, Kanagawa and Shimoda to open offices and shops in Yokohama.
The only *ryogae* so designated was the house of Mitsui which was commissioned to fulfil several functions including financial services for the *bakufu*,
to receive from western merchants proceeds of Japanese exports and to
provide both for the Japanese and for the westerners paper currency of
dollar denomination issued by the *bakufu* in Edo. This paper currency was
exactly the same as that which was issued in Nagasaki from 1857 and
without which the westerners could not do any trade in the treaty port at
all.[6] Captain Sherard Osborn, the Royal Navy commander on board the
Furious, fully explained how it was:

By the old laws of the Japanese Empire, the exportation of their currency, whether
gold, silver, or copper, is strictly prohibited, and to insure it, no European is allowed
to possess native coin. The difficulty, therefore, of purchasing, would be great upon
that ground alone; but in addition to this rule, another exists, by which the natives
are forbidden to receive our coins either. For a while, it seemed there must be a dead-
lock in the market; but it was explained to us that a government bank existed in the
bazaar, where we could obtain paper currency (available only in Nagasaki) in
exchange for our dollars. From that bank we came out with bundles of very simple-
looking strips of card-board covered with cabalistic signs, indicative of their value,
in lieu of the silver we had given – a favour for which the Government charged us six
per cent! With these Japanese bank-notes we paid the tradesmen who no amount of
persuasion could induce to receive silver; and he again, poor fellow, had to present
them at the bank, and receive the amount in the metallic currency of the country,
paying of course a handsome tax for the honour of selling to the foreigners.[7]

The office where Osborn received the bundle of paper currency was not
really 'the *bakufu*'s bank', but it was *kaisho*, that is, the *bakufu*'s office for
commerce in Nagasaki, the only place until June 1859 where the westerners
could obtain paper currency valid inside Japan. It was this business done in
the *bakufu*'s office for commerce that the *bakufu* commissioned Mitsui to
conduct in Yokohama.

When Mitsui opened in Yokohama, they were intending to do banking
business and trade in silk. But the serious fire of 1862 and the decline in

profitability in the silk trade elsewhere in Japan forced them to withdraw. From 1863 Mitsui only did money business in Yokohama.[8] Besides the business for the *bakufu*, as described by Osborn in Nagasaki, Mitsui was of course keen to do any profitable money business. They thought that by being the official agent in Yokohama they would have the advantage of making the government's surplus money (deposited with them to cover everyday transactions) work for them to produce profits. No details of Mitsui's own resources which relate to the Yokohama business remain but some figures are available of the *bakufu*'s reserves.

In February 1867, Mitsui was entrusted by the *bakufu* with the sum of 220,019 *ryo* plus 40,350 Mexican dollars, which makes 250,282 *ryo* in all.[9] In the course of 1867 the sum dropped substantially due to collapse of speculations, standing at 186,740 *ryo* in all. The loss of the *bakufu*'s money totalling 63,542 *ryo* was indeed a grave matter, which resulted from Mitsui's mismanagement of the fund in Yokohama, and had to be covered by emergency resources gathered from the offices deployed in various parts of the country.[10] The balance sheet of Yokohama business done by Mitsui showed a considerable deficit. Mitsui, however, cannot be blamed because treaty port business was highly speculative and volatile.

Figures for the *bakufu* budget were hardly known but it is clear that the *bakufu* was in serious financial difficulty. In the financial statement of the *bakufu* in the year 1863 (which survives), the total expenditure was 7.06 million *ryo* against a total income of 6.92 million *ryo*.[11] The deficit of 0.14 million *ryo* may seem slight but it was indicative of a disastrous trend. In 1863, Shogun Iyemochi, the symbol of the newly found unity between the court and the Shogunate regime, proceeded to Kyoto with an entourage of 3,000 armed men to pursue his own ends, and to rival the anti-*bakufu* and 'expel-the-barbarian' power, mainly led by the Choshu domain. The expedition cost 1.37 million *ryo*, which was nearly 20 per cent of the total annual budget for the whole country. The opening of three ports had placed heavy financial burdens on the *bakufu* government, which among other items had had to shoulder some 60,000 *ryo* (£25,000) as indemnity for the Namamugi or Richardson incident paid in 1863 to the British on behalf of the Satsuma domain. Because of the presence in the treaty ports of western forces there was a feeling of increasing instability among the Kyoto court. This required the *bakufu* to spend more on defence externally and internally, the cost of which stood at 0.55 million *ryo* in 1863.[12] All in all the *bakufu* had to appropriate 1.93 million *ryo*, more than a quarter of the total budget, to meet extraordinary as well as emergency needs. It is not clear which item in the *bakufu* financial statement corresponded to this expenditure. It can however be said with confidence that it was clear by the early 1860s that financially the *bakufu* could not survive.

Despite the restraints of the rice economy, which was the strait-jacket imprisoning Tokugawa Japan, there was remarkable economic growth within the system.[13] Many *ryogae* merchants were prospering and they increasingly became the target of the *bakufu*, who levied heavy loans. As early as 1843 and 1853, the *bakufu* obliged merchants in Osaka, including the houses of Konoike and Mitsui, to raise funds totalling a little less than 3 million *ryo*.[14] The opening of the country in 1859 further underlined the *bakufu*'s dependence upon *ryogae* resources.

In Osaka between 1860 and 1866, the *bakufu* borrowed more than 4.5 million *ryo* from 2,521 merchant houses, mainly those of *ryogae*. Their Edo counterparts were no happier; for, being resident in the seat of power, they were more easily importuned. Some 760 houses of *ryogae* in Edo loaned more than 1.5 million *ryo* to the *bakufu* in the three years from 1865 to 1867. On average, the Edo *ryogae* supplied 2,277 *ryo* per house compared to 1,805 *ryo* in Osaka. However, in cumulative terms, the Osaka *ryogae*, being the wealthiest in Japan, suffered much more than their Edo counterparts. Eventually, between 1860 and 1866, the *bakufu* levied more than 6 million *ryo* upon the *ryogae* community, which exceeded the annual revenue of the *bakufu* in 1863.[15]

This extraordinary state of affairs caused alarm and despondency in *ryogae* circles. The house of Mitsui, which operated both in Osaka and Edo, was seriously affected and strenuously resisted *bakufu* demands. In 1843, Mitsui, who had been ordered to lend 50,000 *ryo*, decided after much dis-cussion among themselves to gift the *bakufu* 10,000 *ryo*, instead of 50,000 *ryo* as a loan.[16] But this could only be done once, because it was a dangerous strategy. Earlier such disobedient merchants would have faced heavy penal-ties including capital punishment. In 1843, opulent houses of *ryogae*, such as Konoike, were never allowed to reduce the *bakufu*'s demand.[17] Furthermore, upon Osaka, and also upon Hyogo (later Kobe) *ryogae*, fell the construction cost of opening Hyogo port to the westerners. Pushing the plan through, the *bakufu* in early 1867 forced a group of more than twenty houses of *ryogae*, headed again by Konoike, to set up a joint-stock company, in which *ryogae* would be proprietors and which would be allowed to issue the *bakufu* paper money as Mitsui did. The capital stock of the company would be 1 million *ryo* which was to be instantly borrowed by the *bakufu*. Fortunately for Osaka *ryogae* houses, the last Shogun Yoshinobu decided to hand back his responsibility for administration to the Emperor in November 1867, when only 10,000 *ryo* had been paid in by *ryogae*.[18] *Ryogae* thus narrowly escaped total collapse and lived to fight another day in a new era.

4 The arrival of western banking, 1863–1868

Western bankers did not immediately see any profitable business in Japan and did not arrive in Yokohama until the spring of 1863 when western merchants were becoming desperately short of specie.[1] The first response to the demands came in March 1863 from the Central Bank of Western India with Charles Rickerby as the acting manager at Yokohama.[2] A month later, in April 1863, the Chartered Mercantile Bank of India, London and China arrived in Yokohama. The manager of the Mercantile Bank, who had transferred himself from Hong Kong, wishfully reported that 'the branch was likely to be successful'.[3] Thus, the western banking invasion of Japan, which was to undermine the old order in Japan and was led by two British overseas banks, started on a modest scale. Before 1868 and the Meiji Restoration, another five banks were added to the number: Commercial Bank of India in September 1863; the Bank of Hindustan, China and Japan and the Oriental Bank Corporation in 1864; the brand new Hongkong and Shanghai Banking Corporation in 1866; and from France came Comptoir d'Escompte de Paris in 1867.[4] These foreign banks had enormous assets if their capital stock is translated into Japanese *ryo*.[5] The largest were Comptoir d'Escompte and the Oriental Bank with capital of more than 90 million *ryo* and 42 million *ryo* respectively.

The future of western banking in Yokohama remained, during the 1860s, problematical. The Commercial Bank of India, which had been active in bringing specie from California to China and Japan,[6] made its business over to the Commercial Bank Corporation of India and the East,[7] while the Bank of Hindustan took over the business of the Imperial Bank of China, India and Japan in 1864.[8] The collapse of Overend, Gurney & Co. in London during the financial crisis of 1866 severely damaged the business of British overseas banks and resulted in the disappearance of the Commercial Bank Corporation of India and the East, the Bank of Hindustan, China and Japan and probably the Central Bank of Western India from Yokohama. It is very difficult for the banking historian whose only source of information is the advertisements in the local newspapers to trace the business of western banks in Yokohama before 1868.

Fortunately the Oriental Bank Corporation advertised regularly in the local papers, some of which survive, giving invaluable details of the business they were prepared to transact in Yokohama. The Oriental Bank advertisements suggest that western banking made available to their customers three sorts of business. The first, and probably most important as well as largest, business was foreign exchange services, which were still beyond the capacities of *ryogae*. The Oriental Bank could grant drafts not exceeding six months' sight on London and those on demand on Scotland and Ireland. In the case of the Oriental Bank, drafts on New Zealand, San Francisco, New York and Paris were also available through its branches, agencies and correspondents. The Bank also issued on behalf of customers circular notes for the use of travellers, or, probably something between the letter of credit and traveller's cheque, which were negotiable in any city of importance throughout the world. The foreign exchange services were used by the *bakufu* missions abroad.[9]

The rest of the business was accepting deposits and granting advances. The Oriental Bank offered two types of deposits, current and fixed accounts. Neither interest nor commission was charged on current accounts. The term of fixed account was twelve months and the holder of the account was given the receipt. For the deposit customer, the Bank gave service of collecting papers payable in Yokohama. There were two methods of advances. The Bank discounted bills, notes and other negotiable papers payable in Yokohama, which had to have at least two approved names on them. Another method was advances granted on bullion and non-perishable merchandise. All transactions were effected in Mexican dollars,[10] but there is no evidence from the foreign banks present in Yokohama before the Restoration of how much business they actually did. There remains no evidence, either, about their business connections with Japanese merchants. As far as Japanese financial arrangements with the foreigners in Yokohama were concerned, the *bakufu* ordered that they would be done exclusively through Mitsui. For western bankers, there would not be any chance of contacting Japanese merchants directly, particularly concerning their domestic demands. Nevertheless, despite these restraints, several of these banks and their staff were destined to play an important role in assisting the early Meiji administration to understand modern money and banking matters.

The Meiji Restoration: monetary confusion and banking experiments, 1868–1881 (first year of Meiji to fourteenth year of Meiji)

Historical background, 1868–1881

Restoration government troops finally, in July 1868, swept away the remnants of the *bakufu*. Edo was renamed Tokyo, becoming the new eastern capital, and the Japanese name for the era was changed from Keio to Meiji, or 'Enlightenment', in the autumn of 1868. Following the example of the Taika Restoration in 645, lands and people heretofore ruled separately by nearly 250 *daimyo* under the Shogunate were returned to the Emperor in 1869. The huge change started a kind of political Darwinism. Qualification for survival was without doubt an understanding of western experiences enabling one to comprehend the exact position of Japan in the world and her most urgent needs. In 1871, after the return of a small delegation to America, the abolition of *han* was carried out, and former *daimyo* were denied an active part in politics. In 1873, the return of the Iwakura Mission from their long western tour resulted in the exclusion from power of those who wished to wage war on Korea. The most prominent of the dissentients was Takamori Saigo, who had been supreme commander of the restoration army but who had no western experiences. There followed a series of uprisings of former *samurai* dissentients culminating in the Satsuma Rebellion of 1877 led by Saigo. Even after, power struggles continued and in 1881 Shigenobu Okuma was ousted from government. Okuma had tried various financial experiments which, despite his courage and enterprise, had been disastrous for Japan. He was outclassed by Masayoshi Matsukata whose mind was filled with western ideas.

5 The first banking experiment, 1868–1872

Ryo to yen, 1868–1871

On 3 January 1868, a coup, plotted by a group of radical court nobility and supported by the powerful domains of both Satsuma and Choshu, ignited a fuse which led eventually to the overthrow of the Tokugawa Shogunate regime. On 27 January, the *bakufu* troops, greatly outnumbering the Satsuma and Choshu forces, were easily defeated on the outskirts of Kyoto. Yoshinobu Tokugawa, the last Shogun, dashed to his battleship and fled to Edo. The victory was a tremendous boost to the allied forces of Satsuma and Choshu, who became known as the 'imperial troops' and who marched briskly eastwards, reaching Edo in two months. The *bakufu* surrendered Edo castle on 3 May. On 22 May 1868, Sir Harry Parkes, the British Minister, presented his credentials to the Emperor in Kyoto;[1] thus, the British acknowledged the legitimacy of the new government, with the Emperor at its head. Although the civil war still continued fiercely in north-western Japan, the Meiji government was firmly established by the end of 1868. Financially, however, the government faced formidable problems.

The coinage system, which dated from the establishment of the Tokugawa Shogunate in 1600, and on which the Japanese people relied, was in a state of chaos. Constant debasement during the Shogunate regime had made the system, which had numerous sorts of coins in circulation,[2] fundamentally unreliable. There were eleven types of gold coins, which accounted for 54 per cent of the total coin circulation in 1869, seven varieties of silver coins, 42 per cent of the total, and six sorts of copper coins. Furthermore, every domain had issued its own paper money, or *hansatsu*, which circulation totalled nearly one-third in value of that of gold coins.[3] In addition, some of the domains privately, or illegally, coined their own money. The situation was more than alarming not only internally, but also externally. As the *North China Herald* reported:

Arrangements having been made for the exchange of Boos (Ichiboos – ¼ *ryo*) against dollars at the rate of Two Hundred and Ninety-three (293) per Hundred, exchange will be given to all Foreigners . . . This announcement was received by many with incredulity and distrust, but the Manager of the Oriental Bank having satisfied himself that the native government was acting in good faith, came to its assistance, . . . *Boos* have fallen, in consequence to a point nearly approaching the government rate of exchange, . . . the disturbing element hitherto present in our circulations of prices, will be soon eliminated, by the establishment of native coin as the only currency.[4]

The Meiji government had already (before this newspaper report) attempted to find a way forward. In April 1868, a month before the imperial troops reached Edo, the government drew and adopted a plan of recoinage. In June 1868, the government set up the Accountancy Office, which was reorganised as the Ministry of Finance in August 1869. However, in spite of the newspaper prediction, it took two years for the government to install advanced western-style equipment in what became the imperial mint. There were two crucial problems.

The first related to difficulties of replacing the traditional method of striking coins with a modern minting system. At the suggestion of the Oriental Bank, and at the request of the British consul, the government built the imperial mint in Osaka with an English-made coinage machine, which had earlier been used in Hong Kong, assisted by two Englishmen who supervised the work.[5] The imperial mint was opened on 4 April 1871, on which occasion the foreign ministers, consuls and other distinguished guests were told that:

The work in question has now been completed, owing to the zealous co-operation of the Oriental Banking Corporation and Messrs Kinder and Waters.[6]

William Kinder, former master of the Hong Kong mint, became the first master of the Osaka mint, and Thomas Waters was the designer and supervisor of the erection of the imposing building.[7] In the mean time, the 'yen' was adopted in 1869 as the formal title of the currency instead of the *ryo*.[8]

Elsewhere, the Japanese were eager to borrow money in London which would enable them to build their first railway. Unfortunately, they were easy prey for the unscrupulous Horatio Nelson Lay who, dismissed in 1864 as inspector-general in the British consulate at Shanghai,[9] somehow became the agent of the Meiji government. Lay's terms for contracting the Japanese loans involved charging the Japanese a rate of interest far higher than that charged in London. When the Japanese discovered the deception they dismissed him and asked the Oriental Bank to do the job in 1870. The Lay affair was a reminder to the Japanese that foreign loans should be avoided and that foreign services in general be dispensed with by the Japanese as soon as possible.[10] Banking was, perhaps, no exception.

Another difficulty also had a profound effect. Until early 1871, the government assumed that the metallic standard of the new currency would be silver, which had previously been used as the means of payment for what small foreign trade there was at Nagasaki. As such the government as early as February 1868 declared the validity of silver Mexican dollars as the officially recognised means of payment at the treaty ports. The situation changed irrevocably in the spring of 1871 when the government received a letter from Hirobumi Ito, under-secretary of the Finance Ministry, who was on an official tour for monetary investigations in the United States. Ito, who had been dispatched to the United States as head of a group to investigate the monetary and banking system there in the autumn of 1870, reported:

That Austria, Holland and some other countries still maintain a silver standard is probably due to the great difficulty of changing the old system. If a system of coinage were to be newly established by any of these countries, there is no question but that the gold standard would be invariably adopted. It will be a wise policy for Japan, therefore, to consider the trend of opinion in Western lands and establish her new system in accordance with the best teachings of modern times . . . If the gold standard is introduced, silver may be fitly coined for a subsidiary medium of exchange, putting a limit to its legal tender amount.[11]

The Finance Ministry was easily persuaded by this letter and agreed to adopt the gold standard. As a result a month after the opening of the mint, 'the Imperial Ordinance of the 10th day of May of the 4th year of Meiji (1871)' was issued which promulgated the new coinage regulations and which adopted the gold standard and the yen. The promulgation of the coinage regulations was, however, only the beginning of a lengthy road to the real establishment of the gold standard in 1897, because, in spite of the Ordinance, gold was in short supply and silver was in fact the chief means of settlements in treaty ports. The 'gold standard' was no more than nominal at this stage.

In the mean time, the fledgeling government had to face another formidable task. In 1868 taxes in Japan were paid in rice or in kind. In order to allow the government to introduce a system whereby tax payers paid their dues in money, it was necessary to start issuing paper currency. On 9 June 1868, the very day when remnants of the Shogunate guards were annihilated in northern Edo, the government started to issue its own notes, or *dajokansatsu*. The total amount of the notes was 48 million *ryo*; 25.33 million *ryo*, 53 per cent of the total, was appropriated by the government for ordinary expenditure for the year 1868/69. The second largest sum, 12.73 million *ryo*, was lent out to those domains which needed money to support their forces fighting on the Meiji government side. Satsuma, whose forces were the core of the imperial troops, was the largest consumer. The rest of the notes, 9.93 million *ryo*, was set aside for industrial and commercial purposes, from which the first experiment in establishing a Japanese banking system would emerge.[12]

The government notes were from 1869 to 1872 joined by three other kinds of notes. First, for one year from October 1869, the ministry of civil affairs (predecessor of the ministry of works, or later the ministry of industry and trade) notes were issued, totalling 7.5 million *ryo*. They were all of small denomination to supplement *dajokansatsu*. Second, between October 1871 and May 1872, the Ministry of Finance issued gold-convertible notes for 6.8 million *ryo* to fill a temporary deficit of the government budget; this business was passed to the house of Mitsui. Third, from January to April 1872, Hokkaido colonisation board issued gold-convertible notes for 2.5 million *ryo*, with which the government planned to develop this huge northern island and thus absorb a large number of jobless, including anti-Meiji government ex-*samurai*.[13]

In the long run the issue of a huge amount of inconvertible government notes was the beginning of a runaway inflation. Although the Ministry of Finance notes and Hokkaido notes were theoretically convertible and therefore non-inflationary, they were effectively inconvertible, because of the shortage of gold. The majority of the government notes encouraged inflation. It was an inflammable situation. The wide variety of the government notes themselves, to which, as will shortly be discussed, the notes of eight exchange companies were added, presented problems not only for the government, but also for the economy. In addition, due to the inferiority of the printing of the government notes, they were easy to counterfeit. To overcome the difficulty, the government in February 1872 resolved to consolidate the various kinds of notes into a single set of new government notes which were to be printed on German-made machines. These new notes would, in theory, in the course of six years replace all others in circulation; in practice it was many years before the government actually achieved its objective.

The 'exchange company', 1869–1872

Organising the *ryogae* houses into a joint-stock company, which the *bakufu* had desperately tried as a last resort, was attempted by the new regime. For the Meiji government, which itself, with taxes paid in rice, had as yet no pecuniary basis, there was no choice but to rely on the wealthy (although overstretched) *ryogae*. In April 1869, the government set up trade boards in each of the treaty ports and in a few other selected places. Under these arrangements trading and exchange companies were installed in Tokyo, Yokohama, Niigata, Kyoto, Osaka, Kobe, Otsu and Tsuruga, the last two being situated north of Kyoto. The government intended that both types of company would be incorporated by those wealthy merchants, and that the exchange companies would supply funds to their trading counterparts.[14]

Resources of the exchange companies were twofold. They had govern-ment loans and deposits, which of course took the form of government notes, or *dajokansatsu*. The loans were made only to the exchange compa-nies in Tokyo, Yokohama, Kyoto, Osaka and Kobe. The total amount of governmental resources was 1.622 million *ryo*. Through these measures, the government was intent on pushing its notes into circulation. The rest of resources had to be tapped by the companies' own efforts. The first and most reliable was their own capital. In the case of the five exchange compa-nies cited above, the amount of capital was 34 per cent in 1870 and 19 per cent in 1872 of the total available resources. The capital stocks and shares were negotiable. Deposits of the five companies were 26 per cent in 1870 and 28 per cent in 1872 of the total available resources. Interest and dividends were to be paid on deposits and shares respectively.[15] As far as the business of the exchange company was concerned, it was similar to that of the *ryogae* except that it was organised as a company on the basis of joint-stock princi-ples. The first modern banking experiment thus commenced as joint-stock banking companies comprised of *ryogae*.

The exchange companies were all allowed to issue gold-convertible notes and, apart from Osaka, they issued gold notes of one or two denominations. Only the Osaka exchange company was authorised to issue gold notes of five denominations up to 100 *ryo*. This special privilege was due to the pres-tige of Osaka as the sole commercial centre of the old Shogunate regime. Furthermore, to facilitate small payments, the Tokyo exchange company was allowed to issue silver notes substituting for silver coins and both the Osaka and the Kyoto companies were permitted to issue copper notes sub-stituting for copper coins, until such time as the ministry of civil affairs could provide its own notes. Of the eight companies, the Yokohama exchange company was the more remarkable, being commissioned to issue Mexican dollar notes which had been issued by Mitsui working for the late *bakufu*. Japanese merchants operating in Yokohama were relieved to have support because those western banks which had survived the 1866 crisis – the Chartered Mercantile Bank, Oriental Bank, Hongkong and Shanghai Bank and Comptoir d'Escompte – were vigorously conducting business.[16] The note issuing facility was a most remarkable aspect of exchange company business, supplying about 50 per cent of all available monetary resources at one time in the early Meiji era.[17]

However, the exchange companies' foundations were seriously weakened in August 1871 when the trade board system was abolished. Nine days later in the same month, the prefectural system replaced the old territorial domains. The measures completed the Restoration by sweeping away the remnants of the old, including the offices of the domains' lords and their trading facilities, on which the trade companies, and consequently the exchange companies, rested. These fundamental changes coincided with the government tightening the issuance of the companies' notes, the most important instrument of their lending capabilities.[18] The situation was entirely detrimental to the exchange companies. In addition, and from the outset of the scheme, influential houses of *ryogae*, core members of the proprietors, did not see the business of the exchange companies as their own.[19] Their unwillingness was probably due to their tradition of independence in business.[20] The exchange companies effectively ceased to operate by the end of 1871, though formally they were still in existence in December 1872. The first banking experiment of the Meiji government thus failed.

6　The national bank system: the American influence, 1870–1881

Banking controversy, 1870–1872

Although the prestigious *ryogae* financial houses resisted the government scheme of organising them into joint-stock companies, they did not object in principle to the idea of transforming themselves into modern banking houses. Witnessing the collapse of the ill-fated exchange companies, enterprising ex-*ryogae* merchants thought that the opportunity had arrived for them to set up their own bank institutions. The movement became quite fashionable from the summer of 1871 when Mitsui took the initiative. In the prospectus submitted to the Finance Ministry, Mitsui designated themselves as 'Mitsui Gumi Bank'. They proposed to issue their own gold-convertible banknotes which they would support by 75 per cent gold reserves. These notes would circulate alongside the government notes. They also claimed that their 'bank' would follow the principles of note-issuing pursued by the Bank of England.[1]

There followed a series of bank prospectuses. In January 1872, enterprising merchants in Tokyo, supported by the new city corporation, submitted a prospectus of a 'Bank of Tokyo', which was to be engaged in supplying funds for developing the new capital city. In February, the house of Ono, another great *ryogae* house, ranking with Mitsui among the Edo *ryogae* community, proposed to establish themselves rivalling Mitsui as 'Ono Gumi Bank'. Then in April, the proprietors in Otsu Exchange Company decided to set up their own bank to be designated as 'Goshu Bank' in order to supply monetary resources to the locality of Lake Biwa north of Kyoto, where there were several commercial centres in the Edo era.[2]

As was suggested by the term 'bank', which all four schemes adopted, they promised to conduct their business upon western practice though they probably did not know exactly what this meant. The Finance Ministry, however, rejected their proposals for setting up their banking concerns. Only the Mitsui scheme, which had large amounts of gold holdings as well as a formidable reputation, was seemingly to be accepted, though before long they discovered that they could not be optimistic about their plan.[3]

Nonetheless, these four abortive bank plans were undoubtedly a reflection of a more fundamental and wider trend of widespread quasi-banking, which followed in the wake of the Restoration. There is no doubt that these demands resulted from the growing need for banking resources. The government understood this, but further controversy arose in the summer of 1871 when the monetary mission, dispatched to the United States of America and led by Hirobumi Ito, returned to Tokyo. Ito found the government inevitably in great turmoil in the aftermath of the abolition of the domain system. In addition, the large prestigious delegation of government ministers and officials, later known as the Iwakura Mission, which hoped to secure treaty revision and study the West, was on the point of leaving Japan in November 1871.[4] Ito arrived back to find the banking controversy raging in Japan but after a few months he left again with the Mission.

Hirobumi Ito, who by the autumn of 1871, however, had already transferred his office from the Ministry of Finance to that of secretary of the ministry of works, raised a strong voice on banking matters. His confidence in his own knowledge of banking resulted from his investigations in America, from where he had earlier written to the Finance Ministry recommending the adoption of the gold standard. In the same letter he had indeed recommended a banking scheme. His idea was borrowed wholesale from the National Currency Act of the United States of America.[5] According to Ito's argument, the banks, to be set up all over Japan, would have bestowed upon them the privilege of issuing their own notes. But they would also be issued with government bonds as reserves. Once the banks started business, they would use their own notes, and the voluminous amount of government notes, which were feeding inflation, would, it was hoped, be withdrawn. The proposed system – according to Ito – would accomplish simultaneously two aims by supplying funds through the banknotes to the growing needs of commerce and at the same time redeeming the government notes.[6]

Ito's programme was fiercely challenged by Kiyonari Yoshida, under-secretary of the Finance Ministry. Yoshida, of Satsuma stock, had already had an extraordinary career. In 1864, in the wake of Satsuma's bitter experiences of the British bombardment of their capital Kagoshima, the Satsuma domain dispatched a group of eighteen young *samurai* to Britain to study western sciences and technology. Yoshida was one of this party. He stayed in London for two and a half years; then he crossed the Atlantic Ocean to New Hampshire where he stayed for three years. This relatively long stay in the West had enabled him to compare the two banking systems. In 1866, during his stay in London, he had fortunately witnessed the Bank of England's role in calming the banking upheaval caused by the Overend Gurney crisis, during which many British overseas banks, including those represented in Yokohama, were ruined and pulled down. This experience, perhaps, together with Anglo-American international comparisons, convinced him that the British understood the implications of banking rules rather better than the Americans. His conclusion was, therefore, that the multi-note-issuing system, such as that under the National Currency Act in America, would not work in Japan. He argued strongly that Japan should establish a sole bank of issue on the model of 'the British-style gold bank'.[7]

The controversy continued vigorously, particularly between Ito and Yoshida, in the autumn of 1871. The scheduled departure of the Iwakura Mission in November 1871, however, obliged the Finance Ministry to take a compromise decision, that a bank with the right of issuing the gold-convertible banknotes would be established with the national bond as the reserve for conversion. Nobody knew whether the scheme would be theoretically correct. The Finance Ministry started to work hard on a draft of the National Bank Decree and so the introduction to Japan of the second banking experiment commenced.

National Bank Decree, 1872–1876

The Ministry of Finance was at this time led by a remarkable group of strong men. The Minister was Toshimichi Okubo, a prominent figure who ranked only next to Takamori Saigo during the Restoration war campaign. After Restoration, however, Okubo became the absolute head of the new Meiji government but sadly was assassinated in 1878. Outside the Ministry, reliable support came from Shigenobu Okuma, a Saga man.[8] Okuma, an able young politician, took a seat from July 1871 on the *dajokan*, or the executive body of the Meiji Restoration government, which was composed of only four members. Okubo joined Okuma in October 1873. The same year, Okuma succeeded as Finance Minister. Being in the office of Finance Minister by 1880 and *dajokan* member of 1881, Okuma now became the most powerful man responsible for the overall financial policies. He was assisted by Kaoru Inoue, secretary of the Ministry and of Choshu stock, and Eiichi Shibusawa, high official at the Ministry and ex-*bakufu* man.[9]

The Ministry of Finance made a priority in drafting the banking decree. Shibusawa was in charge of the task. The drafting of the decree, along the lines of the compromise reached in the autumn of 1871, was fundamentally on the model of America's national bank system. The National Bank Decree, consisting of 28 articles and 161 clauses, the first ever in Japanese history, was thus proclaimed in December 1872.[10] It was stipulated that the national bank would be required to have more than five proprietors and five directors including the president. The board of directors would be authorised to appoint a manager, an accountant and a secretary. The three officers would be entrusted to conduct the daily management of the bank. The sum of each equity would be ¥100, half of which would be requested to be paid in at the establishment of the bank. These arrangements were similar to those adopted in the West.

There was also a series of tight regulations, which thereafter came to characterise the interventionist character of the Japanese financial authorities. First of all, the minimum capital stock was set to be ¥50,000 for a bank based in a city of more than 3,000 population, ¥200,000 for 10,000 population and ¥500,000 for 100,000 population. In order that the bank would be able to respond at any time to withdrawals of deposits, it was requested that reserves be kept mainly in the form of national bonds up to the sum of 25 per cent of the total deposits. For lending the bank was prohibited to advance on the security of its own stock. Lending was to be effected of course by the banknotes.[11] It was in this business of note-issuing that the national bank system would prove to be disastrous.

Article 6, the lengthiest and most elaborate in the Decree, stipulated that the proprietors would first be requested to deliver a sum of up to 60 per cent of the capital stock in the form of government notes, of any kind so far issued, to the Ministry of Finance. In exchange for them, the bank was to receive national bonds of equal sum. Then the bonds had to be deposited with the Finance Ministry, which would finalise the sophisticated process by giving the bank notes carrying its firm name on their faces. The rest of the capital, or 40 per cent of the total, would have to be kept, theoretically, in gold specie. This assumed that two-thirds of total note-issue would be covered by specie reserves. This was an extraordinarily high ratio of the reserve compared with western experiences such as that of the Bank of England. It was also advised that the bank management should never confound the reserves for conversion with those for withdrawal of deposits.[12] Furthermore, the Finance Ministry proceeded to display specimens of formats for 'the prospectus of opening the bank', 'the statute', 'the procedure of electing the directors', 'the annual report', and so on. The Ministry of Finance was thus ready by the end of 1872 to receive applications for setting up the national banks. During the course of the next two years five applications to set up national banks were received. In the mean time, however, the Japanese government had to recognise that creeping inflation, and the suffering which that engendered, which was not squeezed from the system until the mid-1880s, was the price which the Japanese were forced to pay for Ito's panacea for Japanese banking.

Immediately after the Bank Decree, Okuma, Inoue and Shibusawa joined forces to set up a model national bank. They deliberately chose Mitsui for this purpose: the go-ahead for an independent 'Mitsui Bank' was withdrawn by the government. Instead Mitsui was approached in December 1871, with the suggestion that they should send their men to America to learn more about western banking. Mitsui, anticipating their exclusive role in a renewed government banking scheme, dispatched five young partners and two clerks to America.[13] Further, in January 1872, Inoue and Shibusawa strongly urged Mitsui to concentrate upon banking. Mitsui was again easily persuaded to develop banking interests, especially as their main business in cloth and drapery deteriorated considerably.[14] The bank scheme had made good progress under the initiative of the Finance Ministry by February 1872, when the house of Ono proposed to set up their own bank as has already been discussed. The Finance Ministry, of course, declined Ono's proposal, but instead thought it more convenient for their bank plan to add Ono to Mitsui to make the bank more powerful.

However, the idea of a joint venture of two prestigious financial houses was opposed by both houses. Traditionally *ryogae* had never united in this way. In any case their long-standing rivalry had resulted in serious disagreements in every aspect of their business activities which had not lessened even after the Restoration.[15] It took three months' negotiation, until May 1872, to induce the two houses to join the scheme. Eventually, some thirteen months later, the first general meeting of proprietors was held in June 1873 and two chairmen, one each from the house of Mitsui and Ono, were elected. It was thus announced that the First National Bank of Tokyo, or *Tokyo Kokuritsu Daiichi Ginko*, was established. Shibusawa was appointed as the chief auditor to the board of directors. Having deserted his office in the Ministry of Finance, Shibusawa started his career as a businessman. Later he became one of the most powerful and influential entrepreneurs in Meiji Japan, with wide interests in manufacturing as well as in banking and finance.

The First National Bank of Tokyo was immediately followed by four other projects. First, in January 1873, the president and his fellow directors of Yokohama Exchange Co. proposed to transform the company into the Second National Bank of Yokohama with the privilege of issuing Mexican dollar notes. This was agreed and the business commenced in August 1874. Next, in February 1873, merchants and landowners in Niigata, an important rice port on the north coast of the mainland facing the Japan Sea, and a treaty port, made an application to set up a bank. The proposal was agreed to by the Finance Minister and the Fourth National Bank of Niigata opened its doors in March 1874. Another two applications came from Osaka in the spring of 1873. A group of ex-*samurai* and merchants, led by ex-Satsuma *samurai* resident in Osaka, proposed to set themselves up as a bank. It was authorised and started business in December 1873 as the Fifth National Bank of Osaka. Then the last, but not least, application came from merchants led by the house of Konoike, who were to designate themselves as the Third National Bank of Osaka. The first call for payment of capital started in October 1873, but there was serious discord. Eventually in January 1874 the Third Bank was abandoned.[16] It is important to note that the ex-*ryogae* in Osaka, the most important commercial centre before 1868, failed to transform their business to take account of the modern world. Perhaps this was inevitable as Osaka was being challenged by Tokyo, Yokohama, Kobe and other treaty ports, all experiencing the fierce blast of outside competition.

National bank promotion came to a sudden standstill with the failure of the house of Ono in the autumn of 1874. Ono, a component of the First National Bank, had mismanaged their own business and could not respond to the requests of the government to enhance guarantee funds as a security for handling the government money.[17] Mitsui survived. However, more fundamentally, Ono's failure undermined the basis of the national bank business. In June 1874 a fall of the yen against the pound sterling in the foreign exchange market resulted in a depreciation of note currency in general against gold specie. Although at this stage the rate of depreciation of the currency was only 1 per cent, this was indeed the beginning of the slide to runaway inflation which would engage the financial authorities up to 1885. A further misfortune for the national banks was the fact that their banknotes even depreciated against the government notes.[18] The situation was alarming and is well illustrated by the following figures. The aggregate national banknotes, which had stood at a little more than ¥0.85 million at the end of 1873, increased to ¥1.36 million in June 1874. But the decrease of their circulation then started and was accelerated by their depreciation. The aggregate sum dropped to ¥0.38 million in June 1875 and eventually to 0.06 million in June 1876.[19] The supposedly gold-convertible national banknotes were by no means able to stay in circulation. The Banking Decree based on compromise reached in the autumn of 1871 proved to be irrelevant to the situation and theoretically unsustainable with the virtual collapse of the second bank experiment. Something had to be done to rescue the national banking system.

The case for British banking, 1871–1877

Although they had not yet decided what they would do about currency, the financial authorities had certainly realised by the time of the banking controversy the necessity of the joint-stock principle for banking. The Finance Ministry commissioned Genichiro Fukuchi, a competent official interpreter,[20] to produce some literature on western banking. The Finance Ministry published a book entitled *Kaishaben*, or *The Company*, in September 1871. The book, edited by Fukuchi, was the abbreviated translation of passages from the writings of J. S. Mill, Francis Wayland and

Neumann (Dutch economist). It was intent on helping would-be proprietors to understand a joint-stock bank.[21] Simultaneous with *The Company*, the Finance Ministry published a pamphlet entitled *Rikkairyakusoku*, or *Concise Procedure of Promoting Companies*. The author was Shibusawa, whose memoranda, put down during his investigation tour in western countries, were the basis of this writing. The pamphlet was a supplement to *The Company* and was intended to assist the ailing exchange companies and forthcoming banking companies. The two works, however important, were only the beginning of banking enlightenment.

In August 1872, four months before the proclamation of the National Bank Decree, the Finance Ministry employed Alexander Allan Shand, exacting manager of the Chartered Mercantile Bank, Yokohama branch, and of Scots banking background, as adviser to the head of the issuing department.[22] The contract of his employment guaranteed him a tremendously high monthly salary of ¥500 as compared with ¥800 for the prime minister and ¥500 for the rest of ministers on the *dajokan*. Although he was very expensive, Shand soon proved to be extremely competent and helpful for the Japanese financial authorities. Shand's first duty was to produce a textbook on bank bookkeeping. He finished writing the draft by the summer of 1873. It was immediately translated by Finance Ministry officials and published in December 1873 as *Ginkobokiseiho*, or *Detailed Accounts of Bank Bookkeeping*; there were five volumes of this work and it provided the first information on western banking accountancy techniques to be introduced into Japan.[23]

In April 1874, the Finance Ministry announced that the department of issue would offer courses on public finance. Shand was to be the lecturer from November 1874.[24] There were two courses, one introductory and the other standard. In the preliminary course, there were lectures on economic theory, bank regulation, bookkeeping and arithmetic. In the regular course there were lectures on banking, translation, bookkeeping, arithmetic, bank history, bank regulation and commerce. Shand was responsible for lectures on J. S. Mill's *Principles of Political Economy* and his own *Detailed Accounts of Bank Bookkeeping*. These courses only operated for five years until 1879, but they were of great importance. In total 341 students qualified and continued to serve the banking and financial world in Japan, of whom 118 were in the Finance Ministry itself while 42 served in local government and 181 became bank managers or officials.[25]

In October, Shand was asked to undertake the first bank inspection in Japan's history. The failure of the house of Ono in the autumn of 1874 had caused grave doubts about the bad debts which might be affecting the national banks. Therefore, the first inspection, executed by Shand by March 1875, gave priority to searching out bad debts in the accounts of two banks, the First National Bank of Tokyo and the Second National Bank of Yokohama. Besides his investigations into the accounts of the banks, Shand pointed out two other crucial shortcomings in modern Japanese banking. In the first place he strongly argued for a necessary reform in the method of note issue.[26] His argument, which would be reiterated in a proposal made in 1876 to be discussed shortly, certainly made an important point. In the second place, Shand took Shibusawa, the auditor of the First Bank, to task for not allowing more liberal overdrawing facilities. Shand took special measures to advise Shibusawa personally on these matters.[27] Shand's inspection was one of the rare examples of the independent audit. Although the independent inspection was stipulated in the National Bank Decree, it was scarcely executed.

In the last two years of his duties in the Finance Ministry, Shand was ever more active and involved in enlightening the financial authorities and assisting the ex-*ryogae* merchants to transform themselves. The Finance Ministry, without any resources in the form of modern banking textbooks, accepted Shand's advice and published a translation of Arthur Crum's *A Practical Treatise on Banking, Currency and the Exchanges*.[28] Shand himself drew up a manual for national banking in Japan, which appeared in serial form in the ten issues of a magazine published by the Finance Ministry and entitled *Ginkozasshi*, or *Bank Magazine*, between 1877 and 1878.[29] Before he left Japan in 1877 for London, Shand himself wrote a short book, *On Banking*, which was translated as *Ginkotaii* and published in May 1877. The book was a concise introduction to banking which was of course based on British practices.

Shand thus contributed tremendously to the development of Japanese banking ideas and practices. In the summer of 1876, the national bank system, which was already in the doldrums with only four banks established, was about to undergo a major reform. The government tried to assist would-be bank proprietors to set up their banks more easily and also tried to find a way forward politically. Facing up to the situation, Shand strongly criticised the financial authorities under no less than fifty-nine heads. Although his paper was lengthy, citing many western examples and quoting from western economic and banking authorities, his argument was clear enough.

His criticisms were threefold. First, both in the National Bank Decree and in the minds of the financial authorities, he argued, banking and issuing businesses were confused. These two businesses had to be kept separate from each other. This led to his second point, that the note issue must be a monopoly, held by a sole state bank of issue as was so effectively done by the Bank of England. Lastly, he stressed that the specie-convertible banknotes should never be allowed to be linked with the national bonds as the conversion reserves.[30] The financial authorities in Japan at this time were unable to understand much of his argument. Shand's advice was dismissed. These banking lessons, at least with regard to issuing business, had to be learnt by the Japanese authorities themselves. The price they paid in cost and suffering was high.

Banking revisions, mania and inflation, 1876–1879

The replacement of the domains by the prefecture system in 1871 had laid the basis for the new social and political framework. Upon this basis, the 1873 political change, in which the pro-invasion-of-Korea faction led by Takamori Saigo deserted the *dajokan*, further consolidated the power structure. After the Restoration of 1868, the stipends of feudal lords, *samurai* and court nobles were paid by the government and amounted to from 25 per cent to more than 30 per cent of the annual government expenditure. In August 1876, the government announced the issue and distribution of money stipend bonds for ¥174 million, a huge figure compared with ¥112 million for the total note circulation in 1875. The bonds were to be given to the *samurai* and others, the ex-ruling class of the Tokugawa regime, as compensation for their stipends.[31] Thus finally the Meiji government attempted to free itself from a crippling financial burden.

The government had already in early 1873 promulgated a conscription system by which all young men were called up for military service. This provided the government with a real power basis which would quite quickly make the ex-*samurai* redundant. Indeed, the maintenance of the ex-*samurai* had long been a burden for the government, both politically and financially. In 1876, the abolition of the *samurai* class came to the top of the agenda for the government. First in March the government decreed that ex-*samurai* would no longer carry swords. The disarmed *samurai* were outraged; threats were made, which grew into a series of small uprisings in the autumn of 1876 and culminated in the Satsuma rebellion in 1877.[32]

How were the ex-*samurai* bondholders to use their money? To assist in the mobilisation of these resources, the Tokyo Stock Exchange was established in June 1878. But some former feudal lords and ex-*samurai* had large sums of money available, and they needed to be capitalised. The Finance Ministry thought out a clever scheme which would use the ex-*samurai*'s surplus funds and stimulate the stagnant national bank system. In August 1876, at the same time as the issue of the ex-*samurai*'s bonds, the National Bank Decree was fundamentally revised. First banknote conversion into gold specie was suspended. Through this suspension, Japan moved on to the silver standard: in March 1876 silver, which had long been the means of payment in treaty ports, was given a status of standard beyond treaty ports, without any legal changes taking place. Secondly, the maximum ceiling of the capital stock payment by the national bonds was enhanced from 60 per cent to 80 per cent of the total amount. Consequently, the national banks were to be allowed to issue their own banknotes up to 80 per cent of their capital. Thirdly, the existent banks were requested to renew their registration under the amended Decree.[33] The revisions of the Decree were directly related to making easier the setting up of national banks so that they would be able to use, as capital, the ex-*samurai*'s bonds. Although these measures were an attempt to rescue ex-*samurai* they proved to be a Pyrrhic victory.

The first application to renew registration came from the First National Bank of Tokyo in September 1876 and was followed by four successful applications by the end of that year. In 1877, despite the Satsuma rebellion in Kyushu between February and September that year, twenty-three banks were set up; of these, remarkably, three were in Kyushu. Another notable institution of the year was the Fifteenth National Bank of Tokyo, soon to be called simply Fifteen Bank, the proprietors of which were exclusively those of the new nobility, the former court nobility and feudal lords. The capital stock of the Fifteen Bank was the enormous sum of ¥17.8 million, which was in fact commissioned to supply funds to the new Meiji army fighting the rebels. In the mean time, responding to Shand's criticism, the Finance Ministry drew up guidelines setting a ceiling for the total amount of national banknote issue. In October 1877, the Finance Ministry announced the ceiling of ¥34 million calculated on the basis of population and tax in each prefecture. The bank promotion culminated in the establishment of ninety-eight banks in 1878. Yet in 1879 there was another bank promotion in which twenty-seven banks were added to the number. The foundation of the 153rd National Bank of Kyoto in November 1879 brought the total sum of notes issued to a little more than ¥34 million. The Finance Ministry then stopped issuing any further licences.[34] The emergence of 153 banks in three years was a prodigious achievement, although as will be seen it was only one side of the picture.

From the outset of the Meiji Restoration, there was always the potential for inflation as large numbers of inconvertible government notes were constantly in circulation. However, until 1875, the rates of depreciation of the government notes were well below 1 per cent for gold specie yen and around 3 per cent for silver specie yen. The additional issue of national banknotes changed all that. In 1879, when the total addition of the national banknotes to the government notes exceeded ¥34 million, the depreciation rates of the notes reached 34 per cent for gold specie and 21 per cent for silver specie.[35] This was the real danger. Rampant inflation threatened all the achievements of early Meiji Japan. Could Shigenobu

Okuma, who had long been responsible for the government's overall financial policies, find a way out? Money and banking questions came to dominate government thinking.

Business of the national banks, 1876–1881

The location of 153 national banks, of which two had amalgamated by 1879, demonstrates that there were two banking belts on the two great commercial centres of Tokyo and Osaka. From Tokyo one stretched north then westwards into Nagano prefecture and eastwards into Fukushima prefecture. From Osaka another reached south-west along the Inland Sea towards northern Kyushu. There were only a few banks on the other side of Chugoku district. This pattern of banking distribution stayed basically the same at least until 1900.

Of 153 banks, 21 were based in Tokyo and 14 in Osaka. The aggregate sum of capital stock of the banks in Tokyo was ¥23.126, which was 57 per cent of the total national bank stock of ¥40.616 million. The Tokyo share appears to be overwhelming compared with that of Osaka which was ¥1.97 million (5 per cent), but the Tokyo figure included the huge Fifteen Bank of which capital stock was ¥17.826 million. Excluding Fifteen Bank stock the Tokyo share was only 13 per cent. Also excluding Fifteen Bank in the aggregate, the average sum of the capital stock was ¥0.15 million. There were 43 banks which exceeded the average, of which 13 were situated in Tokyo and 4 in Osaka.[36] From these figures, it is safe to say that Tokyo started to overtake Osaka as financial centre at the outset of modern Japanese banking.

The first comprehensive statistical account of Japan, issued by the statistical bureau in 1882, fortunately gives some insight into the class structure of the bank proprietors in 1880. The aggregate sum of national bank capital was ¥42.1 million, of which 44 per cent belonged to the new nobility and 32 per cent to ex-*samurai*. This figure proves that some 18 per cent of the former *samurais'* stipend bonds were successfully incorporated into the national banks. However, it should be noted that 96 per cent of the new nobility's share was concentrated in the Fifteen Bank, or so-called 'Nobles Bank'. The rest of the aggregate capital, or 24 per cent of the total, was possessed by the common people, of which two-thirds was in the hands of merchants in big cities and landowners primarily in rice-growing areas. At the outset the new nobility and ex-*samurai* formed the majority of the shareholders, but the growth of national banking and the increases in capital stocks brought more and more merchants into the system, who would eventually overtake the former as the main body of proprietors in the national banks.[37] However, it should also be noted that the management know-how of the national banks, without regard to who were the majority of the proprietors, was perhaps a direct descendant of the *ryogae*. The increasing influence of merchants in the national banks was undeniable evidence of this.

At the cost of inflation, the national bank business made remarkable progress. On the assets side, the total advances leapt from ¥6 million in 1876 to ¥78 million in 1881. Taking three methods of advancing funds, lending on personal bonds and discounts were more important than lending on securities: this reflected two important aspects of the early development of Japanese banking. First, the growth of discounting spread rapidly with the introduction of telegraphic transfer, introduced in 1879.[38] Secondly, there was a strong demand coming from the two sectors of rice and silk, many of whose traders were also national bank proprietors. On the liabilities side, capital jumped from ¥3.5 million in 1876 to ¥44 million in 1881, the sum well above the ceiling set by the Finance Ministry. This was due to the authorised increases of capital without the right of banknote issue. Deposits also grew in the same period from ¥2.5 million to ¥20 million, but they were only half the size of the capital.

Demands for banking resources came not only from the silk and rice merchants, but also from tax-payers who were now required to pay their tax obligations in money, although they rarely had enough cash to meet their obligations. The national banks also readily lent out their money to customers, or indeed more 'intermediaries', who immediately lent them on to other borrowers. These notorious practices were, however, ignored by the initial lenders, who usually sanctioned the advances on the securities of money stipend bonds or even without taking any securities. These factors joined force to make their advances substantially aggressive. Between 1876 and 1881 advances as percentages of deposits, for example, leapt from 240 to 428 per cent. These astonishing figures suggest that the chief lending resource of the national banks as a whole was undoubtedly capital, itself disproportionately large in the balance sheets. They also meant that the banks with smaller resources had to rely upon those with bigger resources through interbank loans. Through these risky relationships, banking correspondence, or primitive interbank markets, barely emerged. The national banks were, however, soon overtaken in number by another two categories of banks which were about to join the system.

7 The origins of ordinary banking: another bank mania, 1875–1881

Private banking: adaptable *ryogae*, 1875–1881

The 1876 revisions of the National Bank Decree allowed would-be bankers to use the title 'bank', but it was only Mitsui who could immediately take this opportunity to establish themselves as a western-style modern bank. As was seen, Mitsui had earlier in 1872 planned to set up their own bank but were persuaded to support the government scheme of bringing about the national bank system. In addition to this earlier willingness, there was another reason for Mitsui to make efforts to renew their proposal.

When it was established, the First National Bank was accommodated in premises specially built by Mitsui for their own banking purposes. As has already been explained,[1] Mitsui had unwillingly joined the house of Ono in launching the First National Bank. When at the end of 1874 the house of Ono collapsed, Mitsui considered its position. Mitsui wrote to Shibusawa, chief auditor of the First Bank, detailing fifteen complaints including their shareholdings, use of Mitsui premises as the First Bank offices and withdrawal of bank clerks who had been Mitsui employees. Shibusawa, who was intending to take over the management of the Bank, remained unmoved, rejecting most of the complaints and concluding:

As far as the institution [First Bank] has been established carrying 'the bank' as its title, I think that the issue department [for the Ministry of Finance] would not ignore the fact that Mitsui Gumi have treated the Bank as their branch shop. As the situation might be considered to cause certain inconveniences, the Bank should, I think, be put in a position free from such shortcomings when the revisions of the National Bank Decree would be made.[2]

Shibusawa's intention was realised in August 1876 when the National Bank Decree was revised and the First National Bank reregistered under the revised Decree with Shibusawa as president. Mitsui were prepared for this. They had already, in April 1876, drafted the prospectus entitled *The Case for the Establishment of Mitsui Bank* which was accepted by the Finance Ministry. Mitsui Bank, the first private bank, with no decree to authorise it, opened its doors on the first day of July 1876. Some details of this first private bank, the first successful transformation of *ryogae* to bank, are worth mentioning.

In the prospectus, Mitsui were proud of 'the business of the house of Mitsui being existent for several hundred years'.[3] However, they also realised that they had to reorganise their basic business structure if they wished to survive. Mitsui had learnt a hard lesson on the need for strong reserves from the collapse of the house of Ono. Thus Mitsui exerted themselves to amass as large a reserve as possible, developing a single capital stock and basing their business upon joint-stock principles. The ancient, distinguished name of Mitsui Gumi was abandoned without hesitation and the new business launched with the simple name of Mitsui Bank. The capital stock of Mitsui Bank was ¥2 million, half of which was the sum transferred from Mitsui Gumi. Of the rest, ¥0.5 million was possessed by branch houses of Mitsui. The remainder was distributed among the employees. The total number of shareholders amounted to 383, of whom 82 employees bought two shares and 40 one share each. This employees' stock ownership plan was the first such initiated in Japan.[4]

Mitsui Bank started with an enormous advantage over all other banking initiatives in early Meiji Japan. By transforming all the branches of Mitsui Gumi from retail trade to banking business they entered the new sphere with an enviable branch network. It is true that the branches were not in any sense grand 'banking parlours' – they were in effect small retail shops. Nevertheless, the Mitsui Bank proclaimed that it was available to do 'business for the government ministries and departments and the prefectural offices, transaction in bills of exchange, exchange of coins, advances, transactions of bullion and so on'.[5] Mitsui had thirty branches, seven each in the Tokyo area (Kanto) and in the Osaka area (Kinki), six in Chubu, four in Chugoku and two in each of Hokkaido, Tohoku and Kyushu.

For the first three years private banking was monopolised by Mitsui. This was entirely due to the fact that the national banks were still being sanctioned. Therefore, private bank promotion started from 1879 when the authorisation of new national banks came to an end and another nine private banks joined Mitsui, bringing the aggregate sum of capital to ¥3.29 million. During 1880 and 1881, eighty banks, from twenty-five prefectures, made entries into private banking, and the aggregate capital stock amounted to ¥10.45 million, one-quarter of the national bank capital. Thus private banking, or a core of ordinary banking, as it would later be called in Japan, really commenced in the early 1880s. Tokyo had thirteen banks with a share of 34 per cent of total private banking capital, Osaka had eleven banks with 5 per cent share, Nagano, seventeen banks with 13 per cent and Shizuoka, ten banks with 11 per cent.[6] Tokyo private banking soon increased its lead over its Osaka counterpart, and this accelerated the process by which Tokyo became almost the sole financial centre. Private banking demands in Nagano and Shizuoka came primarily from silk and tea sectors respectively. In spite of the rapid growth in private banking, there were still places where banking services were not available. There demands were to be filled by other semi-banking services.

Quasi-banking, 1879–1881

Small companies and in fact shops doing lending business had become common in Japan after 1868, or perhaps even before that. Their owners included ex-*samurai*, landowners, merchants, pawnbrokers and farmers, and they existed in the provinces. Little is known of their businesses but it was undoubtedly indispensable to the economy, particularly business remote from cities, which otherwise had no means of lending or borrowing.[7] It was also certain that their number increased greatly after 1879 when the government stopped approving the establishment of national banks. However important their business was, no statistical evidence was available until 1880.

The statistical year-book, prepared by the government statistical bureau from 1882, for the first time gave some details on quasi-banking which was defined as:

Companies conducting monetary business such as bills of exchange, exchanges of coins, advances, deposits and so on are called quasi-banking companies.[8]

The difference between quasi-banking and private banking related solely to the amount of business done.

Between 1880 and 1881, quasi-banking grew remarkably: the number of banks increased from 120 to 369 in 1881, and their total capital rose from ¥1.2 million to ¥5.9 million in 1881. This was a small figure compared with the capital of national and private banks. But the quasi-banks, though individually small in size, were widely scattered throughout Japan, being, in 1881, located in thirty out of the forty-seven prefectures in Japan. Two-thirds of these banks were concentrated in seven prefectures, that is, Kanagawa, fifty-seven banks; Ishikawa (Northern Chubu), forty-two; Oita, seventy-five; Yamanashi (South-eastern Chubu), twenty-five; Saitama, sixteen; Fukushima, fifteen; and Gunma (North-western Kanto), fourteen. In terms of capital, the two prefectures of Kanagawa and Ishikawa claimed nearly one-third of the aggregate.[9] The six dominating prefectures, except Oita, which had been composed of many small domains and where many ex-*samurai* set up so many companies, were all silk-producing areas. In addition to this, Kanagawa, the prefecture with Yokohama as its commercial centre, had various banking demands from both traditional industries and modern developments arising from and around the treaty port, and Saitama, north-west of Tokyo, was also a big tea-growing area. Thus quasi-banking was an inevitable local response to the need for facilities otherwise unavailable for small businessmen. There were only three quasi-banks in Tokyo and Osaka where the national and private banks were dominant.

As the smallness of capital stocks implies, the promoters of quasi-banking often came from rural districts and had modest resources. They were often merchant-landowners who set up their own banks concurrently with conducting their original business in silk or tea. Were they a kind of credit association to finance the members' own businesses?[10] Quasi-banks, which mushroomed in the early Meiji, were in a sense a temporary facility to serve local needs. They were, perhaps therefore, destined to be absorbed either by larger, genuine, banks or submerged by the emergence of subordinate institutions such as mutual loan associations.

Bank associations and clearing houses, 1877–1881

Once Shibusawa's position at the head of the First National Bank had been firmly established he immediately took steps to organise a bank association in Tokyo, although it is not clear that he had at this time any definite idea of arranging clearing operations. Perhaps he felt that it was his duty as the president of the national institution to give a lead in these matters. He named the association *Takuzenkai*, or 'society of selection'; the words came from the *Analects* of Confucius, his favourite book. The first meeting of the society, on 2 July 1877, at which he presided, adopted the regulations. The first article made plain the intention of the society:

Article 1.   The main purpose of the Society is to cultivate friendship among the members and to try to promote prosperity in business. Activities to promote this purpose are to express their own opinions and arguments on practices of business extending from the present state of banking and commerce in general to situations of banking overseas, foreign trades and fluctuations of foreign exchanges. The discussions are considered to be of some help to our business, but should not be done in pursuit of theories and laws.[11]

The address of Shibusawa at the first meeting exactly coincided with this article.[12]

Although membership was not confined to members of the national banks, the response from other bankers was slight, perhaps because they did not appreciate its importance. Eleven banks joined at the first meeting: six Tokyo-based national banks including the First and Fifteen Banks, four provincial nationals and Mitsui Bank. The Society soon started a cheque-clearing operation. Very different from the western precedent, the banknote exchange was not executed, probably because banknotes had become inconvertible into specie and as such the exchanges were meaningless. The association did not, at this stage, clear bills of exchange, probably due to the fact that there were at this time relatively few bills.

In the three years before 1880, the society more than doubled the number of member banks to twenty-four national and two private banks, but the increase in number was modest compared with the bank promotion of the same period. A more remarkable contribution of the society was an off-shoot of their main activities. The oldest banking journal was issued by the Finance Ministry and existent between December 1877 and December 1878. This was followed by a journal issued by the society from May 1878. The two journals were amalgamated by the society in February 1879 when it commissioned Ukichi Taguchi to publish *Tokyo keizaizasshi*, or the *Tokyo Economist*.[13] The publication of the journal marks the real beginning of serious economic journalism in Japan.

The *Takuzenkai* was soon followed by another bankers' association, *Ginkokonshinkai*, or 'friendly society of bankers', the founding date of which is not known.[14] By 1880 this society had thirteen member banks, including ten national and three private banks. Witnessing the rapid increase in the number of banks and the resultant growth in the number of fellow banks' notes and various bills of exchange in their possession, the member banks of both societies knew that they had to create an efficient system of clearing their liabilities among themselves – which their Osaka comrades had, as will be shown, already started. Both *Takuzenkai* and *Ginkokonshinkai* agreed to amalgamate to create a new association equipped with a clearing house. They merged in August 1880 and set up the Bank Association of Tokyo with a membership of forty-one banks. Clearing operations started in 1887.[15]

Another interbank initiative came from the Osaka bankers, who took a very practical approach in organising themselves into an institution. Osaka bankers were proud of their *ryogae* tradition and were accustomed to handling financial instruments of every sort. As we have seen,[16] clearings of bills of exchange and cheques were not exceptional in *ryogae* transactions. Upon this tradition and practice, they learnt the modern clearing operation from the system adopted by the Bank of England. Thus they joined forces to set up the Osaka clearing house in December 1879. The second annual report by the banking department of the Finance Ministry discloses what they were doing:

We, the member banks in Osaka, open current accounts at the clearing house and hand our cheque books over to it. When A Bank has a balance due from B Bank after their clearance, the clearing house debits the sum from B Bank's account and makes a cheque payable to A bank, which, after being underwritten by B Bank, is given to A Bank. The system is operated through the cheque without using any pieces of coin and is very convenient.[17]

It was indeed the system long used by British banks through the Bank of England accounts and their clearing house in London. The Osaka clearing house was joined by the ten Osaka-based and three Tokyo-based national banks, another two national banks and Mitsui Bank. Three years later, following the Tokyo example, Osaka bankers reorganised their clearing house into the Bank Association of Osaka. The same institutions were also set up in Nagoya and Fukuoka (Kyushu) in 1880. The clearing houses in Japan thus came into operation during the unprecedented bank promotion and at the height of inflation.

8 The search for stability: the last bank controversy, 1879–1881

Okuma's innovation: the Yokohama Specie Bank, or *Shokin*, 1879–1881

As more paper money was added to that already in circulation, serious depreciation continued. Depreciation against silver, the Japanese standard, which had been on average 3.3 per cent and 9.9 per cent in 1877 and 1878 respectively, reached 26.1 per cent in March 1879. Although the financial authorities were alarmed, their energies were otherwise occupied with political conflicts.

In 1878 in the wake of the assassination of Toshimichi Okubo, the most distinguished Meiji leader in the government, serious disagreement arose among the *dajokan* members and Shigenobu Okuma became a target. In order to disconcert his opponents, and allow himself a breathing space, Okuma resolved to make major recommendations. First he suggested that Japan should issue abroad national bonds for ¥50 million, or some £5 million, the proceeds of which would be used to redeem the paper money.[1] This proposal was greeted by a storm of protest and Okuma conceded defeat in the spring of 1880. Horatio Nelson Lay's unscrupulous behaviour was indeed still vividly remembered by the oligarchs. Okuma, in a tight corner, had only one choice left. He suggested the establishment of a Specie Bank. Japanese merchants, centred around Yokohama, had also been lobbying for this.[2] Okuma invited the merchants to set up a Specie Bank conjointly with the Finance Ministry and a prospectus was prepared. It was submitted to the chief minister of the *dajokan* in November 1879 and authorised without delay. The Yokohama Specie Bank, loosely based on the amended National Bank Decree, though without the right of note issue, opened its doors on 28 February 1880, the exact day on which Okuma was forced by the *dajokan* to resign as Finance Minister. The Bank was always known thereafter as *Shokin*, literally meaning 'specie'. The ousting of Okuma was part of a manoeuvre by a group led by Hirobumi Ito to remove him from power and was an omen of further radical changes to come some twenty months later.

46

The main aim of Okuma's Specie Bank was to provide the Japanese economy with a market for silver and gold bullion and specie and thus to bring into circulation precious metals previously hoarded inside Japan, instead of scouring the world for them. Once it was firmly established, it was anticipated that the Specie Bank could mobilise the hoarded specie within Japan, which specie would then be supplied and circulated freely by the Bank. To execute this enterprising plan, the Specie Bank was to do business entirely in specie, mainly silver coins, though in effect the ¥1 silver draft, silver-convertible on demand. The capital of ¥3 million was to be in silver specie, one-third of which was to be provided by the government. Article 49 of the Bank's regulations gave the Finance Minister powers to interfere in its business conduct and in the selection of the president, directors and general manager. Although based upon the National Bank Decree, the Specie Bank was the first institution tightly controlled by the government. John P. Hennessy, the maverick governor of Hong Kong, congratulated Okuma, although this was not enough to save Okuma's political life.[3]

Unfortunately for Okuma's Specie Bank, the depreciation of paper money accelerated, reaching 55 per cent in April 1880. Silver specie disappeared from every corner of the country: the Specie Bank had to abandon its principal business. Indeed it was forced to ask the government to lend out its notes to the Bank, otherwise it would have lost the means of banking business and its business would have collapsed. The government lent the Bank ¥0.5 million in the middle of May 1880, so effectively ending Okuma's expectations of the Specie Bank.

For the three months between May and the end of August 1880, there are no records of the activities of the Specie Bank, but on 23 August 1880 the Specie Bank proposed that the government loan it ¥3 million in government notes to be used as 'foreign exchange money'.[4] With this loan the Specie Bank would try to undertake authorised foreign exchange business for promoting direct exports – usually called *goyogaikokunigawase*. This scheme had already, in the autumn of 1879, been proposed by Masana Maeda, a young official at the Finance Ministry. Okuma ignored the suggestion. After the disastrous situations of the Specie Bank in the early months of 1880 Maeda resumed his efforts to persuade the officials in the Ministry and in the Specie Bank to adopt his system.[5] Between May and August it seems likely that officials both in the Finance Ministry and in the Specie Bank were discussing the direct export programme. The authorisation of the huge sum of ¥3 million was evidence that Maeda's proposal had been accepted by the financial institution.

During the first half of the Meiji era, Japan's staple export goods were silk and tea, both highly vulnerable to seasonal fluctuation. From time to time stocks of these goods accumulated in Japanese warehouses in Yokohama,

Kobe and Nagasaki. A buyer's market forced the sellers to dump their goods at giveaway prices into the hands of foreign merchants. This resulted in heavy losses. Could the government not intervene and cushion the Japanese merchants from such damaging losses? This was the first point Maeda made in his proposal. It would be even better if government intervention could so operate as to encourage a net import of specie. This was the underlying objective of both the government and the Specie Bank. The Finance Ministry and the Bank immediately proceeded to build a workable framework.

In the first place the Specie Bank had to arrange with Japanese merchants, who used to sell directly to foreign merchants, to advance them government notes, which it borrowed from the government, on the security of their exporting goods. Then the Bank's agencies had to be established in foreign financial centres, such as London and New York, the ultimate destinations of the goods. If the plan worked, specie would flow in.

On the acceptance of securities for advances of government notes, the Bank drew bills of exchange on foreign importers on its customers' behalf. These were immediately forwarded to the agent. Upon receiving the bills, the agent quickly collected the payments, exchanging them into specie and remitting it by telegram to the head office in Yokohama. Arrivals of specie at Yokohama effectively meant the completion of repayments by Japanese merchants. Finally, the working of the system required the transfer of specie from the Bank to the government. The authorised foreign exchange business for promoting direct exports, or government intervention in foreign trades, became one of the most important instruments through which the government could gather specie, the basis for the currency. How invaluable the government regarded the system could be seen from the amount of government notes lent out, which were increased to ¥3.5 million in October 1880 and further to ¥4.5 million in July 1881. In the mean time the Bank's agents set to work in New York and London. Indeed, the amount of specie in the government safe started to grow visibly from ¥7.2 million at the end of 1880 to ¥12.7 million at the end of 1881. It was an extraordinary breakthrough for the Japanese, but it was achieved without the co-operation and support of the outgoing Finance Minister, Okuma.

It is clear from the success of the direct export scheme that Okuma had lost control over the financial management of the country. Could Okuma have survived the political struggle if he had understood the importance of Maeda's proposal? The inauguration of the direct export scheme carried government financial policy beyond Okuma's banking ability. It should be remembered that Okuma had no practical experience of banking in the West. He had never been abroad.

From Okuma to Matsukata, 1880–1881

Shigenobu Okuma, who had from the very beginning of the Meiji Restoration government until February 1880 been in high office in the Finance Ministry, was well aware of his responsibilities for the overall financial policies. Resigning from the office of Finance Minister, Okuma submitted a report entitled *A General View of Financial Policy during Thirteen Years 1868–80* (a rare example of his writing) in which he noted:

Having been honoured at one time with the post of Minister of Finance, and since then presided over the direction of our financial policy as a member of the Cabinet, I have been induced to compile a short history of what has been done since the Restoration, adding at the same time some scattered observations on the principles upon which various measures were adopted.[6]

Following the introduction, Okuma reviewed his accomplishments, focusing on revenue and expenditure, paper currency, national debt, banks and taxation. Okuma's general review has not seriously been researched by any banking historians, although contemporary commentators were critical. The *Japan Gazette* of 23 and 30 April 1881, after several months' scrutiny of Okuma's paper, argued as follows:

We venture to aver that perusal of H. E. Okuma's book must create either a most favourable impression, or one of distrust and suspicion amounting to absolute disbelief. There can be no middle course.[7]

Although it suggested two possibilities for the ways in which Okuma's book would be received by the reader, *Japan Gazette* deliberately chose the latter course. It dared to point out an underlying inconsistency of Okuma's understanding of the situations:

On the other side, is the fact, not stated in the book, that the paper currency of the country, reduced in amount, has declined in purchasing value from par when its issue was greatest, to 182 paper for 100 silver when its issue was smallest; and, while a large surplus lies idle in the treasury as a 'reserve fund', maintained for the special purpose of preventing depreciation of currency and other government bonds.[8]

Upon this basis, *Japan Gazette* took Okuma to task for his mismanagement of bank affairs:

If the issuers had to redeem many of them, holding *kinsatsu* [government notes] for that purpose, their profit as bankers would be gone . . . Those who held the notes have undoubtedly had to recognise the feature of the situation, and have perhaps not dared to be very exacting with the military gentlemen [ex-*samurai*]. Their safer and easier course was to pass the notes on at some little loss; this is what they have undoubtedly done. Hence the gradual depreciation of the bank notes. Then these bank notes are declared by the government equal to their own *kinsatsu*. Hence, therefore, a general depreciation of all paper money, and lo! we have the key which we sought, and perceive that these national banks which H. E. Okuma regards as both useful to the country and particularly beneficial to the military class, are responsible for the fact that *kinsatsu* which, four years ago were at par, are now, although their amount has been reduced, at 45 per cent discount in silver.[9]

Japan Gazette, in fact its editor, W. G. Talbot, skilfully elaborated the point that there was a fundamental difference between the government notes and the banknotes. Did Okuma know this?[10] Okuma's ignorance may have been a fatal theoretical shortcoming, which prevented him from proposing an effective banking system.

There were two elements in Okuma's failure in tackling Japan's monetary and banking problems. Okuma was of Saga stock, an important south-western clan, but far less influential than the Satsuma–Choshu clique. He failed in his attempt to join the Iwakura Mission, notwithstanding the fact that the Mission itself was originally his own idea. By missing the opportunity of investigating western theory and practice of banking, he was unable to address Japanese banking problems properly. A. A. Shand was Okuma's most reliable guide and he may not have had the necessary experience to advise correctly. However, it should be noted that, as *The Times* of London observed, 'the enormous difficulties with which he had to contend'[11] in early Meiji might well have challenged the resources of even the most skilled of bankers.

The political downfall of Okuma during the Meiji Fourteenth Year Political Change effectively ended his period as a financial authority. Perhaps he had been too long in the Finance Ministry. When Alexander Shand, who had received a letter from Okuma while still in the cabinet inviting him to be the general manager of the Yokohama Specie Bank, learned the news of Okuma's dismissal he wrote sympathetically, 'the increased leisure, which you will not enjoy, may enable you to mature those plans for the reform of the currency', and added:

These at least are the considerations that occur to my mind, and therefore I cannot altogether deplore the temporary release of your Excellency from the multifarious cares of official life . . . I trust your Excellency may be induced to assume – if only temporarily – the governorship of the Bank, for in that case I have no doubt that it will be successfully founded in a very short time . . . I think therefore it is quite clear that your Excellency may well accept for a time the position of Governor of the Bank of Japan. Such a step would be most advantageous to the interests of Japan.[12]

Neither Shand nor Okuma, nor anyone else in Japan, then realised that Okuma was never to be given a second chance as a financial minister.

In September 1882, at Okuma's request, John Robertson, former Oriental Bank Yokohama agent, wrote from London recommending him to consult W. H. Talbot's brand new *The Currency of Japan* for financial questions. Two names of westerners, or indeed the British, were noted at the end of Okuma's career as Finance Minister. As already mentioned, Shand was invited by Okuma to be manager at the head office of the Yokohama Specie Bank. It was also said that Robertson was about to be invited, probably by Okuma, to assume advisership in the Finance Ministry just before Okuma's downfall.[13] Therefore an Okuma Finance Ministry would have retained a strong foreign element. This would not ultimately have been in Japan's best interests, and might well have been resented by those in the Ministry who formed the anti-Okuma element. By this time, however, a formidable successor was emerging.

Masayoshi Matsukata,[14] born in 1835 the son of a lower ranking, poor, Satsuma *samurai*, was brought up in circumstances of extreme poverty. This taught him invaluable economic lessons. In his early *samurai* career he became an accountant. His early experiences were to prove of great importance throughout his life. After the Restoration and a three-year service as governor of a northern Kyushu prefecture, Matsukata returned to Tokyo in August 1871 on being appointed as deputy head of the tax department in the Finance Ministry. In November 1875 he was appointed as secretary, and head of his department, of the Finance Ministry. In this capacity he had full charge of land tax reform which transformed the system based upon rice tax to one based upon money tax. His practical knowledge of financial affairs in the field gave him an unrivalled insight into the banking problems facing the new Japanese government.

He was also appointed to supervise the arrangements for the first exhibition to be held in Tokyo in 1877 and later to carry out the more ambitious plan of displaying the Japanese exhibits in the Paris *exposition* to be held in 1878. In August 1877, he was appointed concurrently the deputy chairman and secretary-general of the Japanese delegation to the Paris exhibition, with Toshimichi Okubo, the utmost leader of the government, as the chairman, though Okubo did not join the delegation. The delegation left Yokohama in February 1878 for Paris. Matsukata's role as secretary-general was taken over in June 1878 by his young colleague at the Finance Ministry, Masana Maeda.

The nine-month stay in Paris between March and December 1878 was enlivened by the interviews which Matsukata had with the French finance minister, Leon Say, grandson of Jean Baptiste Say. Appreciating Matsukata's jobs on the tax reform, Say strongly recommended Matsukata to establish a powerful central bank in Japan.[15] Say made further suggestions to Matsukata, writing:

The organisation and management of the Bank of France, set up long ago, are difficult to understand, because they have incorporated their inherent customs and traditions, whereas no other bank could rank with the National Bank of Belgium in terms of orderly arrangement and perfect organisation.[16]

Indeed, a banking historian later endorsed Say's words, praising the recently founded National Bank of Belgium as 'the ideal bank of issue'[17] and stating that, as such, its influence was strong with regard to 'the foundation and development of some of the other great banks of Europe'.[18] Say's advice impressed Matsukata considerably. Matsukata decided to leave behind him in France one of his advisers, Wataru Kato, who was commissioned to investigate the establishment, organisation and management of the National Bank of Belgium and its influence on the rest of its European counterparts. Meanwhile, Masana Maeda was building up his ideas about financing direct exports by the Japanese merchants, perhaps on the model of European examples and at the suggestion of Mitsui men in France.[19] Matsukata's visit to France was thus very fruitful, though Matsukata also noticed other, less desirable, aspects of the French financial arrangements, as will later be discussed.[20]

For one and a half years after his return to Japan, Matsukata worked hard. In June 1880, at a time when the Yokohama Specie Bank was nearly brought down in the middle of note depreciation, he submitted a proposal entitled *Zaiseikankyugairyaku*, or *A Concise Exposition of My Humble Opinions on Financial Policies*.[21] Severely criticising Okuma's 'unrealistic' financial policies in the preface, Matsukata laid down his policies on the table of the *dajokan*. The report was divided into three parts. First there were eight articles dealing with the accumulation of specie, with which Matsukata's banking scheme was deeply involved. Secondly there were two articles discussing the protection of the rice price. Finally there were nine articles on the promotion of industries. This paper expressed the genesis and core of the financial and economic policies which were later known as Matsukata's deflationary policies.

As for banking, Matsukata proposed to set up 'a specie bank of overseas exchange' to be engaged in supplying funds to the Japanese exporters. The title of the proposed bank was already familiar to the Japanese and similar to the institution already operating under the name of the Yokohama Specie Bank. Indeed, Matsukata's was a counter-proposal to Okuma's Yokohama Specie Bank. He was intent on making full use of the Yokohama Specie Bank in line with his other scheme which will be discussed shortly. However, we should note that there was an important element in this context. Financing the direct exports of Japanese merchants had never been adopted either by the Specie Bank itself or by the Finance Ministry before June 1880. The adoption of the system by the Specie Bank in June 1880 coincided perfectly with the timing of Matsukata's proposal.[22] Matsukata could see the great merit of financing direct exports, the system on which one of his men on the delegation to Paris, Maeda, had already elaborated. It was from the adoption of Maeda's scheme through which Matsukata could install his initiative in the Ministry of Finance, the pivot of the Meiji oligarchy, that the real direction of financial management would come. The adoption of the system by the Specie Bank was a crucial change for the Bank as well as for the overall financial policy. Matsukata's initiative was thus put in the core of Okuma's financial policy machine as early as in June 1880, more than a year before his accession to the Finance Minister's office. Okuma's arrangements *de facto* collapsed.

In September 1881, Matsukata laid down again before the *dajokan* his second proposal entitled *Zaiseigi*, or *On Finance*, this time his arguments being almost entirely concentrated upon banking. In the proposal, Matsukata drew up the framework for a Japanese banking system, which would be composed of three institutions. 'A central bank of Imperial Japan' was the pivot of the system, which was to be supported by a series of banks such as savings banks and a hypothec bank. The central bank was to be an institution to gather diverse resources and the other banks were to supply them to rising industries. These two types of banks were to become indispensable components of Japanese banking towards the end of the nineteenth century.[23]

Matsukata's proposal on central banking was still tentative. The central bank would be allowed to issue two kinds of notes, *waribikitegata*, or notes issued at a reduced value of the denomination, and *azukaritegata*, or certificates of deposit. No detailed explanations were given about the function and use of these notes. Furthermore, although central banking was to be conducted by the departments of 'public money management', 'ordinary bank business' and 'foreign exchange business', nothing was said about the issuing of notes. Therefore, the issuing business, core of central banking, was still very ambiguous in terms of the instruments it would use and the institution through which it would issue. Matsukata and his fellows did not necessarily intend to set up a new institution for central banking business. They believed that the largest national bank, Fifteen Bank, could be readily converted into an institution for their purpose. No further information is available as to how this conversion would work. Indeed, the plan was abortive. In addition they would try to transform the Yokohama Specie Bank into a department of foreign exchange business of the central bank.[24] In this respect, the central bank proposed here was rather nearer to that outlined in *A Concise Exposition of My Humble Opinions* than to that appearing six months afterwards ('the Bank of Japan' plan). Matsukata and his fellow men were still too hesitant about founding an institution independent of the then existing system.

In October 1881, a month after he put forward his *On Finance*, Masayoshi Matsukata was appointed to be Minister of Finance in the wake of the Meiji Fourteenth Year Political Change. Shigenobu Okuma lost the financial portfolio, although *pro tempore* as the statesman.[25] Matsukata emerged as the financial leader and he was to continue in command of the Japanese financial and banking policies for nearly two decades. Kato, one of Matsukata's men who had been left behind in Europe, returned to Japan. The results of his investigations into European banking systems and institutions were eagerly awaited by Matsukata. In November 1881, Kato was appointed head of the banking department and commissioned to prepare the proposals and regulations of 'the Bank of Japan'. Thus by the autumn of 1881, everything leading to the establishment of a central bank of Japan was in place.

Part III

Matsukata, the wizard of Japanese banking, 1881–1897; the Yokohama Specie Bank (1880) and the Bank of Japan (1882) (fourteenth year of Meiji to thirtieth year of Meiji)

Historical background, 1881–1897

The political upheaval of 1881 reaffirmed the dominance of the 'Satsuma–Choshu clique' which remained in power in Japan for more than thirty years. The opposition, which consisted of the popular Freedom and People's Right Movement and included ex-*samurai* dissentients and farmers suffering in the deflation, was quickly suppressed. The oligarchs drew up their political agenda, based upon the Prussian model. In 1885 the *dajokan*, the ancient governing body, was replaced by a cabinet system. In 1889 the Constitution of Imperial Japan was promulgated. In July 1890 the first general election, with a very limited suffrage, was held and the first session of the Diet was convened in November that year. Japan's foreign policy, primarily concerned with renegotiating the unequal treaties, was not particularly successful. On the Korean peninsula, confrontation was building up between China, Russia and Japan which culminated in the Sino-Japanese War of 1894–5. Fortunately for Japan, shortly before the outbreak of the war Britain, first among the western powers, agreed to the revision of one of the objectionable treaties. Throughout the period, Masayoshi Matsukata presided over the monetary and banking problems of Japan. As a result of the Japanese success in the Sino-Japanese War, a huge indemnity was paid by the defeated Chinese. This gave Matsukata the opportunity to achieve a long-cherished dream for Japan to adopt the gold standard.

9 The Bank of Japan, or *Nichigin*, 1881–1897

The chronic specie shortage, 1881–1885

On his appointment as Finance Minister, in October 1881, Masayoshi Matsukata addressed his staff as follows:

The most urgent financial measure to be taken is to relieve the country of the evils of an inconvertible currency . . . I have a new series of policies which will undoubtedly bring results. It is proposed to carry out these ideas regardless of public opposition.[1]

Although the unrestrained issue of inconvertible notes, from both government and national banks, had stopped shortly before Matsukata's appointment, the total amount in circulation was still ¥153.3 million, which was 93 per cent of the amount in 1878, the worst year during the Meiji inflation. Matsukata's idea was simply 'to try hard to redeem as much as possible of the excess of notes on the one hand and to accumulate as much specie as possible which would be applied for the reserve of conversion on the other hand'.[2] In spite of his confidence the amount of specie was at that time standing as low as ¥8.7 million, only 5 per cent of the total inconvertible note circulation and 16 per cent of the reserve fund specially set up for the redemption of government notes.[3] It was, therefore, understandable that Sir Henry Parkes, British minister, should express serious doubts.[4] Nevertheless, Matsukata persisted.

The first job was not difficult. Matsukata immediately on his appointment decided to abolish the government notes in reserve, which were available for temporary expenditures to take account of any time lag between tax collection and its distribution among the ministries. Matsukata totally prohibited these casual expenditures. Thus the notes in reserve, though only 9 per cent of the total, disappeared by January 1883.[5] This was, however, only the beginning of a series of daring measures.

In order to redeem the remaining inconvertible notes, a huge sum, Matsukata decided that he would prepare a balanced budget. He declared that there would be no increase in government expenditure for three years from April 1884 and furthermore that new taxes would be introduced.

58

Indeed, between 1882 and 1885, taxes on medicines, stamps, brokerages on the rice and stock exchanges, soya sauce and confectioneries were introduced and those on sake and tobacco were increased. However, if you look at figures on both revenues and expenditures during the decade between 1876 and 1885, it can be seen that the balanced budget did not originate with Matsukata.

The most important indication of a balanced budget is a surplus of revenues over expenditures. Unexpectedly the balance of total budgets, that is aggregates of the central and local governments' budgets between 1881 and 1885, showed a deficit of more than ¥8 million as against a surplus of more than ¥10 million during the five years prior to 1880. Taking the figures of 1881 as 100, thereafter the trend of revenues and expenditures did indicate that the post-Matsukata budgets were remarkably deflationary. Furthermore, the price index (1873/77 = 100) fell from 100 to 93 and further to 90 between 1879 and 1881. The hyperinflation had clearly peaked before Matsukata's appointment. Therefore, the deflationary tendency had already been gaining ground even before Matsukata's arrival. Matsukata, whose slogan was 'stringency of the budget', won a war, the issue of which was never in doubt. The only significant change which can be credited to Matsukata was that local budgets started to exhibit constant deficits from 1881, though on a scale of ¥1 to 3 million.[6] Matsukata in effect squeezed the provinces in response to central government demands, which were especially high because of the military expenses on the Korean peninsula.[7]

Probably a more remarkable aspect of Matsukata's policies was *Kangyoharaisage*, or privatisation of firms previously government-owned, which helped decrease deficits of the government budgets on the one hand and was instrumental in consolidating a basis for developing modern industries in the private sectors on the other hand.[8] However, a more important and perhaps essential part of the Matsukata financial policies lay in the fact that they were for the first time able to make it clear what should be done to extinguish inflation.

Matsukata had earlier – in the late 1870s – realised the importance of financing the exports of Japanese goods by Japanese merchants as a direct means of acquiring and accumulating specie essential for the issuing of convertible notes which would substitute the inconvertible government and national bank notes. After the further elaboration of *jikiyushitsu*, the financing of direct exports by the Japanese, Matsukata came to the conclusion that 'in order successfully to effect the augmentation of the specie reserve which was to be applied to redeeming paper money, the most appropriate method would be to absorb specie from abroad by properly engaging in transactions connected with the foreign bills of exchange; and this might be done by making certain necessary revisions in the then existing system'.[9] He then submitted a memorandum, as follows:

Now in operating the plan abroad, there are more methods than one, but they may be summarised as follows: first, to make advances in the form of discounting the foreign bills of exchange on the security of goods exported, and second, in the form of making an indirect accommodation of money on the direct transportation abroad. As for the direct transportation, however, there is hardly at this moment a vessel of our merchant fleet engaged in direct trade with foreign countries (excepting ports in southern China, in Korea and with Vladivostock), so that the scheme is to be set aside for the present as impracticable. The only method available for an immediate purpose would be to carry into successful operation the first scheme, and thereby absorb the specie from abroad.[10]

This statement confirms the *raison d'être* of the Yokohama Specie Bank and indicates the acceptance of the continuance of the Bank as an independent institution, although the Specie Bank was to be placed under the stricter control of the Finance Ministry.

In February 1882, the Finance Ministry announced the *Rules for Transacting Foreign Exchange*, Article I explicitly relating to the Yokohama Specie Bank:

With the object of drawing in specie to the Government Treasury, the Foreign Exchange Fund shall be deposited with the Specie Bank and the said Bank shall transact foreign exchange in accordance with the following Rules.[11]

For this national aim, ¥4 million was to be placed in the hands of the Specie Bank. Also for this purpose, the last article, Article XII, underlined the role of the Finance Ministry:

In order to carry out the transactions set forth in the preceding Articles, the Specie Bank shall appoint special officers to have charge of the work; . . . shall keep the Finance Department, and the consuls in foreign countries, acquainted with the names and copies of the seals of the chief manager and of officers sent abroad, as well as of other higher officers in charge of the business connected with the foreign exchange.[12]

In between these two articles, practical instructions were inserted. First, bill of exchange transactions were most crucial to the business. The applicants who would produce the bills for discounting would be required to be reported to the Finance Ministry. Every bill of exchange should have entered on its surface the yen value as well as the rate of discount, from which the officers of the Finance Ministry could instantly know which transactions were going on and at what price. The rate of discount was of course a matter for the Finance Ministry. The amount of advances in the form of discounting was set in the rules not to exceed 80 per cent of the price of goods. When the bills of exchange were to be forwarded, it had to be witnessed by the Finance Ministry officer, whose seal of examination would be required to be stamped in the 'dispatch book'. The goods for trade were also subject to close examination because the Specie Bank had earlier suffered great losses on account of the inferior qualities of the goods handled.[13]

Industrial promotion policies and the selling of government-owned firms, both strongly supported by the ministry of agriculture and commerce (itself set up in April 1881), were accelerated under Matsukata and for the first time in Meiji history Japan had favourable, if modest, trade balances in the years of 1882, 1883, 1885 and 1886. Even more gratifying, for the first time since the Meiji Restoration there was a net inflow of specie.[14] Thus, from 1881 to 1885, the amount of specie in the hands of the government increased dramatically from ¥8.7 million to ¥42.3 million, which was 87 per cent of the reserve fund and 37 per cent of the total note circulation. The trade balance surplus and its resultant accumulation of specie had a remarkable effect upon the discrepancy between the two values of paper currency and silver specie, which became almost negligible towards the end of 1885 and entirely disappeared in 1886, though the note depreciation against gold specie still remained at around 25 per cent even after 1885.[15] The Yokohama Specie Bank was thus the crucial institution in establishing the Japanese system on a solid foundation. Indeed, the silver-convertible banknotes in which the financial authorities had for a long time put their faith were, for the first time in Japanese history, a reality. Now that the government safe deposits were bulging with silver specie, the spotlight turned again on the central bank.

The Bank of Japan and the issue of silver-convertible notes, 1882–1890

While the direct export financing method of the Yokohama Specie Bank was being reinforced, Matsukata began to prepare for the establishment of a central bank. Under the leadership of Wataru Kato, a task force of three – Kato himself, Shigetoshi Yoshihara and Tetsunosuke Tomita (both high officials of the Finance Ministry) – was organised to prepare a prospectus for a 'Bank of Japan'. These men were the ablest of Matsukata's assistants.[16] The prospectus, produced in the form of the memorandum of Finance Minister Matsukata, was presented to the government on 1 March 1882.

Viewing the financial situation of Japan, the memorandum first pointed out that 'in every direction what we chiefly suffer from is the lack of necessary capital',[17] and, therefore, that the 'financial distress of the country, it would seem, can never be greater than it is today'.[18] The memorandum further emphasised that the difficulties arose because of the differences between the values of specie and paper currency. It was, the report continued, 'almost impossible to use the specie in ordinary transactions'.[19] The disappearance of specie, or, put another way, the depreciation of the paper currency, was causing a general deterioration of the economy as a whole. This was because the financial authorities had failed to respond to the emergency, in effect out of ignorance of 'the imperfections of the [banking] system itself'.[20]

'Imperfection' was present because the national banks were too small in size, were undercapitalised, and only served the needs of small areas. Many of the national banks were largely, at least at the outset, confined to ex-*samurai* and their ex-lords centred often on the former domain's castle town. There was little or no interbank relationship, so much so that 'a flourishing bank in the south-west and another strong bank in the north-east are so far separated in sympathy, that they never think of assisting one another'.[21] Interest rates also varied from place to place. Sometimes interest rates were extraordinarily high, undoubtedly due to the fact that there was no money flow from surplus to deficit regions. The memorandum concluded:

While political feudalism with its particularism and separatism, with its several hundred semi-independent jurisdictions, has been happily overthrown, in financial matters we seem to be now living under a system of bank feudalism.[22]

Matsukata's solution to this problem was 'the establishment of a Central Bank',[23] which would occupy a dominating position controlling the other banks, national, private or whatsoever, and would so bring them together that they could correspond with each other and eventually form sound interbank relationships. Matsukata and his disciples were convinced of the crucial role of the central bank to the financial system of a country, comparing it to the role of the heart in the system of blood circulation in a human body.[24]

The memorandum, before proceeding to propose the regulations of a central bank to be designated 'the Bank of Japan', summarised the roles of the Bank as follows:

The five reasons for the establishment of a Central Bank as stated above are: 1st, to facilitate the circulation of currency; 2nd, to offer assistance to other banks and private companies; 3rd, to lower the rate of interest; 4th, to assume a part of the services in the Exchequer; 5th, to discount foreign bills of exchange.[25]

The memorandum was approved by the government. In June 1882 the government authorised the Regulations of the Bank of Japan which comprised twenty-five articles. There were three notable features. In the first place, they were almost entirely developed on the model of the National Bank of Belgium. The official history, *Nihonginkohyakunenshi*, or *Hundred*

Year History of the Bank of Japan, reveals how rigidly word-by-word or article-by-article the promoters of the Bank of Japan imitated their Belgian predecessor. This was exactly what Wataru Kato, the head of the banking department, learnt while he was in Europe during the late 1870s. In the second place, the Bank of Japan was placed firmly under the control of the Finance Ministry, as stipulated in Articles XVIII, XIX, XXI, XXIII and XXIV, the last of which put forward as follows:

Art. XXIV. The government shall oversee the business management of the Bank, and may not only stop activities which are contrary to the Regulations or By-laws, but also those which in the opinion of the government are contrary to the interest of the state.[26]

This was of course also the case with the National Bank of Belgium.[27]

Finally, although the Regulations were on the Belgian model, they did not follow the latter in one of the most crucial points, that is to say, Article XIV in the Bank of Japan case (the equivalent of Article XII in the Belgian case). The Bank of Japan stipulated in the article that:

The Bank of Japan reserves the right of convertible note issue, though a separate regulation will be promulgated when it is sanctioned to carry out the issue.[28]

The Bank of Belgium was chosen as a model because it was recently established and its rules and regulations reflected banking conditions as they were in the mid-nineteenth century. The Bank of England's regulations founded in 1694 could not be relevant to Japan in 1882. In any case the British kept state interference to a minimum, and their ideas and institutions were too liberal for the Japanese.

In the mean time between the promulgation of the Regulations of the Bank of Japan and the spring of 1884, the specie reserves in the hands of the government increased greatly thanks to the success of the Yokohama Specie Bank in financing direct Japanese exports. Matsukata and the Ministry of Finance could see in the spring of 1884 that depreciation of paper currency, an evil of the Japanese financial world, would be eliminated by the end of 1885. In May 1884, the government issued the Convertible Bank Note Regulations (based on the Bank regulation Article XIV). A year afterwards, in May and June 1885, the Bank of Japan issued the first silver-convertible banknotes for ¥3.8 million – a long-awaited experiment. The sum was a little more than 2 per cent of the total circulation at the end of 1884. The issue was successful as will be seen shortly and marked the real start of the Japanese banking system, of which the Bank of Japan, with the Yokohama Specie Bank as a reliable aide, was in complete control. Perhaps from this successful start of convertible notes, the Bank of Japan was to be called *Nichigin*, the nickname of *Nihon Ginko*, or the Bank of Japan.

Central Banking, 1885–1897

Matsukata believed the key to this success was as follows:

The very essence of the banknote exists in its character of convertibility, it is therefore exactly similar to the promissory note. Nevertheless, when you apply government notes to the conversion reserves for the banknotes, this means that you exchange the convertible with the inconvertible and then the notes will inevitably carry the character of so-called 'forced currency'. The essence of the banknote thus will be lost.[29]

This understanding of the nature of the central banknote was undoubtedly a decisive point separating Matsukata from his predecessor Okuma and certainly brought Matsukata's policy to great success. With the Bank of Japan set to work, the burden of redeeming the inconvertible paper currency, both the governmental and national, became its prime concern. Already in 1883, the Finance Ministry had amended the National Bank Decree depriving the national banks of the right of issue. They were required to transform themselves into private institutions at the expiration of their business terms. This amendment required the national banks to open accounts in the Bank of Japan through which they would have to exchange their own inconvertible notes for silver-convertible Bank of Japan counterparts. Simultaneously the Bank of Japan was officially commissioned by the government to purchase specie on the government's behalf by all means. These arrangements started to work following the successful launch of the Bank of Japan convertible notes. The banking laws of 1883 certainly echo in Japan the legislation in Britain in 1844–5 when the role of the Bank of England as the bank of banks was more closely defined. British banks established thereafter had no right of issue, neither did those in Japan.

From 1885 to 1888, the total amount of notes in circulation increased from ¥153 million to ¥172 million. The increase was due entirely to Bank of Japan convertible notes. Of the ¥172 million, the convertible banknotes were ¥63 million, 37 per cent of the total and further in 1889 reached ¥74 million, 42 per cent of the total. The remarkable success of Bank of Japan convertible notes in only their first four years was dependent on the achievement in accumulating specie. The aggregate sum in the government vault increased between 1885 and 1888 by 120 per cent reaching ¥56 million, of which ¥47 million, 84 per cent, was placed in the hands of the Bank of Japan. The specie reserve of the Bank was further augmented to ¥60 million, 86 per cent of the total.[30] As the bank of issue, the Bank of Japan was firmly establishing itself in the emerging Japanese banking system. This encouraged the financial authorities, who then, as early as 1888, amended the Convertible Bank Note Regulations and enabled the Bank to issue beyond the limit set in the Regulations, up to ¥70 million.[31] This was the start of the authorised excessive issue in which the currency authorities, the Finance Ministry and the Bank of Japan, were to be given a wider deliberation upon money supply to the economy.

Various sorts of financial services for the government were until 1883 done in direct contact between the government and the big private banks, such as Mitsui and Yasuda, and the national banks. This governmental business was profitable as it gave the banks additional monetary resources which some of them desperately needed. The establishment of the Bank of Japan changed the situation considerably. In 1887 a government account office was set up, aiming to transform itself into a more comprehensive treasury system in 1890. The start of the treasury system automatically made the governor of the Bank of Japan *ex officio* the chief cashier of the treasury; thereafter all banks became subordinate to the Bank of Japan in handling government money.

Another important business of the Bank for the government was the issuing of national debts. In December 1883, the government first commissioned the Bank to conduct the business of paying interests and redemption of debentures of a railway company. The national debt business soon became an indispensable part of central banking. By November 1888, the Bank of Japan monopolised the national debt business, which during the nineteenth century culminated in the issuing of military bonds in the Sino-Japanese War of 1894–5. War financing gave birth to another important operation for the Bank, allowing the government to borrow in order to fill temporary deficits.[32] The act, promulgated in 1894, obliged the Bank to supply the government with funds on a short-term basis which would enable the latter to manage itself until it received proceeds of newly issued national debts.

An unexpectedly smooth start of the convertible bank notes, together with new government business, certainly contributed to the development of other elements of central banking. During the first half-yearly business period until June 1883, the Bank opened correspondence with twenty-six offices of ten banks, all of which were big banks such as Mitsui, Yasuda and First National Banks. By 1885, when the convertible banknotes were making their first appearances, the number of correspondent bank offices increased to 147. The Japanese system, headed by the Bank of Japan, was beginning to emerge.

The progress of the status of the bank of banks was also clearly shown in the balance sheets. On the assets side, in December 1887 for the first time since its establishment, ordinary advances, such as loans on securities, discounts and overdrafts, overtook the amount of the paper currency redemption account. It was evidence that the worst stage was almost over for the Bank of Japan as well as for the Japanese financial situation as a whole. On the liabilities side, by 1889 the most remarkable items in terms of volume and significance were government deposits and paper money redemption accounts. Both accounts were overtaken by ordinary deposits only in 1890 and 1897 respectively. As far as the liabilities were concerned, the Bank of Japan was seriously engaged in the redemption operation of paper currency until the end of the century.[33] Although there was apparently some awkwardness in certain aspects of their business, the Bank seemed to have made a good start. However, any type of central banking could not be perfect if it failed to act as 'the lender of the last resort', as banking authorities have always taught.[34] The test of this came as early as in the spring of 1890.

The Tokyo Stock Exchange, founded in 1878, had been playing only a very marginal role in the Japanese financial system before the mid-1880s,[35] but became active as Matsukata's deflationary policies successfully brought about promotion of joint-stock companies. Between 1885 and 1890, the number of companies, both joint-stock and partnerships, increased more than three times, reaching 4,300. Of the total, only 1 per cent of the companies were listed on the stock exchange, but they were all first rate big companies playing major roles in the new industrialisation. Before the enforcement in 1899 of the commercial law drafted in 1890, there were neither laws nor decrees which regulated commercial and industrial establishments and their conduct. Even the companies listed on the Tokyo Stock Exchange had total freedom in their conduct of management.

Investigations carried out by the Finance Ministry disclosed that 73 per cent of the total capital stock of companies licensed to be listed on the stock exchange was paid in. More astonishing was the fact that companies set up between 1888 and 1890, regardless of whether they were listed or unlisted on the stock exchange, had only paid in their capital up to 29 per cent. Furthermore they had borrowed huge sums from banks on the securities of their less than one-third paid in shares.[36] The bad harvest of the autumn of 1889 brought large pecuniary demands as rice had to be imported. Bankers attempted to lessen their commitments and the whole Japanese financial system was plunged into unprecedented crisis. There was no choice for banks but to resort to the Bank of Japan for their relief.

The complaints were first heard from the Tokyo and Osaka Bank Associations and were soon echoed by bankers just about everywhere who were heavily dependent upon banks in the two financial centres. The governor of the Bank of Japan responded quickly to the demands, recommending that the Minister of Finance, Matsukata, adopt 'discounting bills covered by specified brands of stocks and shares'. The governor stressed that:

Although we are not responsible theoretically at all for difficulties caused by the stock market as it happened, we feel it our duty to cure troubles resulting from the commerce in general.[37]

Lending on company shares was prohibited by Article XXII of the Bank of Japan by-laws. The Finance Ministry and Bank of Japan had recourse to adding the term 'discounting' in front of stocks and shares in order to avoid the offence. The willingness of the Bank to take emergency action in this way was clear evidence that they would behave as 'the lender of the last resort' in time of emergency. The Bank of Japan was thus qualified fully and finally as the modern central bank.

As the specified shares and stocks the Bank of Japan qualified, besides government bonds, fifteen brands including those of Yokohama Specie Bank, Nihon Yusen (NYK), Tokyo Marine Insurance, and another shipping and eleven railway companies.[38] These 'last resort' facilities, or the special discounting, soon became the most favoured method of advancing for the Bank. The special discounting amounted to nearly half of total discounts by the Bank from 1890 to 1899.[39] The facilities of course not only helped big banks holding first grade shares and business ties with those first rate industrial firms, but also through their relationships with subordinate banks and companies the Bank of Japan could play the role of ultimate lender in time of stringency and could extend its support to securities markets, which would then inevitably come to rely heavily upon the Bank in the new century.

From 1890 to 1897, the Bank of Japan grew remarkably, bringing the total liabilities/assets from ¥152.3 million to ¥360 million. Advances and deposits increased 2.3 and 4.8 times respectively. Of the deposits 95 per cent, ¥72.5 million in 1897, was governmental, chiefly the proceeds of taxes and national debts. Also remarkable was a decrease in the amount of the redemption account which declined from ¥15 million in 1890 to ¥3 million in 1897. The paper currency redemption operation eventually came almost to an end. The Bank of Japan convertible notes made further progress, increasing from ¥103 million in 1890 to ¥226 million in 1897, which constituted more than three-quarters of the total currency.[40] The Bank of Japan also grew spatially. In 1890, the Bank had only one branch, in Osaka, but by 1897 branches were located in Saibu (Shimoneseki), Hakodate (Hokkaido) and Nagoya, with sub-branches in Sapporo, Otaru (Hokkaido), Kyoto and Taipei, although the last was later withdrawn. The number of correspondents, which had decreased from 147 in 1885 to 111 in 1890, again increased to 213 covering all Japan.[41]

As the monetary system in Japan grew, so did the status of the Bank of Japan as the central bank. In May 1897, the Bank drew up a proposal composed of six articles, including the expansion of branch banking, abolition of the special discounting, the start of direct dealing with ordinary customers, other than banks, and the expansion of foreign business other than that with the Yokohama Specie Bank. The proposal, intended to strengthen the status and working of the Bank, was considered by the Minister of Finance. But the suggestions were mostly dismissed by the Minister, who might have thought they were too unreal. The only outcome was the adoption of direct dealing with the industrial and commercial customers, which was, though, only very short-lived.[42] The proposal certainly resulted from enthusiasm of the central bank staff but was not realistic. The shortcomings were represented by their proposal on the Yokohama Specie Bank, which, by that time, had become a formidable institution deeply rooted in the system.

10 The Yokohama Specie Bank, or *Shokin*, 1882–1897

Its unique role, 1882–1889

Matsukata's deflationary policies were a double-edged sword: effective in curing the depreciations of paper currency and also instrumental in launching the Bank of Japan silver-convertible notes in 1885. On the other hand, they caused severe depression in some sectors of the economy.[1] The consumer price index fell sharply from 41.8 (1934/36 = 100) in 1881 to 32.3 in 1884. The business of the Yokohama Specie Bank was threatened as the export trades, particularly silk, fell away. The Specie Bank incurred the unacceptable loss of ¥1.07 million, which led to a confrontation between the Bank and the Finance Ministry. The consequences of the political coup of 1881 eventually required the Specie Bank to accept, in early 1883, sweeping changes in its management. The government's intervention, enshrined in Article 49 of the Bank's regulations, ensured the dismissal of the founder-president of the Bank, Michita Nakamura, in June 1882. In March 1883, Matsukata's close friend, Rokuro Hara, the former president of the 100th National Bank, was brought in as the succeeding president of the Specie Bank. Thus the Bank, originally Okuma's brainchild, was effectively brought under the firm control of the Finance Ministry, or Masayoshi Matsukata.

Matsukata's assumption of overall control of the Finance Ministry, including the Specie Bank, underlined his determination to promote his banking plans. He aimed especially at redeeming the paper currency and in this, thanks to his sophisticated programme and favourable economic conditions, he was tremendously successful. In this way he built up his un-rivalled status and reputation as the foremost financial authority in Japan and this made it easier for him to intervene in conflicts between the management of the Bank of Japan and the Specie Bank. The Bank of Japan objected strongly to the privileges of the Specie Bank in handling foreign business. Naturally the Specie Bank was eager to protect its special overseas business. Towards the end of the 1880s Matsukata had no choice but to intervene.

In 1887, Matsukata and the Finance Ministry passed a decree entitling the Yokohama Specie Bank to a special status, and making it second only to the Bank of Japan. However, although it continued as a separate institution, the Specie Bank had to surrender several vital elements of its independence. The Decree explicitly stipulated that the Minister of Finance would appoint, if necessary, the deputy governor of the Bank of Japan who would serve concurrently as president of the Yokohama Specie Bank.[2] The Yokohama Specie Bank remained an independent institution, but it was subject to and inseparable from the Bank of Japan. The tight interlinkage was, it was believed, indispensable whenever national issues emerged.[3]

Before 1885, the financing of direct exports by the Specie Bank was dependent upon government notes specially earmarked for this purpose. But after 1885, with the successful note issue of the Bank of Japan, it was the Bank of Japan which supplied the funds. The Bank of Japan unwillingly agreed to give funds to the Specie Bank in 1885 provided that the arrangement would be reviewed in 1889. This reluctance reflected the Bank of Japan's determination to wrest the foreign trade financing business from the Specie Bank. The conflict led, through the intervention of Matsukata, to the dismissal of the governor of the Bank of Japan, Tetsunosuke Tomita. At the end of this struggle the Bank of Japan agreed to give special discounting facilities of up to ¥10 million at 2 per cent interest rate to the Yokohama Specie Bank. By 1889, once harmony between the two banks had been achieved, the basis was laid for the Japanese banking system as a whole.

The expansion of overseas business, 1889–1897

Between 1889 and 1897, the Yokohama Specie Bank enlarged its commitment in terms of total liabilities/assets threefold from ¥32 million to ¥96 million.[4] This expansion resulted from business directed by the headquarters in Yokohama and enthusiastically undertaken in offices in Kobe (1880), New York (1880), London (1881), Lyons (1882) and San Francisco (1886). By 1897 there were also offices in Hawaii (1892), Shanghai (1893), Bombay (1894) and Hong Kong (1896). The overseas offices, originally based in consular offices, were by this time in separate independent premises. Setting up eight agents' offices overseas was certainly expensive, and this kind of expenditure could only be undertaken by the Specie Bank with full government support. Among the eight overseas agents' offices, the London office was promoted to branch status as early as 1884 following the closure of the Oriental Bank,[5] which had previously acted there as the Japanese government's agent. This London branch of the Specie Bank would become an outstandingly important overseas office right up to the outbreak of the Second World War.

Before 1889 the government itself bore the risks which arose from foreign exchange transactions but after being granted special discounting facilities at the Bank of Japan the Specie Bank became responsible for its own risks. They became skilled at hedging in foreign exchange markets. First, in 1889, the Specie Bank transferred ¥0.5 million, that is approximately £85,000, to the London branch to form an exchange stabilising fund there. This move coincided with a major economic crisis in 1889/90, which forced the Bank of Japan to adopt a special discounting measure as stated above. The Specie Bank strengthened its London position by adding £0.6 million to the exchange fund. Though the crisis had passed by the middle of 1890, another disaster loomed that autumn when the United States moved on to a free coinage of silver. Silver prices fluctuated violently for a couple of months. The Specie Bank incurred a heavy loss of ¥1.5 million, mainly due to its large portfolio of bills payable in gold. The underlying and fundamental weakness lay in the fact that the Japanese monetary system was still founded effectively on dual metals, silver and gold. Unfortunately for the Specie Bank, another loss of ¥0.5 million, caused by a failure of one of its customers, occurred in May 1891. These misfortunes impelled the Bank to instigate a thorough review of its business conduct.

In June 1891, the Specie Bank reorganised its foreign exchange business, which had hitherto remained the same since the outset of the financing system of direct exports reinforced in 1882. The Bank reported:

Reviews of foreign trades of the country reveal that Japan exports goods to the United States and France and imports products from Britain. The agents' offices in the United States and France are, therefore, requested to be engaged exclusively in collecting payments of export bills and forwarding them to London. Using them as resources, the London branch should draw import bills on Japan thus covering exchange risks.[6]

Following this observation, the Specie Bank divided the branch network into two groups. The first group, headed by the London branch, was composed of offices in gold-standard areas, and the second, led by the head office, consisted of those in silver-standard areas. Thus all offices were requested to direct their exchange business in consultation with the London branch and Yokohama head office. Although this division was rendered meaningless once Japan had abandoned the silver standard in 1897, the status of the London office remained unaffected. The business of the Specie Bank in London will be discussed later.

It was also in this formative period that some curiously termed accounts began to make regular appearances in the Specie Bank balance sheets. The most noteworthy were 'selling exchange' on the liabilities side, and 'buying exchange' on the assets side. Selling exchange was the sale of foreign bills of exchange, which meant that the Bank was supplying payment instruments to importers. Proceeds of selling exchange joined deposits and other items on the liabilities side to enhance the Bank's lending abilities. Buying exchange was the purchase, or discounting, of foreign bills of exchange, which meant that the Bank was supplying advances to exporters. These devices were a further development of the authorised foreign exchange business. Interest rate, or discounting rate, charged on buying exchange was higher than on inland bills, as the former involved exchange risks. Another strangely termed account on the assets side was 'interest bills'. The bills were so termed as the rate of interest charged on them was stamped on their surface. They did not involve foreign exchange risks as they were payable in yen.

Last but not least, 'rediscounting', although not curious, should be mentioned. As arranged with the Bank of Japan in 1889, the Specie Bank was entitled to enjoy rediscounting of foreign bills of exchange up to ¥10 million at 2 per cent. From 1896, the actual figures in this account exceeded the sum negotiated with the Bank of Japan. Indeed, the Specie Bank found another important source for bank money. In 1897, Parr's Bank, in which Shand was serving, the Union Bank of London and London Joint Stock Bank agreed to accept foreign bills of exchange on behalf of the Specie Bank, which were then able to be offered on the London discount market for rediscounting. Limits of their acceptance were said to be between £0.1 and £0.2 million, though the exact sums are unknown.[7] This connection with the London money market would later become an indispensable source of money not only for the Specie Bank but also for the Japanese monetary base as a whole.

The innovation of foreign trade financing techniques certainly encouraged the Specie Bank to compete with foreign, chiefly British, overseas banks. The increasing competitiveness of the Bank was invaluable to the Japanese economy as a whole, because it was so dependent upon foreign trade. At the beginning of 1896, the Specie Bank decided to offer advances at one-sixteenth lower rate than those imposed by several British overseas banks such as the Hongkong and Shanghai Banking Corporation and the Mercantile Bank of India. The Specie Bank also promised to allow would-be customers to overdraw their accounts up to ¥0.2 million, which the British banks were already doing. In this way the Specie Bank deprived its British rivals of their important customers, such as Nihon Yusen Kaisha (NYK), the biggest and monopolistic shipping company in Japan, Mitsubishi Corporation, one of the biggest trading companies, and even the Standard Oil Co.[8] However, the most formidable competitors were, and would continue to be, foreign, particularly British overseas banks. Only from 1916 did several big Japanese commercial, or ordinary, banks embark upon foreign business. Until after the First World War the Specie Bank was said to be the bank of banks in terms of foreign trade financing and doing business with first rate western industrial companies.[9]

The Specie Bank grew remarkably as the threefold increase of total liabilities/assets implies, surviving the crises and innovating methods of financing foreign trades. On the liabilities side, deposits undoubtedly led the jump in growth from ¥7.1 million to ¥36 million. Selling exchange and rediscounting made substantial progress, growing from ¥3.8 million to ¥12.3 million and from ¥7.8million to ¥20 million respectively. This type of growth was an important factor in strengthening the lending resources of the Bank. On the assets side, the growth was stimulated by buying exchange. The sum increased from ¥14 million to ¥54 million, reaching more than half of the total assets, though advances and discounting also increased considerably. The innovation of financial instruments to encourage foreign trade prepared the Specie Bank for a further expansion under the newly adopted gold standard in the new century. The adoption of the gold standard itself was a result of the Specie Bank's successful business in accumulating and remitting the specie which would enable Japan to base herself upon that standard.

11 Consolidation and expansion, 1883–1897

The liquidation of the national banks and the development of ordinary banking, 1883–1896

The revisions of the National Bank Decree in 1876 had fundamentally changed the *raison d'être* of national banks, but the battle against hyper-inflation, by redeeming government paper money, was already lost. Therefore the revised Decree merely exacerbated the problem because the notes of the national banks were additional to other governmental notes and inflation was further aggravated. In contrast, the successful launch of the Bank of Japan, under the leadership of Matsukata, had convinced the financial authorities that convertible banknotes would come to dominate the circulation. These factors combined to persuade the Finance Ministry to make fundamental changes in the way in which the national banks operated.

The first step was to revise once again the National Bank Decree in 1883 so that the national banks would be able to adapt themselves to the new circumstances. To Article 12 in the National Bank Decree, which stipulated the need to renew the licence after twenty years, a clause was added, saying:

The bank's licence will only be renewed if the bank gives up the privilege of note issue. The bank will then continue as a private bank.[1]

This important change required a national banknote redemption procedure, which, as already discussed, was to be conducted through the Bank of Japan accounts specially opened for this purpose. The Finance Ministry simultaneously took this opportunity of reinforcing their powers in order to keep a watchful eye on the management and business of the national banks as they were transformed.

The next step the Finance Ministry had to take was to draft a bank decree which would regulate the banks other than the Bank of Japan and the Yokohama Specie Bank. While the drafting preparations took time, the redemption of national banknotes progressed. From 1883 to 1890 when the

Bank Decree was promulgated, the amount of national banknotes decreased from ¥34.2 million to ¥25.8 million, the latter of which was 13 per cent of the total currency circulation. The enforcement of the Decree was postponed until 1893, on account of the delay in passing the commercial law in the new Diet, which had come into existence in 1890 following the imperial constitution of 1889. The real challenge for the national banks came between 1893 and 1896 after the First National Bank of Tokyo was reorganised as First Bank, or Daiichi Bank, a private, or ordinary bank. By the mid-1890s the proportion of national banknotes in the total circulation, including coins, was only 6 per cent; 72 per cent of the issue was then in Bank of Japan notes. Between 1896 and 1899, the original national banks disappeared. Of the 153 national banks, 122 were reorganised as ordinary banks, 16 were absorbed by other banks, 9 were voluntarily liquidated and 6 were wound up by the government.

The disappearance of the national banks as such marked the beginning of a new era for Japanese banking. In 1883, of the total national bank capital, 65 per cent was owned by ex-court nobility and feudal lords and ex-*samurai* and the rest by the common people, mainly merchants. By 1892 the former's shares had diminished by 10 per cent, but the latter had increased to 45 per cent.[2] Around 90 per cent of the shareholdings of the Fifteen Bank, representing ¥17.8 million capital, was held by ex-court nobility, former feudal lords and ex-*samurai* during these ten years. Between 1883 and 1892, the aggregate sum of national bank capital increased by ¥4.3 million, 10 per cent of the total in 1883. The increase in capital was therefore brought about by merchants and 'miscellaneous', who had to be so termed as 'it was too difficult to classify them among farmers, manufacturers and merchants'.[3] Those classified as 'miscellaneous' were often engaged concurrently in two or more jobs, such as merchant and farmer, or merchant and manufacturer. Although the national bank mania accelerated from 1876 by capitalisation of money stipend bonds given to the ex-ruling classes, it was the merchants who took the real initiative in developing their businesses. It is therefore also safe to conclude that *ryogae* business and tradition remained powerful in Japanese banking even though the national banks as a group were short-lived and not fully successful.[4]

Private banks and quasi-banking companies, which claimed direct descent from the *ryogae*, were more successful than the national banks. Private banks made tremendous progress between 1883 and 1896, when their number increased from 207 to 1,005, including some half dozen of the converted national banks. In the same period the aggregate sum of their capital increased from ¥20.5 million to ¥89 million, which accounted for nearly two-thirds of the total Japanese banking capital. Between 1883 and 1892 quasi-banks increased from 572 to 680 in number and from ¥12 million to ¥14 million in capital stock, but were later absorbed into ordinary banking. The Finance Ministry had tried twice, in the mid-1870s, to curb this rather wild bank promotion by making regulations to control banks other than the national banks.[5] It was against this background of company mania in the later 1880s, exemplified by the private and quasi-bank promotion, that the financial authorities embarked on preparations for a bank decree together with new regulations on commercial law.

In sharp contrast to the earlier examples of the lengthy decrees for the National Bank, Bank of Japan and Yokohama Specie Bank, the Bank Decree of 1890 was composed of eleven articles only, the first of which defined the ordinary bank simply:

Those who, in their offices open to the public, conduct businesses of the discounts of securities, or the transactions of exchanges, or the acceptances of deposits, or advances, are the banks whatever they may designate themselves.[6]

The contents of the Decree were thus simplified, but there were two notable characteristics. First, it did not set any minimum limit to the amount of capital stock. Why this was so is not clear, but it might be due to the belief that the guidance given when permission was granted to projected banks would be sufficient. Second, it did limit the amount of advances, relating these to the level of capital. These two rules were strongly resisted by the bank associations led by the Tokyo Association. The latter stipulation was lifted in the spring of 1895 by the Finance Ministry in view of the anticipated increases in bank money demands in the post Sino-Japanese War boom. But regarding the deregulation on the amount of capital, the Finance Ministry strongly showed their confidence in their control over the banks.[7] The relaxation, as was expected, resulted in a substantial decrease of average capital which diminished from ¥99,000 in 1883 to ¥87,000 in 1896. To combat the situation, the Finance Ministry legislated the Amalgamation Act in April 1896, but their efforts were in vain. The Bank Decree of 1890, effective from 1894, thus allowed a large number of small-scale quasi-banks to remain in and join the system legally as 'genuine' banks. The continued existence of a large number of small banks thus became a grave problem which the financial authorities would have to deal with in the coming century.

The savings banks, 1883–1897

As did their British counterparts, Japanese financial authorities distinguished the term 'savings' from that of deposits. As early as 1875, the ministry of internal affairs started to accept money of 10 sen (1 yen = 100 sen) to 100 yen at its nineteen offices situated mainly in Tokyo, which money was termed as 'savings' by the ministry.[8] The business was later renamed in 1880 as *ekitei*, or stage savings, and further in 1887 as post office savings. In the mean time in 1885 the savings, collected at the post offices, were to be entrusted to the deposit department of the Ministry of Finance, constituting an important contribution to the government money.[9] The term 'savings' was also applied to small sums, entrusted to financial institutions, usually of very small scale, from the outset of the Meiji government. However small each account at the post office might be, when they came to the Finance Ministry department, their total amount was formidable. Post office savings reached more than 9 per cent of the total national bank deposits in 1883 and nearly 13 per cent of the total ordinary bank deposits in 1897.

Savings business, therefore, became a target even for those seeking to gather resources. Earlier in 1877, Yamanashi Kosan Co., a quasi-bank later registered as 10th National Bank, and 33rd National Bank started to accept savings of more than 5 sen. In 1880, Tokyo Savings Bank was set up as a first specialised institution for the business.[10] Both the 10th and 33rd National Banks conducted savings business as a sideline. Tokyo Savings Bank was followed by another eighteen specialised institutions by 1883 when the Finance Ministry, already contemplating a consolidation of national and private banks into the same category, carried out an investigation into savings businesses. The investigations revealed two astonishing facts.

In the first place, the aggregate sum of the capital of nineteen specialised savings banks was only ¥353,000 ranging from ¥72,000 to only ¥1,000. The average was far less than ¥20,000 and even well below that of quasi-banking companies which stood at ¥21,105 the same year. In the second place, it was uncovered that the savings banks were taking in deposits at from 12 to 15 per cent rate of interest and lending them out at from 20 to 25 per cent. These rates were extraordinarily high compared to 7 per cent on deposits and from 8 to 10 per cent on lending offered by national and private banks in the same year.[11] High rates on both deposits and advances meant high cost of available money resources and risky lending. The disclosure of the extraordinary business conduct of the savings banks obliged the financial authorities to prepare another decree putting them under stricter supervision.

In 1890, together with the Bank Decree for ordinary banks, the Savings Bank Decree was promulgated. The financial authorities, alarmed by what their enquiries had revealed, prepared strict regulations. Article I defined the savings bank as 'a bank to conduct deposit business on compound interest basis for the public'.[12] The deposits had to be no more than ¥5 and would be accepted either in current or term accounts. The minimum sum of capital of each savings bank was ¥30,000. Half of the capital was required to be held in national bonds which would be applied to the reserve for withdrawal of savings. Besides the national bond holding, the business area of the savings bank was strictly restricted to advances on securities and discounting of bills. Any other business was forbidden. Further, for advances, the savings bank was requested to limit the lending term to six months and take only national and municipal bonds as securities. In case of discounting it was allowed to accept the bills which carried two good names on them as under-writers, otherwise it would not be eligible for discounting. The directors had unlimited liability and were still responsible for losses for a year after resignation from the management. The Decree concluded by saying that offences against the regulations could result in fines for the directors of between ¥50 and ¥500.[13]

The extremely stern regulations deterred the setting up of the savings banks. From 1893, when the Decree became effective, to 1895, there were few additions to the existent nineteen banks. However, towards the end of the Sino-Japanese War, the situation changed and anticipated demand for bank money increased, necessitating a certain mitigation of the Savings Bank regulations as well as of the Bank Decree for ordinary banks. In March 1895, two important changes were made in the Savings Bank Decree. First, the reserve ratio against the savings was pulled down from a half to a quarter. Secondly, the restriction on their business area was entirely lifted.[14] The revisions of the Decree had remarkable results. The number of savings banks increased from 23 to 221, that is, nearly 200 banks were added to the system in four years. In the same period, the amount of capital, deposits and advances jumped up from ¥0.5 million, ¥6 million and ¥1 million to ¥6.5 million, ¥33 million and ¥22.3 million respectively. The most vigorous element was of course the growth of advances which rightly reflected the strength of bank money demands in the post Sino-Japanese War period. Nonetheless it should not be overlooked that the savings banks were still weak. The average paid-in capital increased only by ¥10,000 in the same period. Together with the continued presence of small ordinary banks, the large number of savings banks was later to pose a serious problem for Japanese banking.

Ordinary banking in transition, 1890–1897

The preparations for the consolidation of national and private banks into ordinary banks coincided with two successive economic crises in 1890, which seriously affected the money, securities and foreign exchange markets.[15] The crises alarmed some bank depositors who deserted the smaller banks and moved their money to the bigger and, they believed,

more stable institutions.[16] Indeed, some of the banks were in difficulties in
the aftermath of the crises,[17] though the transition of national to ordinary
banking was not seriously affected.

Excluding the Bank of Japan and the Yokohama Specie Bank, there were
three categories of banks in Japan during the 1890s: national, private and
savings banks. The former two were obliged to transform themselves into
ordinary banks. The savings banks, too, on account of the revisions in their
regulations, were in effect doing the same business as their ordinary counterparts although on a very much smaller scale.

The national banks started to convert themselves into ordinary banks
from September 1896 when, as we have seen, Daiichi Bank (the direct successor to the First National Bank of Tokyo) commenced business as an
ordinary bank. During the preceding years, from 1879 to 1889, government
deposits held by the national banks were 25 per cent on average, increasing
to 32 per cent in 1882 but falling thereafter. Government money continued
to diminish and accounted for 14 per cent on average of the total from 1890
to 1896; this was mainly tax revenues temporarily placed with the national
banks and there was no doubt that this financial device enabled the national
banks to improve their position as lenders, especially in the 1880s. Because
they were receiving less and less on deposit from the government this meant
that they would have to increase proportionally ordinary deposits from
other sources. This proved to be extraordinarily difficult. The amount of
deposits fell far short, even in the 1890s, of increasing demands from borrowers. This situation was reflected in the extraordinarily high figure of
advances as a percentage of deposits, which stood on average at 414 per cent
between 1890 and 1896. Shortages of money for lending, that is the gap
between advances and deposits, were supplemented by capital itself, occa-
sional interbank lending and special discounting facilities given by the
Bank of Japan on specially listed brands of securities commenced in the
aftermath of the 1890 crises.

The private and savings bank were not in so tight a situation as the
national banks as far as governmental money was concerned, partly
because these private banks, except only the biggest of them, were rarely
allowed to hold government deposits before 1896. In the years of 1896 and
1897, the governmental deposits rapidly increased on account of the conversion of the national banks into ordinary banks. Advances as a percentage of deposits of private banks were 120 per cent on average between 1890
and 1897. The figure was considerably smaller than that for the national
banks. This was due to the cautiousness of private banks as well as to their
poor lending resources. The big banks such as Mitsui and Sumitomo were
exceptional. In spite of the remarkable growth in their number, the performance of savings banks was poor as far as the core of banking business was

concerned. They were mostly very small. Advances as a percentage of deposits of savings banks were only 32 per cent on average from 1890 to 1897. They were in effect considered by the financial authorities as national bond-holding institutions, although no statistical evidence was available. The strict regulations, however, undoubtedly forced them to keep their assets chiefly in national bonds. This was necessary according to the articles of their Decree but was in any case wise.

It is almost impossible for banking historians to say with any precision to whom the banks were lending money. Nevertheless much useful research into various industries gives some idea of the sectoral lending pattern in this period.[18] In general, banking customers were divided into two classes. The first was traditional borrowers who handled rice, silk or tea. The latter two had vigorous money demands because theirs had been staple export products since the opening of ports in 1859. Producers of these commodities were scattered throughout Japan as were rice growers, although there was a special concentration of tea and silk producers in Shizuoka to the south and Nagano to the north-west of Tokyo. Both these areas supported both national and private banks. The other class of borrowers came from expanding new industries such as those involved in railways, shipping, mining and cotton spinning. Several of these strategically important company equities were eligible as securities for special lending facilities at the Bank of Japan. The main suppliers of resources to these sorts of borrowers were top-ranking national and private banks.

In addition to the reorganisation of the banking world in Japan there was an enormous increase in the number of offices. From 1890 to 1897, banking offices, including both head and branch offices, increased from around 500 to 2,491, of which 1,502 were head offices. In terms of numbers of branches per bank, the savings and ordinary, or private, banks grew between 1893 and 1897 more remarkably than the national banks between 1890 and 1896. Although in relative terms the growth of the savings banks was strongest, they were widely scattered over Japan and they were very small. It was undoubtedly the expansion of ordinary banking which led the growth. The ordinary banks' branch offices increased by 486 in only four years up to 1897. The increase far exceeded the number added as a result of the national bank conversion. Ordinary banking thus came to occupy its rightful position in the Japanese banking system by 1897.

Simultaneously with the progress of ordinary banking, a group of big banks was beginning to emerge. In 1897, banks having more than ¥1 million numbered less than fifty, but they owned 40 per cent of the total capacity of ordinary banking. At the top of the group came Mitsui, Mitsubishi,[19] Yasuda, Sumitomo and Daiichi Banks. Although their aggregate capital was little more than 6 per cent of the total of ordinary banking, the aggregate of their deposits and advances commanded 26 per cent and 14 per cent of the totals respectively.[20] The 'Big Five', dominant in the first quarter of the new century, were already significant as early as the last decade of the nineteenth century.

12 The adoption of the gold standard, 1893–1897

Two incidents in the early 1890s, which were apparently unrelated, exerted pressure on Japan to adopt the gold standard. In the autumn of 1893, India, the largest silver standard country in the world, abandoned silver and made gold her standard metal. The Indian preference for gold was in response to the world trend. Germany was able to adopt the gold standard in 1871 following the gold indemnity obtained from France after the Franco-German War. The bimetallic Latin Monetary Union, composed of France, Italy, Belgium, Switzerland and Greece, fell apart in 1878. These two incidents were probably exactly what Masayoshi Matsukata anticipated when he was in France listening to French Finance Minister Say. Silver, as a financial standard, was judged increasingly risky because its declining value was far faster and greater than that of compensating price rises. An alternative to the silver standard, that is a dual gold and silver standard, did not offer any solution. Indeed, having to juggle the values of two metals led to the nightmare of continuous adjustment. There was another great merit to the adoption of the gold standard. London was the sole international monetary centre which could supply resources to any countries accessible to the market, albeit on the gold standard basis. In order to tap money from this unequalled money market, the gold standard was a necessary prerequisite. The Indian departure from silver, therefore, was more than a great shock to the Japanese.

In October 1893, immediately in the wake of the Indian action, the Japanese government appointed a Monetary Commission. This body was composed of twenty-two members with Viscount Kanjo Tani (minister of agriculture and trade in Hirobumi Ito's first cabinet) as chairman, one secretary and two high officials of the Ministry of Finance, two high officials of the ministry of foreign affairs, the governor of the Bank of Japan, the president of the Yokohama Specie Bank, one representative each from Mitsui and Mitsubishi, four academics, six politicians and a journalist. They were commissioned to find answers for three questions: what were the causes of, and results of, the recent fluctuations in the gold and silver values?; what were their influences on the Japanese economy?; and which metal standard should be adopted, gold, silver or both?

Opening the first proceedings in October 1893, the Commission immediately appointed as a task force a special committee of five members. The president of the Specie Bank was its chairman and the other members included two Finance Ministry experts, Juichi Soyeda and Yoshio Sakatani, both close associates of Matsukata.[1] Under the chairmanship of Kokichi Sonoda, former diplomat in Britain, the special committee worked extremely hard (there were thirty-seven meetings between the autumn of 1893 and the spring of 1895). The Sino-Japanese War over the sovereignty of Korea broke out in 1894 and ended in 1895 in an overwhelming Japanese victory. By the Treaty of Shimonoseki, China agreed to pay Japan 200 taels of gold. This indemnity changed the scene dramatically. Enriched by the Chinese gold, the Japanese dream of adopting the gold standard could become a reality. Matsukata, who had resigned from the office of Finance Minister in August 1892, was recalled in March 1895 to guide the proceedings of the Monetary Commission. The anticipated acquisition of the gold indemnity put pressure on the Commission to decide quickly which metal should be adopted as the standard.

Matsukata's appointment undoubtedly tipped the scales, for it was known that both the government and the Ministry of Finance favoured the gold standard. It is not known exactly when Matsukata first began to favour the monometallic gold standard, but his views on this may have been of long standing. They were reinforced by his stay in France where he knew of the French payment to Germany in the aftermath of the Franco-German War and the dissolution of the Latin Monetary Union. Earlier in 1884, when the Silver-Convertible Banknote Regulation was promulgated, he had suggested privately that gold was the more stable metal and should be made the standard as soon as the gold reserve became sufficient to support the system.[2] Again in 1887, when the value of silver relative to gold was declining sharply, Matsukata sent a letter to the minister of war, advising him that because of declining silver value he should use much more caution in ordering munitions from western countries.[3]

Simultaneously with the proceedings of the Monetary Commission, Matsukata was requesting Sakatani to prepare a draft plan for the adoption of the gold standard. A series of drafts was produced, variously entitled 'Draft on the Monetary System', 'Appendix to the Draft on the Monetary System', and 'Replies to Anticipated Questions on the Monetary System'.[4] Sakatani, a radical gold monometallist, would not have succeeded had not Matsukata been reappointed as Minister of Finance. Between March and June 1895, Matsukata worked very hard sounding out the members of the Commission. Sakatani's ingenious arguments for gold monometallism[5] –

and he was strongly supported by another equally committed young economist, Soyeda – made an important contribution to Matsukata's success in
getting forward his ideas of adopting the gold standard. Matsukata's arguments were strong but it should be noted that the world trend favoured gold
and that the parity between gold and silver was 1:32 compared with 1:16 in
the early Meiji.[6] In this situation, two silver yen could be worth one gold
yen. By a mixture of bullying and cajoling Matsukata was successful in June
1895 in preparing for the adoption of the gold standard. Although there
were small setbacks for Matsukata and gold, in the spring of 1896 when
Matsukata assumed the premiership concurrently with the finance ministership, the gold standard was to be effective from the first day of October
1897.

To respond to the situation quickly and efficiently the Finance Ministry[7]
transferred the general manager of the Bank of Japan to the board of the
Yokohama Specie Bank, which was the only banking institution with a
London office into which the Chinese indemnity money could be paid. One
senior official of the Bank of Japan became the head office manager of
Specie Bank in Yokohama to whom the London branch would remit the
proceeds of the indemnity. Indeed, the remittance had started earlier in the
autumn of 1895, although the mandate of receiving and remitting the
indemnity money was given to the Specie Bank in January 1896.[8] The execution of personnel exchange stipulated in the Yokohama Specie Bank Decree
certainly smoothed the way in which the unprecedentedly huge amount of
specie would be successfully transferred from London to Japan: further reference will be made to this matter.[9]

The adoption of the gold standard not only put Japanese banking on the
same footing as western banking but also gave her an invaluable opportunity of making a debut in the western banking world. In April 1887, for the
first time since the Yokohama Specie Bank's London branch opened in
1884, the *Bankers' Magazine* published a translated version of the Bank's
fourteenth annual business report. It took another eight years for the Specie
Bank to be accepted by the London banking world, and the Japanese government and the Specie Bank tried hard to persuade the Bank of England to
open an account for the Specie Bank. The account was opened only because
of the payment of the huge Chinese indemnity. The *Bankers' Magazine* estimated that in February 1896 some £14 million sterling and in December
that year £9.5 million sterling was lying in Threadneedle Street credited to
the Japanese.[10] The journal believed that the money would be hoarded
'against a note issue in Japan'[11] for the gold standard basis. The journal was
also interested in those Japanese who were manipulating the operation
behind the scene. Remarkably, the *Bankers' Magazine* for the first time in its
history carried successively in 1896 portraits and articles on three Japanese

bankers: Yoshigusu Nakai, London manager of the Specie Bank, in the February issue, and K. Kawada, the governor of the Bank of Japan, and K. Sonoda, the president of the Specie Bank, together in the December issue. In concluding its series on Japanese banking, the *Bankers' Magazine* described the Japanese performance as 'Japan's monetary somersault'.[12] In the mean time, *The Times* for the first time acknowledged 'Japan as a commercial rival', though it was critical of Japanese cheap labour.[13] It could, however, be argued that the adoption of the gold standard marked Japan's appearance on the world stage, some thirty years after the upheaval of the Meiji Restoration – and astonishing progression.

Part IV

The Japanese on the London money market, 1897–1911 (thirtieth year of Meiji to forty-fourth year of Meiji)

Historical background, 1897–1911

The Japanese government remained dominated by the old Satsuma–Choshu clique, but change loomed over the political horizon. For the first time, the premiership was assumed in 1898 by Okuma, a former Saga man and an outsider. The Meiji oligarchs were ageing, and it was inevitable that the party system would take over the role thereto played by the senior statesmen. Thus the first decade of the twentieth century witnessed the emergence of political parties formed by both sides, by the oligarchs and by their opponents. Even the tiny socialist party gained followers as the labour movement emerged. The Peace Police Law of 1900 was intended to keep a sharp eye on anyone who demonstrated left-wing views. That year it was agreed, under a hawkish Choshu premiership, that the ministers of both the army and the navy would be a general and an admiral on active service. This concession was ultimately to prove disastrous. Extraterritoriality was abolished by 1899. The Anglo-Japanese Alliance, a triumph for Japan, was concluded in 1902. As a result Japan could confront Russia over Manchuria, which resulted in the Russo-Japanese War of 1904–5. Amidst wild euphoria Japan claimed a spectacular victory over Russia, but militarily and financially it was a close finish. Banking leadership had been handed over on his retirement by Matsukata in 1900 to a younger generation. Japanese bankers thereafter tended to rely heavily on the British banking system.

13 The 'Siamese twins': *Nichigin* and *Shokin*, 1897–1911

The Bank of Japan and its monetary policies, 1897–1911

While *Nichigin* (the Bank of Japan) was engaged in working successfully towards the gold standard, it was criticised for failing to redistribute fairly the profits resulting from the privileged fiduciary issues of banknotes. Following the publication of a critical article in *Tokyo Keizaizasshi*, or *Tokyo Economist*, several officials of the Ministry of Finance, bank associations and newly elected Diet members all echoed the same cry. Throughout the 1890s the question of the redistribution of the Bank of Japan's profits remained hotly disputed especially in the Diet. In the mean time the Bank tried to demonstrate its ability to serve the nation by extending its branch network to Nagoya, Fukushima, Hiroshima and Kanazawa, making by 1909 nine branches in all. In 1899 it was decided, and enacted into law, that the Bank of Japan should pay a tax at the rate of 1.25 per cent, which rate remained the same until 1923, on outstanding fiduciary note issues. In exchange the Bank was to be allowed to increase the limit of their excessive issue from ¥85 to ¥120 million.[1]

The 1897 proposal by Bank of Japan officials to the Finance Minister on central banking received a negative response from the Ministry[2] but Matsukata's replies as Finance Minister well illustrate the sorts of measures the Ministry were using for their monetary policies. Above all they utilised the facilities of special discounting of bills covered by specified brands of shares and stocks listed on the Stock Exchanges. Although he admitted that these arrangements were 'illegal' in the Bank's regulations and should be dispensed with as early as possible, the Finance Minister also confessed that they would have to continue in order to provide the economy with sufficient resources. In July 1897, shortly after the reply of the Ministry of Finance to the proposal, the number of named brands of equities increased by six to eighteen in addition to all sorts of national bonds, all of which were acceptable to the Bank of Japan. In exchange for the extension of specified securities, it was to be required that the credit ceiling be 60 per cent of the securities market prices and the discount rates were to be 0.008 per cent per annum above the Bank Rate. Both regulations were new.[3] This lending device was renamed collateral facilities, but the essential character remained the same and indeed became more popular. The share of special discounting in the total rose from 52 per cent in 1897 to 95 per cent in 1911, being 73 per cent on average in these fourteen years. Furthermore between 1907 and 1911 their share stood at 53 per cent on average of Bank of Japan aggregate advances.[4]

Before 1903, stocks and shares were major components of the collateral for special discounting, occupying approximately 60 per cent of the total. Then national bonds took their place, averaging 75 per cent of the total and even standing at 94 per cent in 1911. This reflected the second surge of the national debt in Japan's financial history. Even prior to this period of 1897 to 1911, government revenues were heavily reliant upon national debts. The total sum of their issues amounted to 319 per cent of the annual revenue on average during twenty years prior to 1896. The average figure fell to 280 per cent between 1897 and 1911, but the figure from 1901 rose again to 316 per cent. This augmentation was due to Russo-Japanese War demands and foreign loans, as will be discussed shortly, but domestic long-term national debts grew nearly threefold between 1897 and 1911 and it was these domestic national bonds which were lodged as collateral securities to the Bank of Japan by banks for special discounting. In addition to long-term lending, the government had already in 1890 started to borrow from the Bank of Japan on a short-term basis, with the intention of filling the gap until the proceeds of long-term borrowing came in. Therefore, in order to prevent these situations and also in order to avoid dear money, the Bank of Japan first, though provisionally and very timidly, carried out a buying-in operation of national debts for ¥37 million.[5]

The first buying-in operation was a compromise reflecting the conflicting opinions of the governor of the Bank of Japan and the Finance Ministry regarding the Bank Rate. These differences were not resolved and the governor, Yanosuke Iwasaki (of Mitsubishi, brother of Yataro Iwasaki), resigned. As this incident illustrated, the accumulation of national debts inevitably became strongly associated with the manipulation of Bank Rates. From the establishment of the Bank in 1882 until 1896, Bank Rates were changed fifty-four times. But in Britain the Bank of England changed its rate 101 times. During this period the Bank of Japan rate was a little less than 7 per cent on average, compared to the Bank of England rate of 3.5 per cent. From 1897 to 1911, the Bank of Japan altered the Rates thirty-three times while the Bank of England, over the same period, found it necessary to intervene in the money market seventy-nine times. The Bank of Japan rate was nearly 7 per cent on average in these years in comparison with 4 per cent on average for the British counterpart.[6] This substantial dearness of the Rates and the comparative infrequency in the number of Rate alterations, both relative to those of the Bank of England, were Japanese characteristics and resulted from two problems.

First, the Japanese financial authorities had to maintain dear money in order to prevent outflows of capital which would cause decreases of specie reserves and thus weaken the currency basis, eventually causing the collapse of the gold standard. These difficulties led to serious disputes within the Bank of Japan between those who advocated lowering the rates of interest and those who believed rates should be kept high.[7] There was at this time in Japan no interrelationship between individual banks; in other words, there was no interbank money market. All demands therefore for monetary resources had to go directly to the Bank of Japan. The Bank had to respond to the many demands through special discounting facilities, particularly on the security of national debts. Indeed, in the three years from 1909 to 1911 when the accumulation of national debts accelerated, the shares in securities offered to the Bank amounted to 74 per cent in discounting and almost 100 per cent in overdrawing.[8] The ever-increasing national debts were therefore due to the government as well as the banks seizing money from the Bank of Japan.

Whatever instrument was used to supply money to the nation and its economy, *Nichigin* needed a solid currency basis. The Finance Ministry and *Nichigin* commissioned *Shokin*, or the Yokohama Specie Bank, for the business of securing specie. In order to do this, the Specie Bank had no other choice whatsoever but to go to London, and in this sense the system was indirectly relying heavily upon the London money market.

The Chinese indemnity: *Nichigin–Shokin* co-operation, 1897–1903

By the turn of the century, the Yokohama Specie Bank had become one of the biggest banks in Japan with a capital of ¥18 million, advances of ¥45 million and deposits of ¥53 million, compared with the so-called Big Five, that is, Mitsui, Mitsubishi, Yasuda, Sumitomo and Daiichi, whose aggregate figures of capital, advances and deposits stood at ¥14 million, ¥77 million and ¥78 million respectively.[9] In addition to this huge amount of deposits, the Specie Bank had been allowed earlier from 1889 by the Bank of Japan to discount bills in foreign currency at specially favoured low rates. With the aid of these inducements the Specie Bank could afford to maintain thirteen branches including ten overseas branches of which five offices were situated in western countries. The opening and maintenance of independent overseas offices was still beyond the capacity of the Big Five.[10] In terms of both size and experience, no other banks, except the Bank of Japan, could compete in any way with the Specie Bank.

In 1892, one of the high officials at the Bank of Japan, Nobukichi Koizumi, was transferred to the Specie Bank to be its head office manager.[11] This first exchange was soon followed by the transfer of two persons to the Specie Bank in the wake of the conclusion of the Sino-Japanese Treaty of Shimonoseki in 1895.[12] The senior person on this occasion, Tatsuo Yamamoto,[13] was ordered by the Finance Ministry to return to the Bank of Japan in 1898 in order to succeed the fourth governor, Yanosuke Iwasaki, who had had to resign consequent on the difference of opinion on the Bank Rate to which reference has already been made.

Under Yamamoto's governorship, a serious conflict, this time among the directors, occurred regarding the management of the Bank, which was primarily due to Yamamoto's lack of leadership. Several of the directors resigned from the board.[14] Then the director and head office manager of the Specie Bank, Korekiyo Takahashi, who had in the summer of 1895 been transferred there together with Yamamoto, was called back to the Bank of Japan in 1898 to fill the vacancy on the board and to assist Yamamoto as the deputy governor. Takahashi, who was later twice in office as prime minister and eight times as Financial Minister, had had a chequered career. At the age of twelve Takahashi had been employed as messenger boy at the Yokohama branch of the Chartered Mercantile Bank, where Alexander Allan Shand was the acting manager. Then he worked for some years in America as a house boy, returning to Japan in 1868. Thereafter he changed jobs every three or four years until 1892 when he entered the fabric maintenance offices of the Bank of Japan. He was quickly promoted and became the branch manager at Kyushu until his transfer to the Specie Bank in 1895.[15] In 1900, a year after his appointment as deputy governor, Takahashi accepted the office of adviser to the vice-presidency of the Specie Bank. The exchanges of personnel between *Nichigin* and *Shokin* were further accentuated by Takahashi's accession to the presidency at the Specie Bank concurrently with his deputy governorship of the Bank of Japan. In 1911, Takahashi, finally leaving the Specie Bank, started to devote himself to the Bank of Japan as the governor. Between serving in *Nichigin* and *Shokin*, Takahashi emerged as the top financial authority who in effect succeeded Matsukata as the leader of the second generation of Japanese bankers in the new century. Also through Takahashi's career with both *Nichigin* and *Shokin* one could see the close co-operation of the 'Siamese twins'.[16]

The Chinese indemnity business was carried out through these close relationships of the two banks. The Bank of Japan was represented in London by the Yokohama Specie Bank office to which the government had in 1896 given a mandatory authority to receive and remit the indemnity money. Therefore the official document of the Japanese government given to the Chinese representatives carried as one of the Japanese delegates the Specie

Bank London branch manager.[17] All Chinese indemnity business was thus executed through arrangements between the Specie Bank and the Bank of England, at which the Specie Bank now had an account.

The Japanese government outlined its attitude to the indemnity money, resolving, as a matter of urgency, to direct the largest portion of the indemnity to paying off war-related heavy industrial purchases, much of what had already been bought through the London money markets. This was urgent as payment was in arrears. Also, the Specie Bank London manager was requested to ensure that specie remittance be carried out cautiously so that the foreign exchange markets would not be disturbed. Thereafter, a portion of the indemnity money was to be temporarily applied either for purchasing the domestic national debts for lodging in the governmental account at the Specie Bank London branch.[18]

The remittance, thanks to the diligence and care of the Specie Bank London manager, Yoshigusu Nakai, was effected by 1903, disturbing neither money nor foreign exchange markets.[19] In the event, the proceeds of Chinese indemnity money came to ¥364.51 million, a tremendous sum, amounting to some 14 per cent of the Japanese national income in 1903. Of the total 54 per cent was transferred to ordinary accounts of the government budgets for 1896/1902, to be applied for armament and heavy industry purchases – money which had already been spent; 22 per cent was added to the Sino-Japanese War Extraordinary Accounts; and 19 per cent was carried over to the accounts of the imperial household, education, casualties and warship purchases. Two-thirds of the rest, that is some ¥11 million and 3 per cent of the total, was left in the Bank of Japan accounts held by the Specie Bank London branch, which became an additional reserve for the issues of Bank of Japan notes under the title of 'specie kept abroad'. This category of 'specie abroad' held under the control of the Specie Bank London branch became an important barometer of the health of Japanese finance and, therefore, of the economy as a whole right up to 1930.

Shokin: foreign loans on the London money market and financing the Russo-Japanese War, 1897–1911

Despite the large amount of specie received from China, Japan continued to have deficits in the balances of current accounts. In the eight years from 1897 to 1904, there were only three years when there was a modest surplus on the current account. The deficits in 1904 at last reached ¥130 million. The increase of reserves from 1900 to 1903 was primarily due to the proceeds of the Chinese indemnity, but then the reserves declined sharply between 1903 and 1904 from ¥139 to ¥97 million. This meant that, despite the enormous Chinese indemnity, the equivalent of the 1903 specie reserve was swept away by only a year's current account deficit in 1904. The precarious financial situation threatened Japan's ability to maintain the gold standard. Nor could the government contract its own money requirements, for Japan had itself embarked upon an imperialist expansionist programme. Colonial commitments in Korea and Taiwan required more and more military expenditure to develop capital industries such as iron and steel making, engineering, shipbuilding and railways. There was no choice for the Japanese government but to have recourse to foreign loans which Japan had not considered since 1880 but which now once again became a hotly debated issue.[20] In its predicament the government began to consider how to proceed to obtain funds from abroad.

In January 1897, the Bank of Japan arranged with the government to lend to the Specie Bank London branch £1 million (¥9.76 million) so that it could operate more deliberately on the London money market. In April 1897, it was agreed between the two banks that several of the directors and the general manager of the Bank of Japan would sit on the board of the Specie Bank whenever it should be thought necessary. In June 1897 the Japanese government issued on the London money market war bonds for ¥43 million (£4.39 million), which had been issued domestically and were already in the possession of the deposit department of the Ministry of Finance, an ultimate reservoir of post office savings. The Japanese government, through the Specie Bank in London, arranged with Samuel & Co. to organise a syndicate which consisted of the Specie Bank itself, Hongkong and Shanghai Banking Corporation, Chartered Bank of India, Australia and China and Capital and Counties Bank. To the delight of the government the issue was successful.[21]

Eight months later, in February 1898, the government dispatched Korekiyo Takahashi, vice-president of the Specie Bank, to investigate western money markets and enquire into the further possibilities of raising funds there. Takahashi travelled to the United States, Britain and Europe between April and September 1898. He found his most useful contact in London in Alexander Allan Shand, the acting manager of Parr's Bank London office, who had in the earlier Meiji years had a decisive influence on Japanese banking and also been a close friend of Shigenobu Okuma.[22] Takahashi himself was well known to Shand who was astonished to find his former messenger boy as vice-president of *Shokin*. Shand was extremely helpful, clarifying the problem of how to obtain a Japanese loan in London and how to form a syndicate to do so. First, perhaps at the suggestion of Shand, the Specie Bank London position was strengthened in April 1899 by borrowing through the Bank of Japan another £1 million (¥9.7 million) from the government.[23] Then further arrangements were negotiated.

In June 1899, the 'Prospectus of Imperial Japanese Government 4 per cent Loan for £10 million, secured by the customs' duties and redeemable in fifty-five years' was issued. The syndicate included the Specie Bank, Parr's Bank, the Hongkong and Shanghai Banking Corporation and the Chartered Bank of India, Australia and China. Despite the previous success and first-rate backing from banks like Parr's in London, the issue of this huge amount presented problems. Credit at this time on the London money market was tight.[24] The outbreak of the South African War (Boer War) in October 1899 obviously had an unfavourable effect upon the Japanese issue. Indeed, the market price of the loan soon fell below the issuing price. The Japanese government became alarmed. Eventually the government negotiated through the Specie Bank to buy £4.5 million, 45 per cent of the total. Only 10 per cent of the total amount of the loan was subscribed in the open market; the other 45 per cent was placed privately by the syndicate. The 4 per cent loan was therefore not the success for the syndicate and the Japanese government which had been hoped for. Those involved, however, had paid a high price but had gained invaluable experience.

Tensions over the Korean peninsula and Manchuria between Russia and Japan continued and grew during the first years of the new century. Russo-Japanese confrontation over these areas was undoubtedly long-standing and particularly reinforced since the Boxer Rebellion of 1900. In its struggle against what it saw as Russian aggression, Japan was overjoyed to conclude the Anglo-Japanese Alliance, 'a triumphant alliance' as the Japanese called it.[25] The Russo-Japanese War broke out in February 1904, perhaps as a direct result of the Alliance. Takahashi was immediately dispatched to London to negotiate a further loan of £10 million. Again, Shand was the vital Japanese contact. The Hongkong and Shanghai Bank again offered to join the syndicate, though they could only find half the sum in London. Certainly Shand proved invaluable. He found useful names among Parr's Bank correspondents and discovered that Jacob Schiff of Kuhn, Loeb & Co. in New York was interested in the business.[26] Kuhn, Loeb were soon joined by the National City Bank and the National Bank of Commerce in New York. In May 1904, the 6 per cent loan of £10 million, secured by the customs' duties and redeemable in seven years, was successfully launched.

Takahashi continued searching in London for further chances of raising larger sums. An opportunity arose in the autumn of 1904 when market conditions in London were easier. Another 6 per cent loan for £12 million was floated by the same syndicate based in London and New York. The Russian surrender in Lushun in January 1905 strengthened Japan's position and four more loans soon followed at lower rates of interest. In the last two loans, the syndicate was joined by the Rothschilds, and the Americans were not involved in the last loan of 1907. All in all, between 1899 and 1907, Japanese loans totalled £140 million, mostly obtained on the London money market. The actual sum the Japanese government received was ¥1,211,549,929. This amount was more than 70 per cent of the 'Extraordinary War Expenditure Special Account' which the government set up for the Russo-Japanese War. The Specie Bank London office had become therefore the indispensable agent through which foreign resources could be tapped.

In the wake of the Russo-Japanese War foreign loan fever, the Specie Bank continued to be commissioned to float further loans for the government; five were in London and one in Paris before the First World War. The issues totalled £40.5 million, not a small sum, although the Japanese government was no longer as desperate for foreign loans as it had been. In 1908, when the most difficult times had passed, the directorate of the Specie Bank, perhaps at the suggestion of the government, expressed their great debt of gratitude to Shand of Parr's Bank by sending Japanese bonds of ¥10,000 as a token of thanks.[27]

Western money markets, chiefly and notably London, also provided Japan – solely through the Specie Bank – with short-term advances by accepting and discounting bills of exchange which had commenced earlier in the 1890s.[28] Although there remains no material to examine this development more closely, short-term borrowings, particularly on the London money market, were undoubtedly progressing, as will be proved later.[29] The Specie Bank network of branch offices and correspondents expanded remarkably, hand in hand with the success of the Bank in performing national business. From 1897 to 1902,[30] the number of domestic correspondents, in terms of office number, increased from 55 to 144, and the overseas counterparts from 57 to 109. The latter were located in eighty-six cities worldwide, and 144 bank offices in Japan could conduct business through the Specie Bank almost anywhere in the world.

By 1911, the Specie Bank had no less than thirty branches of which twenty-five were overseas.[31] The most important of these were situated in London, Lyons and New York, where the Bank could find resources for the Japanese customers. It should also be noted that the Specie Bank extended their network on the Chinese mainland, where ten branches operated in the north-eastern districts, later 'Manchukuo', and five in the rest of China. This kind of extension was carried out during and after the Japanese military campaigns, particularly after the Russo-Japanese War, and it was certainly a portent of Japan's later thrust into North East Asia. Any serious money business which the Japanese wished to undertake could therefore be transacted by the Yokohama Specie Bank anywhere in the world. This was an enormous achievement.

14 Special banking, 1897–1911

Long-term industrial financing, 1897–1911

The 'special banking idea' had in the late 1870s made its appearance in Matsukata's *On Finance* in the form of the proposed 'hypothec bank' which was to be commissioned to 'specialise in mobilising capital, to promote production and encourage business progress'.[1] It was the acceleration of industrialisation, which commenced in the latter half of the 1880s,[2] which brought Matsukata's idea into prominence. The progress of both light and heavy industries, particularly the latter, demanded heavy investment. To respond positively the government was forced to mobilise any resources it could find. In the early 1880s the Ministry of Finance started to draw up a plan to set up an 'industrial bank'. In 1895, after an interruption during the Sino-Japanese War, the plan was re-examined and a bill was laid before the Diet inaugurating the Hypothec Bank of Japan (*Nihon Kangyo Ginko*) under the Act of 1896.

The Act stipulated that the Hypothec Bank supply funds for the development and improvement of agriculture and manufacturing and that the government would appoint the management to direct the business conducted from the head office, the only office, based in Tokyo. The Hypothec Bank would be allowed to make advances to agricultural and industrial sectors on real properties redeemable within fifty years. Public institutions, such as prefectural and urban corporations, were allowed to borrow without pledging securities, but against their public creditworthiness. With ¥2.5 million paid-in capital, out of nominal capita of ¥10 million and with no right to accept deposits, the Hypothec Bank had to rely upon its issued debentures to secure lending resources. This Bank was the first of the debenture-issuing banks which would become an indispensable part of the banking system in Japan.[3]

The Hypothec Bank operated only in Tokyo; a system was needed therefore through which the Bank could channel its resources nationwide. This was provided in 1896 by the Agri-Industrial Bank (*No-Ko Ginko*) Act and then in 1899 by the Hokkaido Development Bank (*Hokkaido Takushoku*

Ginko) Act. The Agri-Industrial Bank was to be set up independently in each of the forty-six prefectures including Tokyo. The first to open its doors was in Shizuoka Prefecture, where tea production made heavy demands on the banking facilities. Shizuoka Agri-Industrial Bank was followed by forty-five other establishments between 1898 and 1900. In addition to debenture-issuing business, the Agri-Industrial Banks were also allowed to accept deposits and to open branches with the sanction of the Ministry of Finance.[4] The Agri-Industrial Bank debentures were taken by the Hypothec Bank as securities for borrowing. The Hypothec versus the Agri-Industrial banking division was in a sense a compromise between ideas of centralisation and decentralisation of industrial banking. The Hypothec Bank symbolised the former idea. This compromise would have to be reviewed as early as during the first decade of the twentieth century.

Further to provide a subordinate structure beneath the Agri-Industrial Banks the government legislated the Industrial Association Act of 1900. Under this Act, four types of associations, i.e. credit, selling, purchasing and user, could be organised. In the first decade of the twentieth century, the number of associations increased from 21 to 7,308, of which 5,331 were credit associations. Eventually more than half a million people were organised into 7,308 associations.[5] The Hokkaido Development Bank was based in Sapporo but its business included both ordinary banking and debenture issuing. It operated as the Hokkaido version of the Hypothec and Agri-Industrial Banks combined.[6]

Between 1897 and 1911, the aggregate sums of deposits, debentures and advances of the three types of banks grew by 410 per cent, 200 per cent and 360 per cent reaching ¥32.7, ¥174.9 and ¥227.9 million. Most remarkably, the advances of the Hypothec Bank and debentures of the Agri-Industrial Banks increased 950 per cent and 620 per cent respectively. The tremendous increase in the Hypothec Bank advances largely resulted from revisions of limitations on advances in 1910, together with the abandonment of the prohibition against accepting deposits. The Agri-Industrial Bank Act was also revised in the same way.[7] The revisions in the method of advances enabled the Hypothec Bank to lend more easily to the Agri-Industrial Banks and thus strengthened their relationships. Indeed, the Hypothec Bank effectively became the headquarters of the forty-six Agri-Industrial Banks, though the Hokkaido Development Bank took an independent course.

In promoting the Hypothec Bank and its subordinate institutions, it was Juichi Soyeda who was decisively influential and himself drafted the Hypothec Bank Act. A year after the launching of the Hypothec Bank, Soyeda became the secretary of the Finance Ministry. Soyeda, in collaboration with Sakatani, who followed him as secretary to the Finance Ministry, proceeded to prepare a plan to set up an industrial bank and drew the draft, which was enacted as the Industrial Bank of Japan (*Nihon Kogyo Ginko*) Act of 1900. The Industrial Bank was based in Tokyo and its top management was government-appointed. Soyeda accepted the presidency of the Industrial Bank, a post which he occupied for ten years. The capital stock of this Bank was to be ¥10 million, of which one-quarter was to be paid in. Later in 1905 another one-quarter was paid in and further in 1906 it was resolved that ¥7.5 (£0.77) million would be floated in the London money market. The total paid-in capital thus increased to ¥17.5 million in 1911.[8]

Article 9 of the Industrial Bank Act stipulated that it would be allowed to make advances on national and local bonds, debentures and equities, to issue and underwrite national and local bonds and debentures including its own, to accept deposits and depositary securities and to conduct trust business on local bonds, debentures and equities.[9] More details of the business purposes were later laid out by Soyeda himself in a lengthy address at a meeting held by an academic society in 1902.[10] According to his arguments, the Industrial Bank was in sum the bank of mobilising any monetary resources unemployed whether domestically or abroad as well as of giving liquidity to securities already in the hands of various institutions. Mobilisation and liquidation were particularly essential in a situation where securities markets were in their infancy and active only for transactions relating to national bonds. Therefore, domestically, the Industrial Bank could be thought of as a sort of substitute for a securities market. However, the Bank was commissioned to play a more important part abroad.

Reijiro Wakatsuki, who succeeded secretary Sakatani and who later served both as Finance Minister and premier, disclosed the ultimate intention of the establishment:

If the government issues national bonds, it could maintain the level of specie quantity. But this course was not available as the government was forced to follow the policy of 'no more loans, no more tax increases'. Overseas markets are full of Japanese national bonds, the prices of which have only been supported by the policy of 'no more loans'. Therefore it is out of question to float new national bonds abroad. However, there is always a way out. Municipal corporations are to be encouraged to issue loans abroad . . . The government will encourage big cities like Tokyo, Nagoya, Yokohama and so on, which require funds for their works, to issue bonds overseas, so that the proceeds of the bonds could be carried over to the specie holdings of the government and that the municipal corporations instead would receive and employ Bank of Japan notes to undertake their business.[11]

The business was to be exactly the same as that done by the Yokohama Specie Bank since the 1880s, in the sense that the government encouraged non-governmental transactions, itself appropriated the specie and thus augmented its own reserves.[12] It could, therefore, be argued that the Industrial Bank of Japan was an imitation of the Yokohama Specie Bank, heretofore the sole agent for issuing national bonds abroad. When the Industrial Bank first appeared on the London money market in 1902, it operated in exactly the same way as the senior Specie Bank.[13] The plan, put forward by Wakatsuki, was indeed a wonderful device, a further example of Japanese ingenuity.

From 1902 to 1911, the Industrial Bank successfully floated securities on the London money market. The total amount was more than £27 million, made up of £5.104 million (¥50 million) national bonds, £2.77 million of the Bank's own debentures and equities, £5.302 million Tokyo, Osaka and Yokohama municipal bonds and £14 million South Manchurian Railway debentures.[14] It was nearly 7 per cent of national income in 1911 and almost six times larger than the aggregate sum of the Bank's own debentures in 1911. The Industrial Bank was successfully launched and, as the large share of South Manchurian business in its issuing business suggests, this encouraged the imperialistic aspect of Japanese banking.

Colonial banking: the Bank of Taiwan and the Bank of Korea, 1897–1911

Two successive victories in the wars against China and Russia in 1895 and 1905 encouraged Japan to colonise Taiwan and Korea. The take-over in these countries allowed Japan to indulge in imperialist dreams which were to lead eventually to the attack on Pearl Harbor in 1941 and the ultimate defeat of Japan in 1945. All this caused great suffering in both Japan and the other Asian countries.[15] However, the development of Taiwan and Korea required that the Japanese set up money and banking facilities there.

Before 1897 there were no modern financial and banking institutions in Taiwan. In the aftermath of the Japanese take-over, the Japanese government enacted the Bank of Taiwan Act in April 1897. The preface to the Act explained its purposes:

The Bank of Taiwan, as the financial institution for Taiwan, intends to supply commerce, manufacturing and public utilities with monetary resources, develop the wealth on Taiwan, encourage the economy to grow and further extend the business in southern China and the southern sea areas so that the Bank will become the foremost institution for commerce and trade in those countries.[16]

The prospectus of this first colonial bank is indicative of Japanese expansionist policies. The establishment of the Bank was of course meant to fund Japanese enterprise there. The first presidency of the Bank was assumed by Juichi Soyeda who, however, was only to serve briefly as he accepted the presidency of the Industrial Bank.

Article 5 of the Act authorised the Bank of Taiwan to conduct every sort of banking business. Articles 8 and 9 sanctioned the Bank to issue notes of

¥5 and above payable on demand even on a fiduciary basis. Two years later the denomination of the banknotes was lowered to ¥1 and above. The Bank of Taiwan notes became the sole legal paper currency in Taiwan, where previously there had been only silver coin circulation. Further revisions made in the Act between 1904 and 1906, coincident with the Russo-Japanese War, extended the business field of the Bank. First, the metallic standard of the Taiwanese currency reserve was changed from silver to gold as in Japan. Secondly, the Bank of Taiwan was allowed to issue its notes in excess of specie reserve and fiduciary limit, also the same basis as the Japanese counterpart. Thirdly, the limitation of securities investment was lessened so that the Bank could purchase debentures of the newly established Industrial Bank of Japan. Lastly, the prohibition on directors having concurrent business appointments was lifted so that the selection of the directorate could be eased. The concurrent appointment clause was also inserted in the Act of other special banks such as the Hypothec, Industrial and latecomer Korean Banks. The clause might have led to some irresponsibility on the part of the directorate, particularly in the case of Korea and Taiwan remote from their supervising governmental authority. This did later prove to be the case.[17]

The Korean peninsula was like a 'shuttlecock' tossed between the three neighbouring powers of Russia, China and Japan throughout the fourth quarter of the nineteenth century. Two successive Japanese victories in the Sino- and Russo-Japanese Wars temporarily displaced Russia and China by the early twentieth century. In 1904, Japan forced Korea to sign a treaty which eventually developed into the take-over of Korea as a colony in 1910. It was in these turbulent years that Japanese banking gradually strengthened its grip on Korea.

Backed by the army and the presence of Japanese officials, it was Daiichi Bank, the former First National Bank, which was officially granted the right to do business on behalf of the Japanese government, and which first opened offices in Korea. By 1908 Daiichi Bank had fourteen offices in Korea. Five banks, including Juhachi Bank (former 18th National Bank of Nagasaki) and Gojuhachi Bank (former 58th National Bank of Osaka), which had ten and five offices respectively on the Korean peninsula in 1908,[18] also opened offices. All served the Japanese and their businesses, not the Koreans. Reinforcement of Japanese control under the renewed Korean–Japanese Treaty in 1907 resulted in the setting up of the Bank of Khankuku (Korea) in 1909 which took over government business done by Daiichi Bank. Final colonisation of Korea under Japanese imperialism in 1910 transformed the Bank of Khankuku to the Bank of Korea in 1911.

The Bank of Korea Act, legislated by the 1911 session of the Japanese Diet, stipulated that it would be based in Seoul and put under strict supervision of the governor-general, Japan's chief official in Korea. The president and directors were of course Japanese government appointments. The Bank of Korea was to conduct every kind of banking business, including the issue of banknotes, similar to those privileges granted to the Bank of Taiwan.[19]

In 1911 the Japanese overseas bank network was formed by seventy-three offices set up by fifteen banks.[20] Among the number only six offices were in western countries: five were those of the Yokohama Specie Bank and one was that of a small, ordinary bank in San Francisco.[21] Of the rest, that is sixty-seven offices, two were in India under the Specie Bank and sixty-five were in Far Eastern Asia, where Korea accounted for twenty-nine, Chinese mainland eighteen, of which eight were in Manchuria, Taiwan seventeen and Vladivostock one. Of the fifteen banks, five were chiefly responsible for the far eastern Japanese banking network: the Specie Bank had thirteen offices, Bank of Korea ten, Juhachi Bank (which still survives in Nagasaki under the same name) ten, Bank of Taiwan ten and Hyakusanju Bank (former 130th National Bank of Osaka and later absorbed by Yasuda Bank) six. Although the Juhachi and Hyakusanju branch networks were not negligible, it was undoubtedly the Specie Bank, Bank of Korea and Bank of Taiwan that mattered.

The Yokohama Specie Bank expanded its Asian branch network mainly during and after the Russo-Japanese War. This meant that the Specie Bank closely followed the army as the Russian withdrew northwards in Manchuria. The Bank was commissioned by the Bank of Japan to conduct primarily treasury and war-note business. An extraordinary aspect of Bank of Taiwan and Bank of Korea business was seen in figures of advances as percentages of deposits, which showed on average 152 per cent from 1900 to 1911 and 142 per cent from 1909 to 1911 respectively.[22] Their lending capacity was dependent upon their own note issue: both were excessive and, as became clear later, dangerous. Colonial banking thus started to grow, as an additional element of the Japanese system, during the first decade of the century.

15 Banking at the end of the Meiji era, 1900–1911

Five big fish and a mass of minnows: the banks, 1900–1911

In 1901 there were 1,867 ordinary banks in Japan, but a decade later this number had dropped to 1,613. In Britain in 1911 there were about 100 banks following various bank amalgamations. During these years in Japan ordinary banking increased its advances twofold and deposits nearly threefold. Savings banks also increased in number from 419 to 478 while their advances and deposits increased more than three and four times respectively. Advances as percentages of deposits of both ordinary and savings banking showed the same trend. The former declined from 151 per cent to 100 per cent standing at 120 per cent on average, while the latter did so from 80 per cent to 60 per cent, standing at 70 per cent on average. The trend was certainly due more to augmentation of their deposits rather than to their unwillingness to lend, as the above figures indicated.

The regulations in the legislation during the 1890s for ordinary and savings banking were similar. It could safely be said that the only difference between the two banking categories was a matter of scale. Therefore, it may be wise to start discussions from comparisons of three figures of average capital, advances and deposits in order to clarify their positions. In terms of average capital, savings banking grew from 28 per cent of that of its ordinary counterpart in 1900 to 49 per cent in 1911. Although in terms of average deposits the savings banks diminished from 79 per cent to 76 per cent of the ordinary banks, the savings banks enhanced their lending proportional to that of the ordinary banks from 41 per cent to 56 per cent. These figures suggested that the smaller scale savings banks were more aggressive than the ordinary banks and could become a potential danger, especially during the economic boom of the coming war after 1914.

Other circumstantial evidence supports the view that the ordinary and savings banks were very similar to each other. Between 1900 and 1911, there were 724 new banks, while 540 banks disappeared. The savings bank movement recorded 352 entries and 152 withdrawals.[1] Although there were a few examples of savings banks re-registering as ordinary banks and vice versa, the large number of entries and withdrawals suggests that it was relatively easy to set up a new ordinary or savings bank. Promoters even with small means could establish a low-ranking ordinary or top-ranking savings bank.

The large number of banks posed a formidable question, that is, how would the Ministry of Finance be able to execute inspections stipulated in the Bank and Savings Bank Decrees of 1890? By the end of the nineteenth century it had been proved that the strict inspection of all banks would be impossible. Failing to cope effectively with this problem, the Finance Ministry issued a circular notifying banks of possible mismanagement, including unfair favour lendings to directors' firms and irregularities in lending in general.[2] This lack of any strict inspection, or of an independent audit, meant that the system was always vulnerable to abuse.

From the other end of the scale emerged a group of five big banks. They were Mitsui, Mitsubishi, Sumitomo, Yasuda and Daiichi Banks. When Mitsui set up their bank in 1876, they had also established Mitsui Bussan (or Trading) Co. In 1888 they bought the Miike coal mine in Kyushu from the government. This mining enterprise became Mitsui Mining Co. in 1892. These three businesses of banking, trading and mining were the core of the Mitsui house. Later, by 1900, they had a firm industrial basis in electrics, paper, shipping and cotton, which were represented by well-known companies such as Shibaura Manufacturing Works (later Toshiba), Oji Paper Making Co., Hokkaido Mining and Shipping Co. and Kanegafuchi Spinning Co. (later Kanebo). This group of companies became a *zaibatsu*, of which Mitsui Gomei Co., founded in 1909, became the headquarters. Mitsubishi, which had its origins in shipping ventures headed by Yataro Iwasaki during the turbulent years of dying Shogunate and early Meiji era, also developed their business as a *zaibatsu*. In 1887 Mitsubishi purchased Nagasaki Shipbuilding Works directly from the government through its privatisation policies. In 1893, Mitsubishi Goshi Co.[3] was set up with five departments in mining, shipbuilding, banking, real estate and general affairs. In 1919 the banking department became independent as Mitsubishi Bank. Sumitomo, with an old tradition as *ryogae*, had also been involved in copper mining and metallurgical business. These enterprises became a solid basis for Sumitomo to grow into a *zaibatsu*. Between 1887 and 1901 Sumitomo undertook amalgamations in the metallurgy sector, setting up Sumitomo Metal Works which responded vigorously to war demands. In 1909, Sumitomo General Office was created as their headquarters, later renamed as Sumitomo Goshi Co.

Yasuda and Daiichi Banks were somewhat different from the others. They did not have a manufacturing base strong enough to rival the other three. As we noted, Yasuda Bank had emerged from a rather humble *ryogae* established during the last days of the Shogunate regime, a company which always concentrated on developing their banking business. After several amalgamations, which they pursued vigorously, Yasuda emerged as a financial *zaibatsu*. Historically, the Daiichi Bank was more elevated because, as the first example of a national bank strongly supported by the Finance Ministry, it felt obliged to keep itself aloof from other institutions. Later, however, especially during the First World War boom and mainly through Eiichi Shibusawa, their respected and powerful leader, Daiichi Bank gradually built a relationship with many industrial and commercial institutions, and eventually came to be called a *zaibatsu*.

This group of five was really emerging as the 'Big Five' during the first decade of the twentieth century. Between 1900 and 1911 the number of their offices increased from sixty-seven to seventy-five, 2 per cent of the total ordinary bank offices, head offices included. Although the share of their paid-in capital was 7.3 per cent on average during these twelve years, those of deposits and advances were more than 21 per cent and 15 per cent respectively.[4] They were indeed powerful banks, but this did not necessarily mean that the Japanese banking system as a whole was strong. What was significant was the gap between the Big Five and the rest. The lopsidedness of the system, aggravated by the widespread existence of small savings banks, was to prove a formidable problem for the financial authorities.

Tokyo as a financial centre and the 'gentlemen's agreement' on price competition, 1900–1911

Prefectures exceeding the national averages both in terms of paid-in capital and number of ordinary and savings banks were, in 1900, Tokyo, Kanagawa, Niigata, Nagano, Shizuoka, Aichi, Kyoto, Osaka, Hyogo and Fukuoka. Tokyo and Kanagawa were local centres in eastern Japan, Kanto, while Osaka, Hyogo and Kyoto, known as Kansai or Kinki district, were the western counterparts. Aichi was midway between the two centres with Nagoya as its local centre. Fukuoka and Niigata represented localities in Kyushu in the south-west of Japan and in the northern Japan Sea coast respectively. Nagano, north-west of Tokyo, and Shizuoka to the south were prefectures, producing silk and tea, staple export products. In 1911 Kyoto and Shizuoka dropped out of the group of top financial centres. Perhaps the business of the two cities was being absorbed by Tokyo, Osaka and Aichi. The share of the paid-in capital of ordinary and savings banks of these eight prefectures reached nearly two-thirds of the total.[5] Among the top eight, Tokyo was eventually to emerge supreme, with Osaka in second place. In 1900 both Osaka and Tokyo had eighty-five ordinary banks, though the amount of paid-in capital of those in Osaka was half of those in Tokyo. On the face of things Osaka still held first place at the turn of the century against her rising rival Tokyo. But the situation changed during the first decade of the twentieth century.

In 1911 Tokyo had 165 banks, that is 91 ordinary and 74 savings banks, compared to 50 ordinary and 7 savings banks in Osaka. In terms of ordinary banking size, the Tokyo banks eventually overtook those in Osaka, the average paid-in capital of the former being ¥1.1 million against ¥0.65 million of the latter. Furthermore, in terms of paid-in capital of both the aggregate of ordinary and savings and of ordinary banks alone, Tokyo could, by 1911, claim to be the sole financial centre, her shares of 29 per cent and 35 per cent being far larger than the 9 per cent and 12 per cent of Osaka. Charles Kindleberger's theory that a sole financial centre must emerge in any industrialised economy was certainly true in the Japanese case.[6]

In theory, the emergence of the paramount monetary centre tends to lower the rate of interest on both lending and deposits. But, in spite of the rise of Tokyo, interest rates did not move that way. There were perhaps three factors working against the lowering of interest rates. In the first place, as we have already seen, the Bank of Japan Rates were kept high in order to prevent money flowing abroad so that the basis of the gold standard could be secured.[7] Another factor resulted from a structural shortcoming. In 1900 there were 1,802 ordinary banks with a total of 1,374 branch offices. Even in 1911 there were 1,613 banks with 1,784 branches. In the case of savings banks, the number of branches was slightly larger, but these small banks did not have any influence on interest rates. This slow development of the branch banking network, especially in ordinary banking, was responsible for deterring the smooth flow of money inside the bank so that the gap between credit surplus and deficit areas would be minimised and the rates could be lowered. The third factor working against lowering of interest rates was that the large number of independent banks undoubtedly accelerated price competition, thus pushing up borrowing costs and resulting in high lending rates.

Because of fierce price competition it was inevitable that some sort of agreement would be thought by bankers to be advantageous. The initiative came from Osaka, where in May 1901 member banks of the Osaka Bank Association agreed to set the maximum rates of interest on deposit and current accounts. They were followed by their Tokyo counterparts in June 1902, Yokohama and Nagoya in July 1902, Kobe, Kyoto and two others in October 1902.[8] These rate arrangements were all on a 'gentlemen's agreement' basis, but they were certainly effective in lowering banking rates. The average rates of advances and deposit accounts decreased from 13.7 per cent and 6.2 per cent between 1893 and 1899 to 10.7 per cent and 6 per cent respectively between 1900 and 1911.[9] These arrangements did much to eliminate price competition.

16 Banking and the securities market, 1897–1911

There were forty-six stock exchanges by 1898; the first founded in Tokyo and Osaka in 1878. Thereafter numbers dropped and, by 1911, there were stock exchanges at Tokyo, Osaka, Yokohama, Kobe, Kyoto, Nagoya, Niigata, Nagaoka, Hakata (Fukuoka), Kuwana (Aichi), Wakayama, Hiroshima and Nagasaki, making thirteen in all.[1] During the company promotion and general economic boom in the late 1890s, in the aftermath of the Sino-Japanese War, the Ministry of Finance encouraged provincial businessmen to establish their own stock exchanges. Inevitably the mushrooming of stock exchanges led to speculation and abuse.

During this company promotion boom period there were very few listed company stocks, particularly in provincial stock exchanges. The favourite securities became therefore the shares and stocks of their own joint-stock stock exchange institutions which were joint-stock companies themselves and which share listings were peculiarly Japanese. Tokyo Stock Exchange carried on the same sort of business.[2] Additionally, the stock exchanges were also allowed to deal in rice futures, which became favourite targets for speculation. From 1902 to 1906, the government, while encouraging transactions of the many national bonds, was eager to suppress small provincial stock exchanges.[3] By 1911, as we have seen, nearly three-quarters of the stock exchanges had disappeared.

Despite its fragile foundation the securities market in Tokyo and Osaka grew steadily. From 1897 to 1911, the aggregate value of listed stocks and shares in Tokyo soared from ¥564 million to ¥2,095 million, roughly the same sum as the total banking advances. But during this brief period Osaka lost its supremacy. In 1897, of the total transactions, Osaka boasted 41 per cent against the 31 per cent of Tokyo, but by 1911 the position had been reversed, for Tokyo's share rose to 47 per cent while Osaka's fell to 37 per cent.[4] Once Tokyo had established its supremacy its position became unassailable.

Another aspect of the securities market should be noted. The main components of listed bonds were national bonds and company equities, the proportions of both of which in the total slightly decreased between 1897 and 1911 from 61 per cent and 39 per cent to 55 per cent and 38 per cent respectively. The aggregate of national bonds and company equities formed 100 per cent of the listed brands in 1897, but they could not fill the total in 1911, leaving a gap of 7 per cent. This gap meant an appearance of a new type of securities, that is, debentures, which made their debut in 1898, though they did not visibly increase until the Industrial Bank joined the system. Once the Industrial Bank was in business a debenture market was created with the aid of its trust business which it was specially allowed to conduct. On the other hand, the transactions of national bonds and company equities, which had begun in 1890, continued to be supported firmly by the Bank of Japan through special discounting facilities. Therefore, the securities markets, though apparently expanding steadily, were in fact being backed up by special banking facilities generously given by Japan's central banking, which was, in turn, substantially reliant upon the London money market.

War, the Japanese boom years, 1911–1919 (forty-fourth year of Meiji to eighth year of Taisho)

Historical background, 1911–1919

On 30 July 1912 the Meiji Emperor died and on that day the Taisho era commenced. Emperor Taisho, of weak mental and physical health, had none of the charisma of his father. This marked the end of an era, during which Japan had exerted herself to the utmost of her strength in order to catch up with the western powers. In February 1913, the military-clique-led cabinet was forced to resign, for the first time in Japan's modern history, by popular protest from both inside and outside the Diet. This led to the emergence of a male suffrage movement and the vague term 'Taisho democracy', and eventually to the formation of a party-led cabinet with the first common people premiership, Kei Hara. Indeed, because of rising prices, there were serious rice riots in 1918. In international relationships, Japan, with the Anglo-Japanese Alliance still in place, played a modest part on the Allied side in the First World War. The Japanese military, backed by strong anti-western right-wing activists, increasingly showed aggression by taking the opportunity of fishing in troubled waters in China and elsewhere. Shortly after the declaration of war against Germany in August 1914, the Japanese military took over the German territories on the Chinese mainland and presented to the Chinese the notorious Twenty-One Demands. The Russian Revolution of 1917 induced Japan, in co-operation with the western powers, to intervene in Siberia, which extended until 1925. The Taisho era, of less than fourteen years, was a period of tension, but at the same time there was an astonishingly rapid growth of the economy which produced a prosperous banking sector.

17 Bank of Japan money supply, 1911–1919

In spite of frequent large issues of national bonds on the western markets, primarily on London, specie shortages continued to worry the Japanese financial authorities. Since 1904 and the outbreak of the Russo-Japanese War, the Japanese economy had suffered heavy deficits and trade imbalances because of the large amounts of imports of heavy, engineering and chemical industry products, all of which had to be paid for. The good years were 1907 and 1909 but the worst deficit of ¥324 million was recorded in 1905, being 13 per cent of the national income of that year. In both 1911 and 1912, the deficits exceeded ¥100 million. Between 1906 and 1911, the specie reserve diminished by almost one-third. What could be done to remedy this situation?

Between August 1911 and July 1914, the Finance Ministry gave top priority to finding a solution to the specie question and continued to discuss the matter with the Bank of Japan and the Yokohama Specie Bank. In the middle of July 1914, exactly a month before the outbreak of the Great War in Europe, an agreement was reached. Generally the Ministry of Finance, Bank of Japan and the Specie Bank determined that the specie reserve, hitherto largely dependent on the proceeds of issuing national bonds abroad, should be augmented by encouraging economic growth and the increase of exports.[1] Even if this worked it would not be sufficient to meet an emergency, and therefore the Bank of Japan was requested to keep the Rates high so as to keep money inside Japan. The Specie Bank too was strongly urged to encourage discounting of export bills and also to supply the Bank of Japan with specie of ¥15 million per annum as a minimum requirement so that the latter could build up the currency basis.[2] The *Nichigin–Shokin* partnership was again called in to face the fundamental problem. These crucial relationships were again superbly co-ordinated by Korekiyo Takahashi, as president of the Yokohama Specie Bank and deputy governor of the Bank of Japan, concurrently, until June 1911. While Takahashi was governor of the Bank of Japan, between June 1911 and February 1913, the Minister of Finance was Tatsuo Yamamoto, a former colleague of Takahashi's at the

Bank of Japan and the Specie Bank. In February 1913 Takahashi became the Finance Minister. Indeed it was Takahashi who was the pivotal figure in the discussions between the three institutions, though he did not necessarily oppose issuing national bonds in foreign markets.

As G. C. Allen clearly pointed out, 'the outbreak of war completely changed the situation',[3] although this was not immediately apparent as demand for Japan's staple exports, silks, suddenly suffered a sharp fall and prices fell ominously. This was in fact temporary and demand was soon very great.[4] An unprecedented increase in exports stimulated the Japanese economy, which, between 1914 and 1919, found its exports jump from ¥670 million to ¥2,379 million per annum. This prodigious growth naturally improved greatly the balance of trade. In the same period the current accounts recovered from ¥9.5 million deficit to ¥397.2 million surplus, and the general accounts improved from ¥42.1 million deficit to 533.2 million surplus. Thanks to this rapid growth of foreign trade, the national income of Japan grew three times from ¥4,241 million in 1914 to ¥12,834 million in 1919. The growth rate of more than 300 per cent was unprecedented and indeed has never again been seen in the Japanese economy.[5]

One of the most significant financial effects of this tremendous economic growth was the accumulation of specie reserve, which leaped from ¥341.1 million in 1914 to ¥2,045.1 million in 1919, further reaching ¥2,178.6 million in 1920, a figure never again attained in Japan's history during the period on the gold standard.[6] The astonishing amount of specie reserve which accumulated in the hands of the financial authorities for the first time, though for only a little more than half a decade, relieved the Finance Ministry, the Bank of Japan and the Specie Bank of any further worry. In 1919 the total amount of Bank of Japan note issue stood at ¥15,600 million, of which the portion of excessive issue beyond the reserves was 31 per cent, or ¥4,800 million, a sum far larger than the total issue of 1914. This gigantic note issue, firmly supported by the solid basis of accumulated specie, enabled the Bank of Japan to keep their Bank Rates at a reasonably low level, not exceeding 6 per cent between July 1916 and November 1918, which again was a rarity in the Bank's history.[7] This resulted in lowering market rates and ensured fierce price competition as will shortly be disclosed.[8]

The extra supply of Bank of Japan notes contributed in three ways to the rapid growth of the economy, domestically and externally. First of all, intent on supplying funds to strategic industries, the Bank of Japan gradually expanded those securities eligible for their special discounting facilities. In 1915, a Tokyo municipal bond and Hypothec and Industrial Bank bonds were added to the list. Further in 1916, ten municipal bonds, including those of Tokyo, Osaka and Kobe, and two foreign bonds were included.

Eventually in November 1917, a fundamental revision was made on the special discounting facilities. There were two notable aspects to the revision. As the deputy governor of the Bank of Japan explained:

Regarding our special discounting facilities we have decided this time to adopt the deliberate selection system of customers on the basis of their creditworthiness, replacing that of simply listing up and announcing of securities brands eligible for the facilities. The system follows mainly the model of the Bank of England, in that the Bank of Japan would allow special discounting facilities to customer 'A' on securities regarded good on the market, but it might reserve the right to reject similar facilities to customer 'B' on the same securities.[9]

The Bank of Japan was clearly swayed in determining how to allocate special discounting facilities from the securities themselves to their holders, that is, by the customers' creditworthiness. Therefore the Bank, which hitherto had made their list of eligible securities public, decided to keep them out of the public domain.

This alteration in the way the Bank business was ordered led to another notable measure which could be considered to compensate for the earlier change of custom. Before the revision the types of securities available for discounting included five national bonds, twenty-nine municipal bonds, seventeen banking bonds and four equities. The revision in November 1917 added 110 further securities, bringing the total to 165. Another accepted category of securities comprised nineteen industrial debentures, including electricity, cotton spinning, shipping, shipbuilding, steel-making, paper-making and the South Manchurian Railway. The emergence of this category was a reminder of the progress of new industries accelerated by the First World War boom. The boom was also reflected by equities which increased from four to twenty-six, including those of electricity, gas works, cotton spinning, sugar refining, chemicals and private railways. In the case of the railways remarkable progress was being made in several big cities after the nationalisation of trunk lines in 1906. Banking bonds, which hitherto had been composed of seventeen types of the Industrial and Hypothec Banks, were also joined by sixty-five bonds of the Agri-Industrial Banks set up in forty-six prefectures and a colonial development financing company based in Korea.

All in all some 60 per cent of the additional securities were those of banking and financial bonds. Of the rest, cotton spinning ranked first in the list, holding a share of 24 per cent, followed by electricity and gas with 18 per cent, railways with 16 per cent, shipbuilding with 9 per cent, sugar refining with 9 per cent and shipping with 7 per cent.[10] They were the staple and strategically crucial industries, which themselves grew and thus helped economic growth to accelerate. The Bank of Japan excessive note issues were therefore essential in both promoting and sustaining the boom domestically.

By using the Yokohama Specie Bank and the Bank of Taiwan, the Bank of Japan found two outlets for its excessive note issue. Between 1914 and 1918, nearly two-thirds on average of the total Bank of Japan advances were given to the Specie Bank and the Bank of Taiwan. During these hectic years, foreign exchange transactions, in which these two Banks were most vigorous, were the hungriest money eaters. In order to meet their demands, even proceeds of national bonds were from time to time applied.[11] The second biggest consumers were foreign investments. For the first time in Japanese history, yen bonds of foreign countries were floated by syndicates of banks in Tokyo and Osaka, albeit only for a short while between 1916 and 1917. The countries which were involved were Britain, France and Russia, all of which were in the midst of the Great War.[12] Less satisfactory outlets, to which reference will shortly be made, were the Chinese, with which the Bank of Taiwan, Bank of Korea and the Industrial Bank of Japan were engaged.[13]

In the mean time in September 1917 specie exports were prohibited in Japan. Following the western countries, Japan effectively departed from the gold standard. The departure coincided with an eclipse of hitherto-growing exports. Could the World War boom continue?

18 The expansion of special banking, 1911–1919

The Yokohama Specie Bank and foreign trade financing, 1911–1919

The Yokohama Specie Bank enlarged its commitments nearly fourfold in terms of total liabilities/assets from ¥378.3 to ¥1,465.6 million between 1914 and 1919. On the assets side, the figures of buying bills and interest bills grew remarkably from ¥135.2 and ¥36.6 million to ¥538.1 and ¥165.1 million respectively. The growth rates during these five years were 431 per cent and 451 per cent respectively. The aggregate amount for the two items, symbols of foreign trade financing of the Specie Bank, was well over half of the total assets. On the liabilities side, deposits grew by nearly three times to ¥516.6 million. Rediscounting facilities at the Bank of Japan also increased at the same rate to ¥136.1 million. However, in both relative and absolute terms, the growth of interbank borrowing was most remarkable, jumping from ¥54.2 to ¥456.3 million from 1914 to 1919.[1]

It was during these hectic years of 1914 to 1919 that the overseas branch network of the Specie Bank reached maturity. Between 1914 and 1919, the number of branches increased from twenty-three to thirty-six, of which six were in Japan and thirty were overseas. Of these overseas branches fourteen were on the Chinese mainland, including seven in Manchuria, six in the western countries, two in South America, five in the Straits of Malaya and Australia and three in India. There were no branches in Africa. By far the most important branch was that in London, which handled extensive interbank borrowing.

In 1914 the Bank of Japan prepared a report, which underlined the importance of the London money market and demonstrated how energetically the Specie Bank was endeavouring to exploit it. From the opening of its account at the Bank of England in 1895 and business with major banks in London from 1897[2] the Specie Bank had by 1914 successfully infiltrated the London money market. According to the report, there were three important entries into the London market. First, the Specie Bank could rediscount at London banks foreign bills of exchange which it was holding mainly through buying exchange. The Bank could secure by this method to the extent of ¥50 million to approximately £5 million. Secondly, the Bank could borrow in London on the security of national bonds and another type of foreign exchange bills, the latter of which were documents against payment and as such were not available for rediscounting. In this way the Bank could obtain the sum of up to ¥10 million. Thirdly, the Bank could draw two sorts of finance bills on London. One type was the bills drawn on London banks. Usually the bills were £2,500 or £5,000 payable thirty, sixty, or ninety days after sight. The Bank pledged equities and debentures as fixed collateral securities with London banks, which were drawees of the bills. Another type was the bills drawn by the Specie Bank head office on its London branch. These were accepted by London banks and then were sold, or discounted. The bills were usually £5,000 or £10,000 payable three or four months after sight. In fact, all procedure for the last sort of finance bill was executed by the Specie Bank London branch. It prepared the printed forms of bills, which even had printed on their faces the sums of £5,000 or £10,000. The date spaces were left blank and so could be filled in at any time. The London branch was thus able to draw the bills for any date to suit. This type of bill was termed inside the Specie Bank a 'special bill'. Finance bills gave the Bank ¥10.5 million, of which more than 80 per cent was procured through the latter type.[3]

In conducting the London business, the Specie Bank negotiated with Parr's Bank, Lloyds Bank, London Joint Stock Bank and Union of London and Smith Bank. Later the business was joined by Heine & Co. in Paris. The Bank of France, too, allowed the Lyons branch of the Specie Bank to over-draw its account at the former to the extent of 10 million francs, or some ¥4 million. Lyons was one of the important centres of the silk trade. New York also became available by this time, though unfortunately the banks involved are not known. The Specie Bank could thus raise resources in Paris, Lyons and New York up to ¥14 million.[4] Money from London, Paris, Lyons and New York counted for nearly a quarter of the average sum of deposits during the Great War. For the first time since its foundation, free from the specie problem, the Specie Bank energetically absorbed resources from these financial centres and supplied them to the rapidly growing economy in Japan, especially to the foreign trades.

It is almost impossible for the banking historian to know exactly to which sectors of the economy the bank was supplying money. Thanks to surviving records of the Specie Bank,[5] we can discover something of its sectoral lending during these hectic years of rapid growth. The Specie Bank increased its share of export financing from 34 per cent in 1910 to 44 per cent in 1919. Both before and during the war boom, Japan's vital staple exports, silk and manufactured cotton, were generously financed by the

Specie Bank. The Bank's share of their financing fell slightly from 1910 to 1919, but still in the latter year a tremendous sum was given by the Bank to finance the export of both silk and cotton from Japan.

On the import side, metal, machinery and raw cotton were vital, although, because of bad harvests at home, in 1919 rice and soya beans featured. The total share of the Bank in import financing rose to more than 40 per cent in 1919. The foreign trade financing share of 40 per cent and above by one bank was itself a tremendous achievement even if the Specie Bank was firmly supported by the Finance Ministry and the Bank of Japan. However, it should not be overlooked that the Specie Bank share was slightly declining and so left room for other institutions. Indeed, the serious competitors of the Specie Bank were foreign, particularly British, overseas banks until 1916. Thereafter, as we will see, ordinary Japanese banks began to penetrate international banking.

Sustained economic growth with the resultant accumulation of a specie reserve during the war boom effectively eliminated the shortage of specie, a problem which of course the Specie Bank had been designed to correct. During these carefree years, the Specie Bank was headed by Junnosuke Inoue, a first-rate financial expert, the third generation in line after Matsukata and Korekiyo Takahashi.

Inoue was in striking contrast to Takahashi, who was of lower class *samurai* stock and without a university education. He was born in 1869, a year after the Restoration. Graduating from the law faculty of the Imperial University, Inoue entered the service of the Bank of Japan in 1896, only, a year later, to be dispatched to study in Britain. He arrived in London towards the end of 1897. Despite the recommendation of the Japanese Embassy, he was refused permission to join the Bank of England as a temporary member of staff. He then turned to Alexander Allan Shand of Parr's Bank who ensured that he was accepted as an apprentice at Parr's Charing Cross branch. For some eighteen months, at the very time that the Chinese indemnity money was being remitted to Japan by the Yokohama Specie Bank London branch, he worked hard at both Parr's and the Specie Bank and returned to Japan in the spring of 1899. By the summer of 1906 he had been promoted to general manager of the Bank of Japan in Tokyo but later he was transferred to become the New York manager. On returning from New York in the spring of 1911, Inoue was invited to join the board of directors of the Specie Bank, leaving the employ of the Bank of Japan. Shortly thereafter he was elected vice-president of the Specie Bank and by the autumn of 1913 he became president.

He led the Specie Bank for several years of rapid growth until 1919 when he became the governor of the Bank of Japan.[6] Inoue's service in both *Nichigin* and *Shokin* was certainly a reflection not only of the close relationship between the two institutions, but also of Inoue's own abilities. Inoue was the last to serve in both institutions. Later the two Banks had become too well established to accept this sort of interdependence. Inoue was, therefore, the last example of the banker who was of the Takahashi-type elite.[7] In one sense the war boom ended the good old days of co-operation between *Nichigin* and *Shokin*.

Long-term industrial financing in transition, 1911–1919

One type of the industrial banks, that is, the Hypothec Bank and its *de facto* subordinate the Agri-Industrial Banks, available in every prefecture, as well as the Hokkaido Development Bank, all grew during the wartime boom between 1914 and 1919. Their combined lending resources of deposits and debentures, as well as their advances, expanded enormously to nearly ¥600 million each in 1919. The growth of the Industrial Bank of Japan was even more remarkable. The combined lending abilities of deposits and debentures increased nearly fourfold to ¥277.6 million, and the advances threefold to ¥169.3 million. The growth of these banks, however, was not necessarily entirely a result of the war boom. Furthermore, two types of the banks started to develop different categories of banking business during the boom period..

By the original regulations of the Hypothec Bank Act the Bank was required to confine its business to advances in the agricultural and industrial sectors and to lend only on the security of real property. But by 1910 there was some relaxation of this rule. This easing of restrictions was followed by complaints from urban property holders who, finding that they could not claim to be agriculturalists or industrialists, could never borrow money on the security of their real estate. This type of complaint came particularly from those urban residents in big cities other than Tokyo, who could only borrow at high interest. The 1911 revision of the Hypothec Bank Act abandoned the rules relating to the limitation of property which could be used as security. In order to make the revision more efficient, the resource side of the Bank was strengthened by simplifying the procedures of issuing bonds of smaller, and therefore more marketable, denomination. Further in 1914, light railways were to be sanctioned as eligible securities for Hypothec Bank advances. These facilities became more extensive in 1918. In addition, in 1917, industrial associations were to be allowed to enjoy discounting and overdrawing facilities at the Hypothec Bank.[8]

The new facilities opened up a wider range of business opportunities for the Hypothec Bank. It was natural for the Tokyo-based bank to look for closer contacts with the Agri-Industrial Banks which were deployed in every prefecture, although competition between the Hypothec Bank and

Agri-Industrial Banks became very keen, especially after May 1917 when the former was allowed to open a branch in Osaka. This development meant that the Hypothec Bank was in direct competition with the Agri-Industrial Banks. There could only be two alternatives, either a clearer division of the business or amalgamation. The arguments, which had already been vigorous before the war boom, suggested that amalgamation would be preferable although this did not result in immediate or successful legislation.[9] However, it did seem as if the Hypothec and the Agri-Industrial Banks would look increasingly favourably on amalgamation. The Hokkaido Development Bank, remote upon the northern island of Japan, though of the same category as the Hypothec and Agri-Industrial Banks, was not involved. The Hokkaido Bank was a special case concerned with ordinary banking following the relaxation of almost all restrictions on their business conduct. Since the hesitant start of this bank they had been encouraged to undertake domestic and long-term industrial finance banking.

Before and during the First World War the regulations governing the Industrial Bank of Japan were revised so that it would be able to conduct a far wider range of business on the lines of the Hypothec Bank. In March 1911 the Industrial Bank was to be allowed to discount bills, give advances on property and transact securities and buy and sell bullion. These changes enabled the Bank to undertake ordinary banking business. In February 1914 the Bank was permitted to undertake foreign exchange operations, which were thought essential for a bank floating various sorts of Japanese debentures abroad. This sanction enhanced its status and made it similar to the Specie Bank. Further in June 1917 it was permitted to make loans to industrial associations, particularly those situated in urban areas, which had previously done business entirely with the Hypothec and its subordinate Agri-Industrial Banks.[10] The future of both the Hypothec and the Industrial Bank seemed to be with ordinary banking.

In the mean time, the Industrial Bank was authorised by the Finance Ministry to do three important jobs. First, in December 1916, when a German proposal for peace, albeit abortive, was announced, the securities market collapsed both in Tokyo and Osaka. The Industrial Bank, assisted by the Bank of Japan, supplied emergency loans of up to ¥15 million to stockbrokers in the Tokyo and Osaka Stock Exchanges in collaboration with two ordinary banks.[11] This operation would lead to another of larger scale in the early 1920s.[12] Secondly, the Bank supplied ¥5.8 million to support the shipping and shipbuilding industries which, from the latter half of 1918, began to suffer from a constant fall in shipping rates and ship prices. To do this, the Bank was allowed to open a temporary office in Kobe, which soon became permanent, as the second of the

Bank branches. The first branch office had been opened at Nihonbashi, in the very centre of Tokyo. Further, the Bank assisted several shipping firms to set up conjointly a *Kokusai Kisen Kaisha*, or International Shipping Co., in July 1918.[13] This was the beginning of a long-term commitment, for shipping remained depressed and assistance was required for some years.

The third commission related to Chinese investments, which had become important as early as 1904 when the Industrial Bank initiated this business, the first of its sort in Japan's financial history. But during the First World War, Chinese investments became large and important. Between 1913 and 1914, the Industrial Bank invested, through a Japanese company, ¥6 million into Chinese railway schemes. Between 1917 and 1918 there were two important developments. First, the Bank was allowed to issue government-guaranteed debentures to the extent of ¥100 million, the proceeds of which were to be applied for Chinese investments. Using the money, the Industrial Bank, in collaboration with the Banks of Taiwan and Korea, organised a huge loan to China, the so-called 'Nishihara Loan', amounting to more than ¥180 million between January 1917 and September 1918. This loan was done on behalf of the government, although this did not become public, partly because of the uproar in the aftermath of the notorious 'Twenty-One Demands' against China.[14]

Although both the Hypothec and Industrial Banks started as long-term industrial financiers, they were by the end of the war boom very different from each other. The Hypothec Bank undoubtedly started moving towards ordinary banking through the anticipated amalgamation with the Agri-Industrial Banks, even though debenture issuing was a privilege not allowed in ordinary banking. Contrary to the Hypothec Bank, the Industrial Bank of Japan remained a 'special' bank. The Industrial Bank had earlier, in 1906, opened its first branch in Seoul. This was soon taken over by the Bank of Khankuku, the forerunner of the Bank of Korea. Until 1918 it opened only three branches in Nihonbashi, Osaka and Kobe.[15] The small number of banking offices meant that the Bank did not rely on deposits of ordinary customers as did other banks. Curiously the head office of the Industrial Bank was situated at a site remote from the banking centre, within the inner moat surrounding the palace, but this headquarters site was much nearer to the Finance Ministry than any other bank. This location suggests that the Bank was entirely a creature of the government. As it did not have any overseas offices, the foreign business of the Bank was done through the Specie Bank offices abroad. This reliance on the Specie Bank overseas branch network was further evidence that it was in a sense a dummy institution of the Specie Bank.[16] Thus the Industrial Bank always remained a special bank.

Aggressive banking in Korea and Taiwan, 1911–1919

During the war boom, colonial banking made extraordinary strides. The Bank of Taiwan increased its capital fourfold, its deposits more than five-fold and advances nearly sevenfold. The Bank of Korea was even more remarkable. Capital grew fourfold, deposits elevenfold and advances tenfold. This extraordinary growth inevitably brought about some remarkable features of their banking business.

Advances as a percentage of deposits of the Bank of Taiwan increased from 104 per cent in 1914 to 133 per cent in 1919, standing though at 101 per cent on average. Looking into the local figures available only for this period, it is found that the percentages were 200 per cent in Taiwan itself, 87 per cent in Japan and 257 per cent overseas or other than in Taiwan and Japan.[17] The Bank was moving a large amount of its resources to the Chinese mainland, the Malayan straits area and even beyond. This money flow of the Bank can also be perceived from the development of its branch network. Between 1911 and 1919, the Bank increased the number of branches from eleven to thirty-five, of which fourteen were on Taiwan and four in Japan. The rest were on the Chinese mainland and in Singapore, Bombay, London and New York. As far as Taiwan Island was concerned, the Bank did not need to be worried about the lending programme because it was authorised to issue its notes on a fiduciary basis and even to go beyond its limit, that is, to issue excess paper. On average, a little more than half of Bank of Taiwan notes were issued in excess of specie and fiduciary basis from 1914 to 1919. But Bank of Taiwan notes were confined to Taiwan. Therefore the Bank had to rely on the other sources as far as overseas lending was concerned.

The Bank of Taiwan borrowed heavily from the Bank of Japan during the boom years. But it was not sufficient for the Bank of Taiwan which therefore had to search for other resources. It obtained money in two other ways, the first of which was interbank borrowing. During the war boom, the Bank borrowed ¥445 million in this way, more than 97 per cent of which was concentrated in three years from 1917 to 1919. In the year of 1919 alone, the Bank took in more than ¥293 million, an amount far higher than the deposits for that year. Even at the end of 1919, the unpaid balance of interbank borrowing still stood at ¥44 million. Another supply of money was exploited thanks to the call loan market which was rapidly emerging towards the end of the Great War. The Bank started to use the call market in 1919 when it took in a call loan of ¥1,254.5 million.[18] Both interbank and call loans were not necessarily on a short-term basis, but there was no guarantee that the Bank of Taiwan would not use the money obtained for longer-term lending and investments. This created a potential for instability in the business conduct of the Bank of Taiwan which would eventually create a banking crisis of major concern. Although an inspector, a Finance Ministry appointee, was working constantly in the Bank, as in the other special banks, it was very doubtful that serious inspections were being executed regularly to prevent possible danger.[19]

Even so the Bank of Korea was far more aggressive in making advances than its Taiwanese counterpart. Its advances as a percentage of its deposits were 153 per cent on average in the boom. It lent half as much as it had deposited. The figures of the average percentages at three localities between 1917 and 1919 were 198 per cent on the Korean peninsula, 49 per cent in Manchuria and 78 per cent in Japan.[20] In 1919, the Bank of Korea had forty-nine branches, of which twenty-four were in Korea, fourteen in Manchuria, three in Siberia and eight in Japan.[21] The Bank of Korea was primarily concerned with financing Japanese-led industrial transport and other developments in Korea itself, which meant that other areas were starved of resources. For the Bank of Korea, financing the colonisation of the area was a top priority in contrast to the senior colonial Bank of Taiwan, which played a broader role in helping to finance developments over large areas of South East Asia in addition to projects on their own island.

How did the Bank of Korea obtain the resources to do this business? The Korean Bank Act included the stipulation that excessive note issue would, in certain circumstances, be acceptable. In 1917 the sum of ¥10 million was sanctioned, another ¥10 million was added in 1918 and a further ¥30 million in 1919.[22] Indeed, between 1917 and 1919, some two-thirds of the average total note circulation of the Bank was issued under the excessive issue stipulation. Korean Bank notes of course penetrated into Manchuria, where they were made legal tender by the Japanese authorities. These resources were lent directly by the Bank of Korea and indirectly through the *Chosen Shokusan Ginko*, or the Korean Development Bank, and *Tokyo Shokutaku Kabushikikaisha*, or Eastern Development Co.[23] In addition to the colonial system, three Japanese banks, including Daiichi Bank with thirteen branch offices, were operating on Korea in 1919. It is important to note that Korea, together with Taiwan, although firmly under Japanese control during the hectic time of the war boom before 1918, was nevertheless well supplied with effective modern banking networks by Japan. It should be noted that neither the Bank of Korea nor the Bank of Taiwan were controlled by an efficient and satisfactory inspection system.

19 Ordinary and savings banks, the search for strength, 1911–1919

Ordinary versus savings banking: amalgamation, Big Five and overseas business, 1911–1919

Between 1911 and 1919, the number of ordinary banks dropped from 1,613 to 1,340 while savings banks increased in number from 478 to 656. These changes resulted from the revisions in the Savings Bank Decree in 1915 and the Bank Decree in 1916 when the Finance Ministry reinstated the banking department, previously in existence between 1880 and 1891, the main purpose of which was to carry out inspections. This move by the Finance Ministry became ever more urgent because the banking system in Japan was burdened by many small and therefore fragile institutions. However, despite the reinstatement of the banking department, the Finance Ministry failed to institute effective inspections which would have eliminated the malpractices and irregularities of dubious banks. Perhaps the large number of banks discouraged the Ministry? Indeed, from 1916 to 1919, only 131 ordinary and 98 savings banks were inspected by the Ministry, though nearly all special banks were examined.[1] The Ministry clearly preferred supervision to inspections. This attitude of the Finance Ministry was to lead inevitably to a disaster, as will shortly be disclosed.

Revisions in the Savings Bank Decree in 1915 enabled the Finance Ministry to keep tighter control and allowed them to impose punishment for mismanagement on the directors of savings banks. At the same time the revised stipulations allowed the banks to accept wider varieties of savings. The relaxation of savings acceptance made it easier for smaller banks to enter the savings banking sector, thus increasing the number. On the other hand the revisions in the Bank Decree in 1916, similar to the savings counterpart, made supervision stricter and severely prohibited concurrent businesses conducted along with banking. Smaller scale ordinary banks, hitherto doing concurrent business, were therefore forced to withdraw from the ordinary banking field.[2] Through these revisions the Finance Ministry envisaged more explicit division of business between the ordinary and savings banks.

There was another movement which helped to contract the total number of ordinary and savings banks. During the first decade of the twentieth century, 683 banks disappeared, of which only 12 per cent were amalgamated with others. Before 1910 the disappearance of banks was mainly either through failures or a voluntary winding-up of business. In the second decade of the century amalgamation at last started to gain momentum. Between 1911 and 1919 531 banks disappeared, of which 24 per cent, involving 128 banks, was the result of amalgamation. The amalgamation movement was becoming stronger particularly in the three years of 1917 to 1919 when 96 banks were absorbed. The main cause of this movement was the guiding hand of the Finance Ministry which was anxious to make the existing banks larger and stronger. The amalgamation movement ironically led to an increase in the number of savings banks, which could still be launched with relatively little capital.

Although displaying different trends, ordinary and savings banks made great strides, as did special banks, increasing their capital threefold. Deposits and advances of ordinary banking increased fivefold and fourfold respectively, while remarkably, those of savings banking increased sixfold and sevenfold respectively. Furthermore, in terms of advances as a percentage of deposits, savings figures were rising from 65 per cent in 1911 to 83 per cent in 1919, averaging 75 per cent. In comparison, the figures for ordinary banks declined from 111 per cent to 90 per cent, being 104 per cent on average. Clearly, savings banks were receiving money demands from a lower strata of small industries. Additionally, mutual loan associations, pawnbrokers and every sort of small money lenders were mushrooming during the war boom.[3]

The Big Five – Mitsui, Daiichi, Yasuda, Mitsubishi and Sumitomo – were also making extraordinary progress and leading the financing of industries during the boom. Without any amalgamations, they emerged with an increased capital share among ordinary banks, having a little more than 7 per cent of the total in the previous years but 16 per cent on average between 1911 and 1919. In absolute terms, their growth was far more striking. Against the 220 per cent of the total ordinary bank capital growth, the Big Five recorded 420 per cent growth.[4] Mitsui Bank, the capital of which was enhanced from ¥20 million in 1911 to ¥60 million in 1919, made the greatest gains. It was followed by Mitsubishi which jumped up from ¥1 million to ¥30 million. This tremendous increase in the capital was effected to celebrate the independence of the banking department of Mitsubishi Goshi Co. as Mitsubishi Bank in 1919.[5] They were followed by Sumitomo Bank increasing from ¥1 to ¥ 26.2 million, Daiichi from ¥10 to ¥22.7 million and Yasuda from ¥5 to ¥17.5 million.[6] The Big Five, with a capital share of 16 per cent, commanded 24 per cent of the total ordinary bank deposits and 21 per cent of the total advances on average in these years. The rapid growth of *zaibatsu* business thus firmly underlined the importance of the Big Five in the system.

A Finance Ministry survey of foreign banks operating in Japan from 1900 gives us a sketchy idea of foreign banking.[7] Only six foreign banks survived the first decade of the twentieth century in Japan. The Anglo-Japanese Bank, which had arrived in Japan in 1906, dropped out in 1913, making its business over to the Commercial Bank of London.[8] The two senior British overseas banks were the Hongkong and Shanghai Banking Corporation, the only foreign bank represented in all three major ports of Yokohama, Kobe and Nagasaki, and the Chartered Bank of India, Australia and China, which did business through their Yokohama office, their Kobe office having been closed in 1919. The others, all newcomers, included the Russo-Chinese Bank, founded in 1895, which opened its only office in Yokohama in 1899 but which merged with the Banque de Nord in 1910 to form the Russo-Asiatic Bank.[9] The Americans arrived with the International Banking Corporation, founded in Connecticut in 1902, which set up offices in Yokohama and Kobe.[10] Then the Germans came in 1905 with the Deutsch-Asiatische Bank founded in 1889, based upon Shanghai, but with offices in Yokohama and Kobe. These five foreign banks were joined by another three, that is, the Franco-Japanese Bank founded in 1912 as a Franco-Japanese joint venture, Park Union Banking Corporation in 1919 which was taken over by the Asian Banking Corporation in 1922[11] and the American Express Co. in 1919. These late arrivals did not prove to be serious rivals.

Did the foreign banking presence in the major ports affect Japanese banks' willingness to embark upon overseas business themselves? It was a challenge, although independent overseas banking was risky as well as expensive. Therefore most of the Japanese banks seeking foreign contracts did business either through the Yokohama Specie Bank or the foreign, particularly British overseas, banks. From 1900 several top-ranking Japanese banks started tentatively to conduct overseas banking themselves.

In August 1898, Mitsui Bank dispatched a delegation to investigate overseas banking. Arriving in New York, they visited National Park Bank of New York, the Mercantile National Bank of New York and the clearing houses in New York, Boston and Philadelphia. Crossing the Atlantic Ocean, they then moved over to London where they closely investigated the business conduct of the National Provincial Bank, London Westminster Bank and Parr's Bank. In Britain, guided by Mitsui Trading Company officers, they also visited docks and warehouses in London and Liverpool. Returning to Tokyo, Mitsui Bank delegates prepared a report of more than a thousand pages entitled *Gomeikaisha Mitsuiginko Obeishuchoin*

Hokokusho, or *Report of Mitsui Bank Delegates dispatched to the United States of America and Britain.*[12] Receiving this excellent report, Mitsui Bank proceeded to conclude their first correspondent arrangement with Barclays Bank. By 1919 Mitsui Bank had established a correspondence network with nineteen foreign banks including Barclays and Parr's in London, the National City Bank of New York, Disconto Gesellschaft in Berlin and Credit Lyonnais in Paris. In the mean time, in 1913, Mitsui Bank revised its regulations so that it could undertake overseas business more easily. Furthermore, by 1916, permanent representatives were at work in New York and London. In 1917 the first overseas branch was opened in Shanghai.[13]

Sumitomo Bank was in some respects more aggressive than Mitsui. In 1898 Sumitomo dispatched a high official abroad to examine banking in Britain, Germany and France. Returning from the inspection tour, the official, though 'knowing the difficulties of challenging *Shokin*',[14] dared to propose the opening up of overseas banking. On the basis of the proposal, Sumitomo Bank arranged correspondent contracts with the London office of a German bank and with Lloyds Bank in London in 1903. Osaka *ryogae*, with their traditional enterprise, proudly stepped forward during the war boom when in 1916 Sumitomo opened an overseas branch in San Francisco. Previously *Chuo Shogyo*, a small concern, had opened an office there in 1911.[15] By 1919 Sumitomo had opened branches in Shanghai, Bombay, Hankou, New York, Seattle and London. Thus until 1919 Sumitomo became the only Japanese ordinary bank which without any governmental support opened branches in western countries.

In the Sumitomo case, it should be noted that the Bank was following Japanese immigrants to North America. Japanese emigration was increasing in the last quarter of the nineteenth century. When the Japanese government invited applications for 600 Japanese emigrants to America, 28,000 people applied. At the turn of the century, the United States had 86,000 Japanese all told, of whom 62,000 were in Hawaii, which became part of the United States in 1898, and 24,000 in the western states, chiefly California, Oregon and Washington.[16] Japanese emigrants to North America came mainly from south-western Japan, particularly the prefectures of Hiroshima, Yamaguchi and Kumamoto, where the Sumitomo Bank was more strongly represented than any of the other big banks. Two branch establishments on the west coast of the United States were therefore the result of a follow-the-customer policy. Sumitomo, however, had to proceed carefully on account of legal difficulties in each of the states of the United States. Sumitomo therefore had to establish local banks incorporated under the state laws. As a result the Sumitomo Bank of Hawaii was set up in 1916 (reorganised as the Sumitomo Bank of Hawaii Ltd in 1919) and the

Sumitomo Bank of Seattle, Washington state, was established in 1919, but the San Francisco office failed to be independent under the state laws.[17]

Mitsubishi Goshi Co. initiated their overseas business in 1916 when they opened a London branch. Before then, their overseas business was done entirely through the Yokohama Specie Bank and Hongkong and Shanghai Banking Corporation. In 1917, a year after the commencement of the London business, an overseas branch was opened in Shanghai which then gave impetus to Mitsubishi to restructure their entire business organisation. In 1917 Mitsubishi Goshi separated its shipbuilding and iron and steel departments as independent companies, that is, Mitsubishi Shipbuilding Co. and Mitsubishi Iron and Steel Co. In 1918, in the same way, Mitsubishi Mining Co. and Mitsubishi Trading Co. were started. Last but not least, Mitsubishi Bank was born from the banking department of Goshi Co. in 1919.[18]

The coincidence of industrial reorganisation of *zaibatsu* and overseas banking development, demonstrated by Mitsubishi, well illustrated a fundamental cause of Japanese overseas banking aggressiveness. Each of the three banks developing overseas commitments had large groups of industries which were expanding during the war boom of 1915 to 1919. Financing successfully as well as efficiently their ever-growing requirements for buying raw materials and selling manufactured goods could only be done safely by using their own banking facilities. Therefore it was natural that the remaining two of the Big Five, Daiichi and Yasuda Banks, without strong industrial infrastructures, did not require a direct presence abroad. However, it should also be noted that Daiichi Bank continued to open offices on the Korean peninsula even after its national commitments had been cancelled because a Korean bank was established by the Japanese government.

In 1919, at the end of an unprecedented boom, Japanese banking had some seventy overseas branch offices. Sumitomo, Mitsui and Mitsubishi had nine offices in all, and there were several small-scale ordinary banks having an overseas presence. Otherwise the Yokohama Specie Bank and the Bank of Taiwan accounted for more than half the branches of banks overseas. In terms of physical distribution, the Chinese mainland became the chief arena for Japanese overseas banking, where there were some twenty-nine offices. Further north in Russia there was one at Vladivostock. To these Japanese bank branches had to be added another group of banks locally set up in China by Japanese capitalists, totalling twenty-seven in 1919 with thirty-two branch offices and aggregated paid-up capital of ¥14 million, equivalent to 2 per cent of their ordinary bank counterpart.[19] The Japanese banking invasion of China, an omen of a later political development, became increasingly apparent through the hectic years of the boom.

The development of interbank markets and the interest rate cartel, 1911–1919

The amalgamation movement became strong towards the end of the boom; thereafter the total number of all types of banks decreased. However, because branch networks of ordinary and savings banking increased in this period by more than 1,800, there were 4,437 branches in 1919. By 1920 the branch network, which remained basically unchanged until 1959, was complete.

Tokyo and Osaka strengthened their positions as rival financial centres during the war boom period, which ended in 1920. The aggregate of Tokyo and Osaka ordinary and savings paid-up capital commanded 43 per cent of the total in 1919 against 38 per cent in 1911, though, as far as Tokyo–Osaka rivalry was concerned, it was Osaka that took the opportunity, recovering her share from 9 per cent of the total in 1911 to 15 per cent in 1919, whereas Tokyo's share declined by 1 per cent to 28 per cent. Their aggregate shares in the ordinary banks at last exceeded half of the total, reaching 52 per cent in 1919.[20] The supremacy of the two banking centres was also confirmed by the magnitude of bills transacted in the two cities. The sums amounted to 72 per cent of the total in 1911, rising to 76 per cent in 1919.[21]

It was around the two financial centres that the first meaningful interbank market was emerging, albeit as a precarious form of bill broking. Bill broking business, on the model of the British market, had made its appearance earlier in 1899 when Tokisaburo Moroi (uncle of famous industrialist Kanichi Moroi who developed cement manufacturing) started intermediary transactions in bills in Tokyo. Bill broking on Japan's money markets was of two types, that is, call loans which meant lending on the interbank market, and call money which meant borrowing on the interbank market. Moroi's initiative was followed by Seibei Fujimoto in Osaka in 1902. In 1907 Fujimoto reorganised his business into a joint-stock ordinary bank concern, Fujimoto Bill Broker Bank, which was allowed to do any kind of banking business sanctioned under the Bank Decree of 1890, including bill broking. By 1916, the midst of the war boom, at least fourteen specialist bill broking firms were operating in Tokyo, Osaka and Nagoya, and the same year the Bank of Japan opened an account for the leading firm, Fujimoto Bill Broker Bank, a formal appreciation of the usefulness of their activities.[22] The acknowledgments were well-founded in the fact that the never-ending demands for money for foreign trade were certainly due to their operations in financial centres, particularly in Tokyo and Osaka. For the Bank of Japan, which had already supplied huge sums to the Yokohama Specie Bank and Bank of Taiwan, the emergence of bill broking firms was a great relief. Further, in 1919, when the Bank of Japan introduced a method to stamp foreign bills of exchange, that is, to produce bills carrying acceptance stamps by the Bank of Japan, they became a booster to the bill market, though the war boom was coming to an end.[23]

By the beginning of 1919 there were at least sixteen bill broking firms operating in Tokyo, Osaka and Nagoya markets where ordinary banks, stockbrokers, insurance companies, seven textile companies and various sorts of trading companies joined as lenders and borrowers in call loan transactions. Bill brokers usually contacted lenders and borrowers on the telephone, which was already extensively available in several big cities.[24] The sum transacted on each occasion ranged from ¥20,000 to ¥1 million, the average being between ¥50,000 and ¥100,000. Usually the borrowers were requested to offer trustworthy securities such as commercial bills, national bonds, debentures, certificates of deposit and so on, but overnight transactions and those with special banks were not necessarily subject to offering securities. Furthermore, and precariously, there were so-called 'long-term' call loans, the length of which stretched only to three months. Long-term call loans were mainly given to special banks, notably to the Bank of Taiwan.[25] These long-term unsecured call loans weakened the system, which was still dominated by small-scale banking.

By the end of 1918, the balance of call loans stood at ¥312 million and call money at ¥100 million. Of the total call loans, Tokyo accounted for ¥141.2 million and Osaka for ¥145 million; of the call money, Tokyo accounted for ¥6.9 million and Osaka for ¥90 million. The aggregate of both lending and borrowing of Tokyo and Osaka amounted to well over 90 per cent of the total.[26] Osaka's supremacy over Tokyo in the call market reflects the former's recovery as the second money market in Japan. Among sixteen bill broking firms, there emerged the 'Big Four' by 1918, that is, Fujimoto Bill Broker Bank and Masuda Bill Broker Bank, both based in Osaka, and Yanagida Bill Broker and Yamane Bill Broker, both based in Tokyo. Money transacted by these four firms totalled ¥4,464 million in 1918, nearly ¥15 million per day, that is, 6 per cent of Mitsui Bank total advances in the same year.[27]

The emergence and rapid growth of the call money market was merely one of the indications that money demands were ever growing during the war boom. The search for monetary resources was of crucial importance. Additionally, the gradual spread of branch banking and the constant entries of new banks intensified competition and pushed up costs of gathering lending resources, or in other words deposit rates. Many newly set up banks were seeking to obtain resources to finance their concurrent, or parent, business from which they made their entry into the banking sector. Much banking business was done by 'gentlemen's agreement'; even larger banks in big cities including Tokyo and Osaka were keen to operate on this basis. Plenty of smaller, second- and third-rate banks, even those situated in big cities, did not hesitate to offer higher interest rates if they thought they could attract deposits. Two of the special banks, the Bank of Taiwan and the Industrial Bank of Japan, despite the agreements they had signed, installed 'trust deposits', the rates of interest of which were much higher than those paid on deposit accounts.[28]

Price competition was thus accelerating and the banks began to encounter difficulties in the middle of 1918. To avoid disaster the Finance Ministry and the Bank of Japan felt it necessary to increase the Bank Rate in order to cool the money market and bring the fierce price competition under control. In the autumn of 1918 the bank associations of Tokyo, Osaka and Nagoya were urged to restore order by introducing punishment clauses for those who failed to maintain the accepted rates of interest on deposits. The three bank associations concluded in December 1918 their new agreements on deposit rates, which were soon followed by the rest of the bank associations.[29] As far as banking deposits were concerned, the agreements reached in 1918 at last harnessed Japanese banking. Importantly, though, the compulsory agreements did not extend to the call money market except in Tokyo. As a result, smaller, lower-ranked banks and one of the special banks, the Bank of Taiwan, both of which had suffered from considerable losses of deposits following the abandonment of their policy of offering higher interest rates, had to make recourse to the call market particularly at Osaka in order to fill the shortages.[30] Their heavier reliance upon the call market meant that money borrowed on a short-term basis was used for long-term lending. This mismanagement led to a later crisis.

20 Other financial sectors in the boom years, 1911–1919

The war boom stimulated every sort of institution which was in any way involved with money and banking in Japan. Post offices which had operated for a long time, almost since 1868, were by 1900 holding, in the form of small savings, the equivalent of 10 per cent of total banking deposits. These moneys were in effect kept in the trust fund department of the Finance Ministry. They continued to increase in the early 1900s and throughout the war boom. Indeed by 1919, post office savings became the largest resources for direct government needs, amounting to ¥731 million, equivalent to nearly 13 per cent of the total banking deposits.[1]

Another kind of organisation, also important in gathering small savings, was the *mujin*, or mutual loan associations. Already during the first decade of the twentieth century, mutual loan business was progressing and some organised themselves into company form. In 1914 approximately 830 companies with ¥9.6 million paid-up capital were operating. The Finance Ministry determined to set guidelines for mutual loan business in order to protect subscribers and to ensure that their resources were secure. The result was the Mutual Loan Business Act of 1915 which stipulated that the mutual loan company should have a minimum of ¥30,000 nominal capital of which more than half was to be paid in. Subscribers were required to pay instalment money regularly and the company could lend part of the money by lottery, allowing those subscribers who wished to draw lots. These companies were also allowed to buy national and municipal bonds and the debentures and equities of first-rate companies specified by the Finance Ministry, make advances to member subscribers and make deposits of idle money at banks and post offices. During the boom years from 1916 to 1919, the number of firms, both private and joint-stock, increased from 136 to 206, of which 136 were joint-stock, and the paid-in capital increased from ¥2.6 million to ¥4.1 million. The sum received as instalment money and that paid out through lottery, both accurate indicators of business activities, grew remarkably. The former, in effect savings, grew from ¥17.7 to ¥68.8 million, and the latter, in effect advances, from ¥15.2 to ¥59.7 million.[2] Mutual loan companies, the predecessors of mutual banks, thus started to feature in the Japanese banking system.

From 1911 to 1919 the insurance sector expanded, increasing the number of companies by twenty-one to eighty-three, the net premium nearly four-fold to ¥156.4 million and the total assets more than fourfold to ¥556.7 million. Between the two divisions of life and non-life (accident) insurance, the former was larger in 1919 in absolute terms, but non-life insurance companies were more aggressive. The non-life insurance sector, composed of twenty-seven companies, overtook the life insurance sector in terms of number of companies, embracing forty-two firms in 1919. Non-life paid-up capital, or 'fund' in insurance terminology, increased more than threefold from ¥56 to ¥191 million, compared to the life sector whose capital was raised from ¥13.4 to ¥27.5 million. The total assets increase of the non-life sector recorded more remarkable results of a 5.6-fold increase to ¥215.6 million compared to a 3.9-fold increase of the life sector to ¥341.1 million. The strength of growth shown by the non-life sector was an undoubted reflection of the boom in which the flow of goods overseas expanded on an unprecedented scale. Indeed, Mitsui *zaibatsu* set up their own non-life insurance company, Taisho Marine and Fire, specifically to conceal their commodity flows from Tokyo Marine, which was closely linked to their rival Mitsubishi. It is arguable whether capital or total assets would be more suitable and accurate as performance indicators of the insurance business, but even if we use the larger figure, or the total assets, for comparison, the sum of ¥556.7 million was a little more than 5 per cent of the total banking resources of capital, deposits and debentures issued. Although the insurance sector was progressing remarkably, it was still in its infancy.

The securities market, aided by the Bank of Japan special facilities, also expanded during the boom. The value of listed stocks and shares on the Tokyo Stock Exchange increased from ¥2,000 million in 1911 to ¥5,600 million in 1919; at the same time the number of securities listed jumped from 241 to 684. There were two important developments during this period. First, the listed securities became more diversified although national bonds and company equities of course remained in the lead position, but the proportion of company debentures and municipal bonds increased meaningfully and there were, temporarily, even some foreign bonds. Second, before the war boom, of the two leading securities, national bonds had boasted a dominant share of 55 per cent of the total value listed against equities at 38 per cent. The boom reversed the position in which the share of equities leapt up to 54 per cent with national bonds going down to 31 per cent. On the Tokyo Stock Exchange, the number of equities listed and the aggregate face value increased in the same period from 179 companies and ¥756 million to 498 companies and ¥3,053 million respectively. In addition to Bank of Japan special facilities, there was another factor which supported the growth of the securities market. Several *zaibatsu* firms, previously holding exclusively their entire amount of equities, offered a small fraction of their shares on the open market. This single action was positive and encouraged the market.

In the last phase of the boom of 1917 to 1919, there were at least ten securities dealers.[3] Nomura Tokushichi Co., set up in Osaka in 1872 and directly descended from *ryogae*, had the longest tradition. In 1904 Nomura firmly established a modern securities business in Osaka; in 1917 the firm was reorganised and in 1923 it set up an off-shoot, Osakaya Securities Co. Nomura Co. also, in 1918, commenced banking under the title of Osaka Nomura Bank, although banking and securities business was in 1925 separated from the securities department, which eventually became Nomura Securities Co.[4] Towards the end of the boom Fujimoto Bill Broker Bank started worrying about the future of their banking business which was almost entirely dependent upon short-term borrowing and long-term lending. Finally, in 1933, banking was abandoned and the business renamed Fujimoto Bill Broker Securities. It emerged as Daiwa Securities Co. in 1943 when it merged with a trust company whose banking department had been sold to Yasuda Bank.[5]

In 1897 an ambitious young clerk of a merchant house established himself as an independent stockbroker, adopting his own name in the firm title, Koike Goshi, in 1907. In 1911 Koike Goshi took over a small ordinary bank, renaming it Koike Bank and later Koike Securities. On the other hand Koike Goshi changed its title to Yamaichi Goshi, further renaming itself as Yamaichi Securities, which later in 1943 acquired Koike Securities constituting Yamaichi Securities Co.[6] Kawashimayashoten securities firm was started in 1918 by a young running broker. Two years later the Industrial Bank of Japan separated its securities department as Nikko Securities Co. The Bank had long been considering the separation of the model of the National City Bank of New York, which had a securities subsidiary company. Later in 1944 Kawashimayashoten and Nikko merged to form Nikko Securities Co.[7]

Nomura, Daiwa, Yamaichi and Nikko were all of banking origin. This was undoubtedly due to the fact that the stock exchanges were basically sustained by Bank of Japan special discounting facilities enjoyed exclusively by banks. Therefore it must also be added that the close relationships between banking and securities business, on the two levels of firms and money-raising facilities, would convey securities market fluctuations more easily to banking and vice versa. The system, which already had the weakness of mushrooming small banks, was destined to carry with it another potential danger.

Crisis and the road to war, 1919–1937 (eighth year of Taisho to twelfth year of Showa)

Historical background, 1919–1937

The Washington Conference of 1921–1922 which refused equal status to Japan in terms of naval power, and the abrogation of the Anglo-Japanese Alliance, which had sustained Japan from 1902, played into the hands of the small, vocal military clique in Japan which held strong anti-western fascist views. The emergence of the Union of Soviet Socialist Republics following the Russian Revolution of 1917 frightened many in Japan and weakened the already feeble socialist movement there. On the Chinese mainland, the Japanese military radicals never failed to display aggressiveness, deepening their involvement in the invasion of north-east China. Militarism gained force and the party-led government lost their ground. Of twelve prime ministers between 1920 and 1936, five were targets for assassination and three were murdered. This terrible trend was well illustrated by the two abortive military coups of 15 May 1932 and 26 February 1936 and culminated in the founding of Manchukuo in 1932 and the war against China from 1937. The isolation which the Washington Conference agreements brought about in the aftermath of the abolition of the Anglo-Japanese Alliance had far-reaching repercussions. The political and military crises were certainly exacerbated by the disaster of the Great Kanto Earthquake of 1 September 1923, which did great damage to Japan's economy and indirectly brought about the Japanese banking collapse of 1927 which preceded that on Wall Street of October 1929, which in turn resulted in world-wide recession.

21 Post-war collapse, 1919–1923

Banking casualties and emergency measures, 1919–1922

The wartime boom in Japan was inevitably succeeded by recession. The turning point was 1919 and towards the end of the year foreign trade became sharply depressed. During the first quarter of 1920, imports exceeded exports by ¥260 million. This was a heavy blow, suggesting comparisons with the deficit year of 1905 when, during the Russo-Japanese War, the largest deficit during the first decade of the twentieth century was recorded. Japanese exports had ceased to sell abroad. Textiles were seriously hit and even silk, usually in steady demand, was by January 1920 unable to find good markets. The Japanese mercantile marine was badly affected as shipping rates fell by nearly two-thirds during the course of the year.[1] The collapse of foreign trade affected the holdings of specie reserve which in Japan between 1919 and 1922 decreased from ¥2,045 to ¥1,830 million, an 11 per cent fall. More worrying, specie kept abroad, chiefly in London, which reflected most closely Japan's foreign trade position, fell 54 per cent, from ¥1,343 to only ¥615 million during the same period.[2] Japan's disappearing specie was a matter for serious concern.

Bank of Japan interest rates, which had been at their lowest ever at 5.11 per cent in March 1917, were twice raised in an attempt to cure heated money markets and soaring prices and by March 1918 were at 6.57 per cent. In October and November 1919 the rates were further raised, eventually to 8.03 per cent, where they remained for more than five and a half years, a record. As a result call money market rates soared from 9.125 per cent in January to 12.77 per cent in the middle of March 1920.[3] Tight money pressed hard on banks and bill brokers who were urged by their customers to lend, so that foreign trade payments already in arrears could be paid. On 15 March 1920, 'Black Monday', both securities and commodities markets simultaneously collapsed. Settlements for commodities transactions suddenly came to a standstill. Exporters could not find banks to discount, or buy, their foreign bills of exchange, and importers had to meet cancellations of goods ordered or had great difficulty in collecting payments. Securities prices plunged sharply on Black Monday: the Nihon Yusen share price which was previously ¥228 fell on 15 March to ¥192, a 16 per cent drop, and that of Kanebo fell from ¥563 to ¥470, a 17 per cent drop.[4]

Bill broking firms, heavily involved in both the securities and the money markets, were inevitably in great difficulties. First, two big firms, Masuda and Fujimoto Bill Brokers in Osaka, suffered a severe run in early April 1920. Then the pressure spread to Tokyo towards the end of the month when ordinary and savings banks were under threat. Between April and July 1920, 57 bank head offices and 102 branch offices had runs on them and 21 banks were forced, temporarily, to close their doors. No banks failed as a result of this panic, but many of those temporarily closed were permanently damaged both in terms of pecuniary resources and creditworthiness.[5]

During the course of heavy runs, the Bank of Japan supplied emergency loans to those banks which required reserves to sustain deposit withdrawals amounting to ¥85.33 million.[6] The Bank also provided emergency money for the securities market and those infrastructural sectors the collapse of which would undermine the banking system as a whole.[7] Reviewing the banking panic, the Bank of Japan pointed out the mismanagement of banking business, the risky lending, either uncovered by securities or covered by doubtful securities, priority lending to directors of the banks concerned, and irregular and careless audits.[8] This devastating criticism really hit the mark, but it should be questioned how seriously it was received by financial authorities and bankers.

Although it is not clear how the Finance Ministry regarded the comments of the Bank of Japan on banking mismanagement, the Ministry were quick to respond in allowing the Bank of Japan to assist tottering banks. The legislative framework was tightened so that both ordinary and savings banks would be forced to strengthen themselves in order to be better able to face up to difficulties yet to come.

In August 1920 the Finance Ministry made an essential amendment to ease the amalgamation process so that ordinary banks and savings banks could come together. Furthermore the Bank Decree relating to amalgamations was to be exempted from the tight regulations of commercial law. Anticipating cases of ordinary and savings banks joining force the Decree was revised, and this enabled ordinary banks taking over savings banks to succeed to the savings business and continue in it until the expiration of the savings contracts with the customers of the former savings banks.[9]

Eight months later, the Finance Ministry passed the brand new Savings Bank Act of 1921. This was aimed at eliminating abuses by banks which either made loans to savings banks without adequate security or drained them of funds. Indeed, there were many cases of the banks using the savings banks as deposit-collecting machines. The new Savings Bank Act defined the savings bank as one which would accept deposits of not less than ¥10 on a compound interest basis. In other words, the minimum was raised from ¥5 to ¥10. The minimum capital stock was to be raised from ¥30,000 to ¥500,000 and the savings bank would have to be a joint-stock company. The reserve fund to be applied for the withdrawal of savings was also raised from one-quarter to one-third of the amount. More restrictive was the method of portfolio management. While the holding of securities authorised by the Finance Ministry and the advances on them were encouraged, other lending was to be subject to strict guidelines. For interbank lending, the savings bank was prohibited to lend any one bank a sum exceeding either 10 per cent of its own aggregate savings or 25 per cent of the aggregate of the borrowing bank's capital and reserve. For non-bank lending, the savings bank was prohibited to lend the customer a sum exceeding either 10 per cent of the aggregate of its own paid-up capital and reserve or 20 per cent of the borrower's capital stock. Although the tax levied on savings banking business was halved, the new Savings Bank Act was very restrictive. It also ensured a complete break between the ordinary and savings banking business.[10]

Indeed, the result of the amended Bank Decree and the new Savings Bank Act was spectacular. The amalgamation movement, which will be discussed shortly, was at last given a signal to go. Even more notable was the change in the number of ordinary and savings banks. More than 400 banks became ordinary banks and a considerable number of banks withdrew from the savings bank movement. Most of the savings banks became ordinary banks. Unfortunately, notwithstanding the new laws, many small, weak banks remained.

In November 1922, Junnosuke Inoue, the governor of the Bank of Japan, reiterated to a meeting of bankers in Osaka the points raised by the Bank report. The governor stressed the needs of sound banking and warned the bankers that without due care a serious disaster would fall upon the Japanese banking system as a whole.[11] Unfortunately Inoue's remarks were only too prophetic.

All set for amalgamation, 1919–1923

In September 1927, to commemorate the fiftieth anniversary of its foundation, Mitsui Bank created a research institution, *Kinyukenkyukai*, or the Institute of Banking and Financial Research. Thereafter, the Institute contributed greatly to the advancement of banking research and encouraged young researchers in banking science.[12] One of the earlier contributions was the publication of an important survey on the bank amalgamations up to 1932, which remains one of the first quality studies on the subject. The survey proved that the years 1919 to 1923 were only a prelude to the great bank amalgamation movement from 1920 to 1932, but the early period set the tone for what was to come.

Between 1921 and 1923, 389 banks, both ordinary and savings, amalgamated and 218 banks disappeared.[13] In these years the total number of ordinary and savings banks dropped from 1,963 to 1,837, a decrease of 126. Never again would the number of banks in Japan be as high. Towards the end of 1922, another financial panic spread from Kyoto and although the magnitude was less significant than that of 1920, it reinforced the pressure towards amalgamation. The result of the Kyoto crisis was an upsurge in the number of amalgamations. Of 389 banks participating in the mergers, 158 banks, or 41 per cent, did so in 1923. Of the 218 banks which disappeared through mergers, 92 banks, or 42 per cent, did so in 1923. *Daiginkoshugi*, or the 'becoming-the-larger-bank principle', became important.

The tendency was most strikingly illustrated by one of the Big Five, Yasuda Bank, which, almost accidentally, took the lead in this field. In September 1921, the founder and supreme leader of Yasuda Bank and *zaibatsu*, Zenjiro Yasuda, a legendary figure who had emerged from the poverty of the Shogunate era, was assassinated by an insane man at his villa on the shore of Kanagawa. In order to fill this great gap, Yasuda Bank approached a high-ranking officer of the Bank of Japan, Toyotaro Yuki. Yuki had entered the Bank of Japan in 1903 and had been appointed manager in Osaka in 1918. It was Korekiyo Takahashi, then concurrently prime minister and Finance Minister, who introduced Yuki to Yasuda *zaibatsu*. Yuki subsequently assumed the managing directorship at Yasuda Hozensha, headquarters of Yasuda *zaibatsu*, and remained active in Yasuda until 1928 when he deserted Yasuda to become the president of the Industrial Bank of Japan. Later in 1937 Yuki briefly took the office of Finance Minister before moving to the Bank of Japan as governor, where he stayed throughout the Pacific Wars.

It was under Yuki's headship that Yasuda pioneered an era of very large banks. There were twenty-two banks in the early 1920s which were in Yasuda's sphere of influence, having built up a close relationship through either assistance loans during crises or support when setting up their business. Of the twenty-two, ten banks were selected for their profitability, business performance and location. After the selection and the conclusion of the agreement among the merging banks, Yasuda Hozensha set up in April 1923 a *Hozen Ginko*, or 'Virtue-maintaining Bank', with paid-in capital of ¥5 million which was entirely held by the Yasuda family, Yuki and an ex-managing director of Hozensha. The Bank was advertised as displaying the goodwill of Yasuda that the amalgamation would be 'strictly' on equal terms. Therefore, as the first step, eleven banks including Yasuda Bank trusted their whole equities to Hozen Bank. When the amalgamated Bank[14] was about to start business, the Great Earthquake hit Tokyo and Yokohama, causing devastation. The opening of the new Bank was postponed until November 1923 when Hozen Bank was renamed and emerged as Yasuda Bank.

This merger brought Yasuda Bank to the supreme position among the Big Five. The paid-up capital jumped from ¥17.5 million in 1919 to ¥92.75 million in 1923, deposits from ¥129 to ¥568 million, advances from ¥119 to ¥519 million and branches from 22 to 210. Apart from the number of branches, the second ranking was Mitsui Bank with capital of ¥60 million, deposits of ¥418 million and advances of ¥384 million. As for number of branches, Yasuda's 210 branches were an astonishing achievement compared to the second bank, Sumitomo, with only 43 branches. Thereafter Yasuda became the target of the rest of the Big Five. First, in terms of deposits, Mitsui and Sumitomo caught up with Yasuda in 1929. Next, in the number of branches, Sanwa Bank, the amalgamated version of Konoike, Yamaguchi and Sanjushi Banks, all based in Osaka, overtook Yasuda in 1933. Lastly, regarding advances, Sumitomo beat Yasuda in 1938. However, the paid-up capital of Yasuda was never challenged by any other bank before 1945.[15] Thus an era of gigantic banks in Japan was pioneered by Yasuda at the time of the Great Earthquake.

Special banking in retreat, 1919–1923

Specie exports, a vital element of the gold standard system, had in 1917 been prohibited in Japan, as elsewhere in the major western countries. In the wake of the Great War, as early as 1919, the United States again adopted the gold standard. Following this, two successive European conferences, held at Brussels in 1920 and Genoa in 1922, resolved that a return to the gold standard would be favourable for the member countries, but that none of them would do so before 1924. Looking at the progress of western preparations for returning to the gold standard, the Japanese government constantly laid on their table the question when and at what rate Japanese currency should resume convertibility, but no resolutions were carried.[16] Heavy deficits in current trade balances resulting from an excess of imports over exports in the early 1920s and the dwindling of the specie reserve abroad, mainly kept in the Yokohama Specie Bank London safe, were threatening *Shokin*, the most senior special bank. Indeed, for the first time since the reinforcement by Matsukata in the aftermath of the 1881 crisis, the Specie Bank was forced to reduce its activities. Its total liabilities/assets decreased from ¥1,466 million in 1919 to ¥1,294 million in 1923. Buying exchange, or discounting foreign bills, the most significant business of the Specie Bank, dropped from

¥583 million in 1919 to ¥421 million in 1923.[17] Special banking difficulties really began.

The industrial wing of special banking also faced problems. The Hokkaido Development Bank, the Hypothec Bank and the forty-six Agri-Industrial Banks had long been subject to discussions on whether they should merge. The discussions were analogous to those on the national bank system in the early 1870s; it was a struggle between centralisation and decentralisation. This pattern of confrontation was laid before Diet committees twice, in 1907 and 1918, but nothing came of this. In the wake of the war boom, creeping depression at last overwhelmed anti-amalgamation factions through the fact that a larger resource with lower interest rates would be imperative and this could be attained only through mergers of the smaller Agri-Industrial Banks with the Hypothec Bank, the headquarters.[18] In 1921, the Hypothec/Agri-Industrial Bank Amalgamation Act was passed.

The Act was aimed at the absorption of the subordinate Agri-Industrial Banks by the Hypothec Bank so that the former would in effect become branches of the latter and the former's debentures would be renamed as the latter's at their merger.[19] The legislation was so encouraging for the Agri-Industrial Banks that nineteen allied themselves with the Hypothec Bank by 1923. Therefore the results were remarkable increases of business for the Hypothec Bank. The advances jumped from ¥285 million in 1919 to ¥633 million in 1923, compared with the ¥394 million of the twenty-seven still independent Agri-Industrial Banks. The deposits increased sixfold in the same period to ¥60 million, nearly half of the aggregate of the independent banks. The debentures grew nearly twofold to ¥544 million, far more than double the independents' aggregate. Through the amalgamations, the Hypothec Bank made another outstanding stride towards ordinary banking at the same time as it was retreating from the special banking arena.

At the other end of the special banking arena stood the Industrial Bank of Japan. During the same period the Industrial Bank increased advances from ¥169 to ¥308 million, deposits from ¥45 to ¥70 million and debentures from ¥233 to ¥305 million, which shows that the strength of growth was much weaker than that of the Hypothec Bank. The relatively poor performance of the Industrial Bank reflected a special aspect of their business. First, in April 1920, the Bank was commissioned to lead a rescue operation for the collapsing securities market. The Bank organised a strong syndicate composed of fifteen first rate banks, including the Yokohama Specie Bank, Bank of Taiwan, Bank of Korea, Daiichi, Mitsui, Mitsubishi and Fifteen Banks. They raised ¥40 million to assist the securities market, which was able to resume transactions a month later thanks to this rescue.[20] This marked only the start of their assistance commitments.

In June 1920, the Industrial Bank was again commissioned by the government, this time to lead a larger national bond underwriting syndicate of banks based in Tokyo, Osaka and Nagoya, including the Specie Bank, Banks of Taiwan and Korea, Daiichi, Mitsui, Mitsubishi, Fifteen, Yasuda, Kawasaki, Sumitomo, Konoike and the rest of the leading banks. Then the Industrial Bank invited applications for assistance loans from various sectors which totalled ¥92.115 million. The following sums were actually distributed to various sectors of strategic importance which were having difficulties in the aftermath of the boom: telecommunications and electricity, ¥8.65 million; paper and flour, ¥8 million; shipping and shipbuilding, ¥7 million; chemical and brewing industries, ¥6.8 million; mining, ¥5 million; textiles, ¥4.12 million; railways, ¥3 million; iron and steel and machinery, ¥1.675 million; sugar refining, ¥0.6 million; and miscellaneous, ¥2.95 million. In addition the Industrial Bank specially supplied their own resources to shipping and shipbuilding, copper mining, silk and small industrialist sectors which were particularly ailing in the depression. For instance, the Bank gave shipbuilding and shipbuilding companies from ¥30 million to more than ¥50 million every year between 1921 and 1925, among which International Shipping Co. was the most favoured borrower as the Bank itself was among the founders under the governmental assistance.[21]

Worst hit by the depression of 1920 were the Banks of Taiwan and Korea. Their difficulties were well represented by their deposit trend which showed substantial decreases between 1919 and 1923, with the Bank of Taiwan deposits falling from ¥287 to ¥202 million and those of the Bank of Korea falling from ¥189 to ¥163 million. In the case of the Taiwan Bank, the collapse of both securities and commodities markets partly destroyed their usual reservoir of monetary resources, a considerable portion of which was interbank deposits from bill brokers on very short-term bases. Once bill brokers withdrew their money from the Bank of Taiwan, a large amount of long-term lending immediately proved to be in dead loans. For the Bank of Korea, the situation was more or less the same. As far as settlements effected on Taiwan Island and the Korean peninsula were concerned, both Banks could take the easy way out of issuing more notes. But the problem was that they were both actively engaged in foreign trading which necessitated settlement in hard money, or at least by Bank of Japan money. The Bank of Taiwan's difficulty was believed to be due to the fact that it had been too deeply involved with Suzuki Trading Co. shortly before the Great Earthquake. Bank of Japan special accommodation for the Bank of Taiwan was outstanding at ¥117 million, surprisingly nearly 30 per cent of total Bank of Japan lending. Also at the same time the Bank of Korea was borrowing ¥17.5 million from the Bank of Japan.[22]

22 The 1923 catastrophic earthquake, 1927 financial disaster and the new Bank Act, 1923–1927

The Great Earthquake of 1923, metropolitan banks in ruin, 1923–1926

On 1 September 1923, at 11.58 a.m., a severe earthquake of 7.9 on the Richter scale hit the Pacific coast of Japan at Tokyo Bay in the area known as the southern Kanto district. This was the Great Kanto Earthquake, the most serious natural disaster ever to fall on Japan. The number of people affected was 3.4 million, of whom more than a hundred thousand died out of a total Kanto population of 11.8 million. Deaths were particularly heavy in Tokyo and Yokohama, which accounted for 65 per cent and 32 per cent of the dead and for 82 per cent and 17 per cent of the missing respectively. The government later estimated the aggregate amount of assets destroyed to be ¥4,570 million, which was 38 per cent of the national income of 1923. More than a third of these were burnt to ashes in the Great Earthquake.

The disastrous earthquake had major consequences for the Japanese banking system. On the day of the Great Earthquake, there were 542 bank offices in Tokyo comprised of 168 head offices and 374 branches, of which 285 offices, or 63 per cent, were burnt down. In Yokohama, where most of the banking offices in Kanagawa prefecture were concentrated, all forty-two offices, save for the Specie Bank head office, disappeared completely. In Tokyo, of the eighty-four member banks of the Tokyo Bank Association there survived only eight banks without serious damage including the head offices of the Hypotech Bank, Industrial Bank and Mitsubishi and the Tokyo branches of the Specie Bank, Bank of Taiwan and Sumitomo. The main building of the Bank of Japan was partially destroyed by fire.[1] The situation was as follows:

Meanwhile, on account of not only destruction and burnt-down offices but also disorder and unrest of the people in the city, almost all banks quit operating. Besides the Bank of Japan, only Daishin Bank dared to continue their business. Otherwise, even the big banks remained closed until the expiration of a seven-day moratorium.[2]

The most terrible situation confronting the financial authorities and banks was the loss of all records detailing advances, losses of securities

147

against which they allowed advances and the resultant disastrous fall of equity, bond and debenture market prices. On 7 September 1923, the privy council promulgated by decree a moratorium sanctioning the suspension of any pecuniary repayments arising from private transactions effected in the areas affected by the earthquake except payment of salaries and wages until the last day of September 1923.[3] On 27 September, three days before the expiration of the moratorium, the Decree of the Compensation by the Bank of Japan of Losses arising from Discounts of Bills related to the Earthquake was proclaimed. The Decree defined the Earthquake Casualties Bills as 'bills payable in the stricken districts (Tokyo, Kanagawa, Saitama, Chiba and Shizuoka Prefectures to be designated as those areas), or drawn by those operating offices at the districts at the time of the earthquake or payable by the said parties and thereafter discounted by banks before First Day of September Taisho 12th Year'.[4] In addition to the Casualties Bills thus defined, the Decree also included the renewed Casualties Bills and several sorts of liabilities similar to the former.[5] The Decree obliged the Bank of Japan to make special accommodations against the Casualties Bills.

It was estimated that the aggregate Casualties Bills amounted to ¥2,100 million, but even for the Bank of Japan this was only a guess. Bank of Japan special accommodations eventually totalled ¥430.81 million, a little more than one-fifth of the estimated aggregate. The details are known of only about fifty-seven debtors whom the Bank of Japan termed as 'big debtors', though their total sum exceeded half of the Bank's special accommodations. Fifty-seven firms and financial houses were borrowing from ninety-six banks which applied for Bank of Japan special accommodations against Casualties Bills in their possession. Remarkably, the top five firms accounted for ¥117.36 million, or 54 per cent of the big debts. Among the five, Suzuki Shoten, or Suzuki Trading Co., claimed ¥71.89 million, that is, 33 per cent of the big debts and 17 per cent of total Bank of Japan special accommodation. Suzuki Co. was actively engaged in the sugar and camphor trade, the staple products of Taiwan. Suzuki's business grew rapidly, though precariously and excessively, through the boom, fed by generous bank lendings. Second to Suzuki was Kuhara Shoji, or Kuhara Trading Co., the direct antecedent of Hitachi and closely related to that of Nissan Motor Co., whose debts stood at ¥22.2 million. These top two debtors were followed by International Shipping with ¥8.04 million, Hara Gomei Co., silk trader, ¥7.72 million and Takata Shokai, cotton trader, ¥7.51 million.[6]

The list of banks having been allowed advances on the Earthquake Casualties Bills reveals another astonishing fact. There were ten banks which held Casualties Bills of more than ¥10 million. At the top of the list was the Bank of Taiwan. The Bank held a tremendous amount of the Bills, totalling ¥115.225 million, far more than one-third of the 'big debts', and more dangerously nearly 60 per cent of the sum was given to Suzuki and 18 per cent to Kuhara. This was alarming, and the Casualties Bill procedure was *de facto* one of financing the Bank of Taiwan and Suzuki. In the face of the Bank of Taiwan case, the rest of top-ranking bank financing was almost eclipsed. Following the Bank of Taiwan were Fujimoto Bill Broker Bank with ¥37.214 million, Bank of Korea ¥35.987 million, Yasuda Bank ¥25 million, Murai Bank ¥20.429 million, Fifteen Bank ¥20.073 million, Kawasaki Bank ¥19.373 million, Ohmi Bank ¥13.423 million, Hayakawa Bill Broker Bank ¥12.624 million and Toyokuni Bank ¥10.724 million. Although the Bank of Korea and Toyokuni Bank were involved in Suzuki business, their debts were negligible. More precarious and risky were two banks in particular, Murai and Fifteen. Murai Bank was literally a house bank of the Murai family whose business had expanded rapidly during the war boom. Of the Bank's Casualties Bills 80 per cent originated from Murai family business. More than 40 per cent of the holding of Fifteen Bank came from one particular firm, International Shipping having long faced serious problems since the depression in the aftermath of the war boom. In addition to these top ten dangerous banks, there existed numerous risky names in the list of ninety-six banks prepared by the Bank of Japan.[7] Therefore the only problem was how speedily they would be able to get rid of their Casualties Bills. However, the situation in which they were placed was not at all easy.

The Ministry of Finance, very anxious about the situation, decided to set up a commission to consider the fundamental structure of the banking system. The Commission on the Financial Structure was appointed in September 1926 and the first general meeting was about to be convened in the autumn of 1926. In the mean time the total amount of Casualties Bills diminished from ¥430.816 million in September 1923 to ¥206.8 million at the end of 1926, a decrease of more than 50 per cent. But the position in December 1926 was by no means satisfactory. There were still twenty banks which could not liquidate their Casualties Bills. The Bank of Taiwan had more than ¥100 million while the Bank of Korea retained ¥21.6 million, Murai ¥15.5 million and Ohmi ¥9.7 million.[8] It was against this gloomy situation that the Taisho era ended on 24 December 1926 with the death of the Emperor. The new era of Showa commenced on 25 December 1926 with Hirohito as Emperor. On 26 December, the second day of the Showa era, the Fifty-second Session of the Imperial Diet was opened to consider measures to cope with the threatened banking crisis.

Over-ambition in Taiwan and banking collapse in Japan, 1927

The Fifty-second Session of the Diet faced two formidable questions, the Earthquake Casualties Bills and the restructuring of the banking system.

First, on 26 January 1927, two bills to provide national bonds to compensate for the losses caused by the Earthquake Casualties Bills were laid down before the Diet. The two bills were to facilitate the final disposition of bad debts by issuing national bonds which could be exchanged with Earthquake Casualties Bills falling in the hands of the Bank of Japan and others. Only two days before the opening of their debates on the bills, the medium-sized Imabari Shogyo Bank, fourth ranking in Ehime prefecture in the west on Shikoku island, closed its doors due to runs caused by rumours. A week later, the tiny Fukaya Shogyo Bank, operating in Saitama prefecture, north of Tokyo, collapsed. These failures did not attract any special notice.

Meanwhile debates in the Diet were increasingly heated as members argued whether the two bills would favour some particular firms rather than others. It was suspected that the firms favoured were the Bank of Taiwan and Suzuki Trading Co. The opposition party at that time, Seiyukai (Society of Political Friends), pressed the Kenseikai (Constitutional Government Party) government led by Premier Reijiro Wakatsuki, with Naoharu Kataoka as Finance Minister, to disclose the names of bad debtors. The Wakatsuki cabinet barely survived the attack but did succeed in getting the bills through on 4 March 1927.[9] Bank closures continued.

The opposition brought the matter of disclosures of bad debtors before the budget committee, pressing the government harder than ever to give details of Earthquake Casualties Bills, particularly those of Suzuki which were, rightly, considered critical. Otherwise the opposition party persisted in its determination to refuse to pass the budget bills. Before the committee held on 14 March 1927, Finance Minister Kataoka countered:

Suzuki is no more than one ordinary firm. At this moment the budget bills have nothing to do with the disclosure of bills and notes related to this one particular firm. If you say the bill has something to do with the case, that is your opinion and not mine. Even if there might have happened to be any relationship between them, I do not think it good for the business world as a whole to disclose these things which will only spread doubts in the public mind.[10]

The excited Finance Minister blurted out:

Indeed, around noon today, [Tokyo] Watanabe Bank at last collapsed. This is most unfortunate . . . The affair would somehow require rescue measures. – But to assist the financial world generally, we have no choice but to push on with measures I have mentioned earlier.[11]

Although the Tokyo Watanabe Bank was in a grave situation, it had not actually closed its doors when the Finance Minister gave his reply to the committee. Inevitably the Finance Minister's unfortunate slip of the tongue did cause heavy runs and the Watanabe Bank was forced to close its doors the following day.

It has generally been believed that the 1927 banking crash began on 15 March 1927 when Tokyo Watanabe Bank closed . However, in retrospect, as we have already clearly noted, the crisis had been brewing since the Great Kanto Earthquake. Indeed, it grew slowly but steadily. Looking more closely at the course of incidents, from the outset of the year 1927, perhaps we can identify four waves. The first wave came towards the end of January 1927 until 8 March 1927 and engulfed six banks including Imabari Shogyo and Fukaya Shogyo Banks. Their total paid-in capital amounted to a little less than ¥5 million, which was a small sum. These six banks had thirty-six offices in all, remote even from local financial centres.[12] Their small business was not enough to divert the attention of the financial authorities and the Diet, who were absorbed in debates on the Earthquake Casualties Bill questions.

Then a week later came the careless remark of the Finance Minister. The closure of Tokyo Watanabe Bank on 15 March 1927 was immediately followed by the collapse of another two Tokyo-based banks by 19 March. By 24 March nine banks including Murai Bank had disappeared. This second wave submerged twelve banks with ¥19.4 million paid-in capital and 106 offices. The stormy Fifty-second Session of the Imperial Diet ended on 25 March 1927 when the government was relieved to be released from the persistent pressure from the opposition. But peace was short-lived. The third wave of failures started on 31 March and lasted until 13 April, pulling down four banks with ¥8.5 million paid-in capital and forty-three offices, far greater casualties than those in the first wave.

Eventually, on 14 April 1927, Premier Wakatsuki decided to bring these financial matters before the new young Emperor and discuss them in the privy council, the advisory body. Wakatsuki believed that the difficulties concerning assistance to the Bank of Taiwan, and the problems of the Suzuki Company in Taiwan, could be overcome.[13] The first meeting of the privy council was convened on 14 April to discuss whether ¥200 million should be given to the Taiwanese rescue. The privy council laid the matter on the table until 17 April 1927 when the prime minister's request was rejected by nineteen votes to eleven. Feeling satisfied with the result, the most senior and influential councillor, Miyoji Ito, stood up to explain his disapproval as follows:

In sum I dare to say that the prevalent crisis is resulting from mismanagement of domestic and foreign affairs by the present cabinet . . . All in all, the present proposal is offensive against the stipulations and spirits of Articles 8 and 70 of the Constitution. I believe that the responsibilities of the cabinet bringing such constitutionally offensive matters to His Majesty should not be overlooked.[14]

The privy council rejection of the prime minister's plan to give further aid to the Bank of Taiwan was to have far-reaching consequences for Japan which spread well beyond her banking system.

The following day the Reijiro Wakatsuki cabinet resigned *en masse*. On 18 April 1927, the Bank of Taiwan closed its doors in Japan although it remained operational on Taiwan. There followed eleven bank closures, including Ohmi Bank, until 21 April when the gigantic Fifteen Bank, or so-called 'Aristocratic Bank', as its owners were almost exclusively aristocrats, was forced to close its doors. In all, the four-day banking crash pulled down twelve banks with ¥104.5 paid-in capital and 134 offices. As there was no government at the time, the privy council stepped in by promulgating a decree, a moratorium for three weeks starting from 22 April 1927. Thus the banking crash culminated in the so-called 'Showa Second Year Financial Crisis'.

Later, between April 1928 and July 1929, the Bank of Japan research department carried out detailed investigations into twenty cases of closed banks, which some forty years afterwards were disclosed for the first time and made available for banking historians.[15] The reports enable us to make some case studies of the closed banks, of which four examples will be given here.

Bank failure was regarded as a rather routine phenomenon in Japanese banking history since the years of the national bank system and so the case of Imabari Shogyo Bank did not at first glance attract attention. However, closer examination reveals some interesting features. Imabari Shogyo's closure was not only the first bank failure in the Showa era, but also exemplified the cases that followed. Imabari Shogyo fell into difficulties immediately in the wake of the cotton recession in the autumn of 1926 and was forced to close on account of heavy runs upon it. Investigation disclosed that as a bank, they were in fact lending out 30 per cent of their resources to their directors' concerns. Even worse, the advances were made either on their bank stock or without taking any securities at all. Astonishingly enough, bank inspection was seldom done so that matured advances were not even renewed.[16]

Tokyo Watanabe Bank was in the second rank, among Tokyo-based banks, with ¥5 million paid-in capital, ¥37 million deposits and ¥38.5 million advances, which figures were approximately double those of Imabari Shogyo's. Watanabe Bank was entirely owned by the Watanabe family who invested their own money in various concerns, to which Watanabe Bank was lending the enormous sum of 74 per cent of the total advances. Advances were allowed without accepting any securities at all. Furthermore, 80 per cent of non-Watanabe interest advances were also unsecured. Akaji Savings Bank, which closed on the same day as Watanabe Bank, was effectively a subordinate banking concern of the Watanabe Bank.[17]

Then came the culmination. The Bank of Taiwan, at the very core of the

1927 banking crisis, had ¥39.3 million paid-in capital, ¥92.8 million deposits and ¥544.9 million advances at the time of closure, and it was the largest holder of Earthquake Casualties Bills. The Bank, albeit one of the special banks, fell because of the rejection of special treatment by the privy council. The Bank of Japan carefully examined the business conduct of the Bank of Taiwan and revealed four important points. First, there was a tremendous increase in advances, particularly in the two months of February and March 1927, resulting in a disproportion between deposits and advances at the time of closure. The second point was that there was too much concentration of advances in particular firms, of which Suzuki Co., as already shown, was prodigious. Third, there were too many bad securities. Nearly two-thirds of fixed loans were allowed on equities, bonds and debentures whose market values lessened greatly over the years following 1920. Fourth, the Bank was too heavily dependent upon external resources other than deposits. The proportion of deposits in the total resources decreased from 89 per cent in 1919 to 14 per cent in 1926. One of the main resources in the latter year was call money, reaching 76 per cent of the total.[18] The long-term lending out of short-term borrowed-in money was indeed a dangerous business which the careful banker must avoid and which the Bank of Taiwan had long pursued.

The failure of the Fifteen Bank was shocking for the public especially as, on the surface, there was no particular reason for the failure. The Bank had recently absorbed three banks in Osaka, Kobe and Tokyo respectively, intending to be a nationwide bank in terms of branch banking. Although it may be said that the amalgamation of three banks might also be the absorption of their bad debts, the fundamental aspects of their business which the investigation revealed were no better than the cases above. Remarkably the Matsukata family business took 50 per cent of big loans and 30 per cent of the total lending of the Fifteen Bank. The Matsukata family, whose head, Masayoshi Matsukata, fortunately did not survive to witness the disaster, were the largest proprietors of the Bank. Additionally, advances, except discounting, were made without securities.[19]

In summing up these four cases, we can deduce several common characteristics from the failed bank management. The banks concentrated too much money in a too few firms, particularly those of directors and shareholders. In supplying such a big amount, the banks failed to secure the guarantee of reimbursing their loans. In addition the banks either ignored or even sabotaged all or part of the procedures of auditing their business conduct. These three aspects of business behaviour were apparently a product of their aggressive performance nurtured during the war boom, as the governor of the Bank of Japan had earlier feared[20] although it is understandable that it was hard to contract the over-expanded businesses.

Especially in the circumstances in the aftermath of such a terrible situation as the Great Kanto Earthquake, it is right to say that the governor's warning should have been listened to earlier.

Indeed, the cost the Japanese banking system had to pay was tremendous. Between 24 January and 21 April 1927, thirty-four banks were forced to close the doors of 319 offices. Even after the moratorium, by September 1927 another ten banks had closed their doors. According to an examination carried out by the Finance Ministry in the summer of 1927, the number of closed, nearly closed and officially suspended banks reached 126.[21] The aggregate sum of the paid-in capital of the thirty-four banks closed by the moratorium was ¥127.7 million, 6.7 per cent of the total. By the time the moratorium was in effect, ¥609 million, 5.4 per cent of the total deposits, was withdrawn. This money undoubtedly found its way to bigger, therefore safer, banks and even beyond banking, that is, to post office savings, which indeed increased in the wake of the banking crash.

Another Finance Ministry examination reveals that only twelve of the thirty-four banks could reopen their doors by the end of March 1928, and that five of the twelve relied heavily upon Bank of Japan assistance. Four of the rest never opened their doors again. Seven banks merged with other banks, of which six medium-sized banks based on big cities were absorbed by Showa Bank, specially established in November 1927 for rescue purposes conjointly by influential banks including the Big Five. Therefore, in March 1928 eleven banks were still in the process of reopening or liquidating. Among them, of course, the Bank of Taiwan and the Fifteen Bank were given priority. These two Banks would re-establish themselves, albeit as smaller, weaker institutions and with tremendous assistance from the government and the Bank of Japan. All in all, throughout the crisis the Bank of Japan gave the closed and tottering banks some ¥2,000 million as emergency loans, which accounted for 18 per cent of total Japanese banking deposits.[22] The circumstances necessitated a review of the Japanese banking structure as a whole by the financial authorities to investigate seriously every aspect of banking conduct.

The resignation of the Wakatsuki cabinet, forced by the privy council decision, was followed by a government headed by General Giichi Tanaka, a military man. Tanaka had very little understanding of economics; his interests lay in aggressive military behaviour. It was the Tanaka cabinet that sent, in May 1927, the Shantung expedition which became the first step in Japanese military aggression on the Chinese mainland. This led within five years to the founding of the puppet regime of Manchukuo and eventually to the war against China, the devastating results of which Tanaka, fortunately for him, did not live to witness.[23] The privy council rejection of the Wakatsuki cabinet's plan was thus far reaching.

Post-mortem, the 1927 new Bank Act, 1926–1928

The Commission on the Financial System was appointed on 21 September 1926 and its first general meeting was convened on 12 October 1926. However, every sort of preparation had earlier been embarked upon by the Ministry of Finance. Gotaro Ogawa, representative on the Diet and himself an active member of the Commission, left a detailed account of preparations and debates leading to the legislation of the new Bank Act, entitled *Reasoning of the New Bank Act*.[24] The preparations for setting up the Commission on the Financial System and its agenda started in April 1926 when a preliminary committee for the Commission was organised. The membership of twenty was exclusively chosen among Ministry of Finance high officials with the Ministry's secretary sitting as chairman. The first meeting of the preliminary committee was held in April 1926 and decided their agenda, simultaneously appointing a task force under their command. The members of the task force were selected one each from the Bank of Japan, Mitsui, Mitsubishi, Daiichi and Sumitomo Banks. Their first meeting was called in the middle of July 1926.

The task force was commissioned to draw draft reports on three subjects: the improvement of money markets, especially those for bill discounts and securities, the resultant effects of lowering interest rates and the improvement of the ordinary banking system.[25] The head of the banking department of the Finance Ministry, a member of the preliminary committee, elaborated the subjects before the task force. He disclosed the Ministry's desire to create discount and bond markets on the model of the London and New York money markets. They envisioned that the discount and acceptance houses would operate as efficiently on the markets in Japan as they were doing on the London markets. Although they believed they were imitating both the British and the American systems, it would appear that they did not know the differences between the two. Indeed, both the discount house and the acceptance house were typical British products. It may perhaps be said that their western image was extracted from the British money market system.

Since the banking controversy in the 1870s, British banking had seemed worthy of emulation in the minds of Japanese financial authorities and bankers. Their liking for 'British banking' was due to two factors, British banking hegemony over the rest of the world and the prevalence of study of British banking among Japanese bankers, economists and university scholars. Alexander Allan Shand, to whose activities reference has already been made, remained, in the minds of Japanese bankers, the canny Scot into whose hands banking, with all its challenges, could be safely entrusted. It should be remembered that Shand, at the request of Okuma, had undertaken the first inspection of Japanese banks in 1874 following the collapse of the house of Ono.[26] There remains much evidence that Shand was still highly regarded by the Japanese, including Korekiyo Takahashi.[27]

One of the members of the task force, Teruo Akashi, Daiichi Bank manager and later president, put forward in an interview held some twenty-five years afterwards:

Although the banking system was copied from the American [national bank system], the guiding spirits were those of British banking. The British banking is conducted by those sound methods and spirits, especially of the Scotch [sic].[28]

Toyotaro Yuki, then the managing director of Yasuda Bank, later Finance Minister and governor of the Bank of Japan, and Nariakira Ikeda, then managing director and later president of Mitsui Bank, governor of the Bank of Japan, Minister of Finance and of commerce and industry and a privy councillor, also looked to British banking as sound banking and as such as worth copying.[29] 'Follow the British' was a fashionable feeling prevailing among the bankers and financial authorities at a time when the Japanese banking system was confronted by a serious restructuring problem. However, it is an axiom that the reality is sometimes far from the ideal. Indeed, the Japanese reality made it impossible to develop British-style institutions. The Ministry of Finance was in sober mood when the head of the banking department concluded his instructions to the task force, commenting that the forthcoming proposals must be 'manageable by the Ministry of Finance'.[30]

The *ad hoc* committee, composed of five practical bankers, soon agreed that the top priority was the ordinary bank. They immediately set to work, holding meetings regularly at the Bank of Japan office. As early as 14 August 1926, they produced a draft proposal entitled 'Definite Policies for the Improvement of the Ordinary Banking System in Our Country'.[31] In a preface to the draft proposal, the committee put forward their basic observations:

Ordinary banks in our country have frequently conducted their business badly. There has been excessive competition among too many small banks with slender means; bankers have been ignorant of the need for reserves to back deposit withdrawals and generally ill-informed about the working of deposit banking; there has been over enthusiastic lending of bank resources in either particular or long-term outlets against securities of real estates in favour of related businesses; there has been serious negligence in establishing a thorough audit system both inside and outside the banks.[32]

These serious criticisms were not in fact new. The governor of the Bank of Japan had expressed similar misgivings in the early 1920s, which the investigations carried out by the Bank in the aftermath of the 1927 crisis revealed to have been thoroughly appropriate. The defects in the system were therefore well understood by the better-trained bankers, though no one had succeeded in disciplining the system before the collapse.

The draft proposal on the improvement of ordinary banking was soon followed by those on discount markets (4 September 1926), securities markets (16 September 1926) and lowering of rates (1 October 1926). Four draft proposals were examined by the preliminary committee for the consideration of the first meeting of the Commission on the Financial System. The Commission deliberately widened its range of subjects and decided to discuss twelve items including central banking, colonial banking, industrial and agricultural financing, pawnbroking, savings banking and trust business. Even so ordinary banking remained the main focus. The proposal for the improvement of ordinary banking together with substantial amendments was submitted to the Minister of Finance in November 1926. The proposal was elaborated in the Ministry until February 1927 when the bill of the Bank Act was laid before the Fifty-second Session of the Imperial Diet. The discussions took only three weeks and on 8 March 1927 the bill was passed as the Bank Act of 1927 together with some minor necessary amendments in the Acts of Savings Banks, of the Agri-Industrial Bank and of the Hokkaido Development Bank.[33]

The Bank Act of 1927 was promulgated on 29 March 1927 and was to come into effect on 1 January 1928. Although certain amendments were made following the Diet discussions, the *ad hoc* committee's recommendations were incorporated into the Act. For the first time, it was stipulated that the ordinary bank be of joint-stock form, with limited liability, and any other style of company be illegal (Article 3). The bank resources regulation was far more strictly set forth. The minimum capital amount was to be ¥1 million, and in specially designated cities the amount must be more than ¥2 million (Article 3). Simultaneously with the enactment, Imperial Decree No. 327 specified Tokyo and Osaka as the designated cities. Further to strengthen resources, banks were requested to set aside 10 per cent of profits each year as the reserve fund until the cumulative sum reached the level of the capital amount. The stipulation therefore was in effect to oblige each bank to double the amount of capital (Article 8).

Then the Bank Act turned to the relationships of the banks with industries on two levels. First, the Act prohibited the banks to conduct any other non-banking business except trust and safe deposit businesses. This prohibition clause emphasised that ordinary banks would not be allowed to act as 'house banks' as did so many collapsed banks in 1927. The business of banking was therefore limited to the acceptance of deposits, advances of money, discounting of bills and transacting of foreign exchanges (Article 1). Secondly, the managing director and chief manager of the banks were forbidden to occupy concurrently similar posts in any other firms (Article 13). The new Bank Act made it a routine task for the banks to audit twice yearly their whole business and prepare the reports to be ready for the examination of the Ministry of Finance at any time (Article 12). For the external audit by the Finance Ministry, the banks were requested to prepare their general business report, statement of balance sheets, statement of profit and loss accounts and statement of the disposal of surplus funds, the forms of which the Ministry specified. The Bank Act, superseding the Bank Decree, which consisted of only eleven articles, came to have forty-seven articles, accompanied by detailed regulations with specimens of various reports and statements, thus keeping a close watch on every corner of banking business and imposing heavy punishments if any offence was proved.

The financial authorities thought it not necessarily sufficient to leave the supervision of the banks to the Ministry of Finance. Could the auditing be undertaken by the Bank of Japan? The Commission on the Financial System decided that the Bank could do the job.[34] In May 1928, an inspection section was set up in the department of banking at the bank. The aims were as follows:

to examine whether business activities of a bank are sound or not, which is a quite different task from that of the Finance Ministry's. While the Ministry as a superintendent authority investigates into the affairs, the Bank of Japan does the job by looking into economic activities, not by questioning the legitimacy of activities.[35]

Even after this decision, though, some of the members of the Commission were concerned as to whether the Bank of Japan examinations would mean interventions in bank activities. Some also asked which sort of banks would be subject to the examination: only agent banks of the Bank, its correspondent banks or all banks? It was eventually resolved that the banks subject to the examinations would be those appointed as agent banks by, and having correspondent arrangements with, the Bank of Japan. In the mean time the examination section was promoted to the independent department at the Bank. The number of banks falling in the category was 197, and the Bank of Japan executed the examinations from the autumn of 1928 to the spring of 1935.[36]

It was astonishing that 809 out of 1,422 banks in March 1927 were unqualified for the ordinary bank category under the new Bank Act capital amount stipulations. During and after the 1927 crisis, the number of banks continued to decrease, but there were still 617 unqualified out of 1,283 banks in January 1928. The unqualified banks had to meet the requirements by the end of 1928, otherwise they would have to be either liquidated or obliged to merge with a qualified bank. The new Bank Act therefore stimulated the last surge of bank amalgamation.

The Commission on the Financial System continued to sit and proceeded with its previously agreed agenda. Following the enactment of the Bank Act, the Public Pawnbroker Act was promulgated in March 1927, widening opportunities for ordinary people to have access to borrowing facilities. In April 1927 the Bank of Japan Convertible Note Liquidation Act was enacted so that the Bank could officially eliminate those banknotes destroyed in the earthquake, consolidate the diversified notes and confirm the amount of notes outstanding in circulation. Further in March 1931, the Mortgage Security Act was enacted so as to give liquidity to lending made on the security of real estates before the Great Kanto Earthquake. In April 1931, the Savings Bank Act was amended to encourage those banks to amalgamate and to diversify their portfolios and so ensure that savings banks operated on the principle of 'one bank in one prefecture'. Lastly, in April 1931, the Mutual Loan Business Act was also revised so that the mutual association be of joint-stock form. Notwithstanding their lengthy proceedings over five years, the Commission neither reached any agreements nor drew any conclusions on the two remaining important subjects, that is, the discount and securities market questions. The restructuring of ordinary banking had eclipsed the two questions. Indeed, ordinary banking remained the core of the financial system as a whole, though non-banking sectors were gradually enhancing their importance.

23 Financing heavy industries, 1927–1937

The depression, amalgamation and securities investments, 1927–1937

The 1927 bank crash in Japan was followed by several depressions exacerbated and prolonged by the Black Thursday collapse on the Wall Street securities market at New York on 24 October 1929. The wholesale price index (1934–6 = 1) fell from 1.075 in 1927 to 0.748 in 1931; thereafter a slow recovery started, with the price rising to 1.036 in 1936 and further to 1.258 in 1937. Industrial production was severely hit, but the recovery, stimulated by demands for war materials, accelerated during the mid-1930s to 1937 when industrial production reached 190 per cent of the 1931 level.[1]

During the decade up to 1937, there was a steady fall in the total number of banks, including special banks, from 1,425 to 462, with a reduction of paid-in capital from ¥1,886 to ¥1,455 million. Advances fell continuously from ¥11,145 million in 1927 to ¥9,969 million in 1934 but then recovered to ¥12,328 million in 1937. Deposits and debentures showed more flexibility, being between ¥11,000 and ¥16,400 million and between ¥1,740 and ¥2,300 million during the decade respectively. The situation of the banking system was a reflection of general economic depression following the 1927 banking crisis and the commencement of world depression. It was also a reflection of a particular factor in the system, that is, the bank amalgamation movement. The two elements formed the basis of banking performances in the decade from 1927.

The progress of the movement to absorb the prefectural Agri-Industrial Banks continued apace. There were only thirteen left in 1937. Special banking advances as percentages of the aggregate of deposits and debentures were between 101 per cent and 116 per cent in the period, standing at 107 per cent on average. The figures for the Hypothec Bank were lower than 100 per cent except in the years of 1927, 1928 and 1937, and advances as percentages of deposits for the Yokohama Specie Bank, non-debenture issuer, were far below 100 per cent throughout. The Banks of Taiwan and Korea and the Industrial Bank of Japan were keen to lend. The Industrial Bank was specially asked by the government to assist ailing and depressed industries.[2] The numbers of savings banks also fell, from 113 to 72, but in terms of capital and advances, savings banking could not compare with ordinary banks, although their deposits did compare with ordinary banking deposits. Widening differences between sustaining deposits and dwindling advances had to be filled, therefore, with securities investments, which indeed grew from 1927 to 1937 by 256 per cent against 179 per cent for ordinary banking.[3]

Ordinary banks, now more properly joint-stock commercial and the key constituent of the system, fell in number from 1,280 in 1927 to 377 in 1937. The loss of 903 banks eliminated a large number of smaller and weaker banks. Because they were the core of the system, and as such the main supplier of industrial financing, their lending behaviour followed the trend of the general depression. In 1927 they were lending a little more than ¥8,000 million but this dropped to a little less than ¥6,000 million before slowly recovering to a little less than ¥8,000 million in 1937. Compared with advances, the recovery of deposits started earlier in 1931 and grew more speedily. In ordinary banking, as with savings banks, there was a widening gap between advances and deposits.

The sharp reduction in the number of banks was due to the movement towards amalgamation in the decade following 1927. It was widely accepted that banks would need to be larger to protect themselves and their customers and to finance industries, among which heavy and chemical sectors were most eager. This, because of the harsh experience of the 1927 banking crash, became a common goal for both financial authorities and bankers. The new Bank Act of 1927, through Article 17, made mergers and particularly absorption of subordinate savings banks easier. In fact in September 1927 the Ministry of Finance issued a special notification entitled 'The Recommendation of Amalgamations'.[4]

A detailed survey on the amalgamation movement, executed by the Institute of Finance and Banking Research, discloses that the half decade following the 1927 banking crisis was crucial to the movement. From 1927 to 1932, 1,082 banks participated in mergers and 668 banks disappeared, which means that nearly 111 banks vanished each year in comparison to 81 banks per annum in the preceding years of 1921–6. This also meant that more than two-thirds of banks existent in 1927 were engaged in the amalgamation movement in one way or another during this period.[5] Closer examinations of the movement reveal two levels on which it was done. An overwhelmingly large number of mergers was carried out among smaller banks based upon provincial cities. This process was much encouraged by the new Bank Act which, as has been explained, set the minimum amount of capital and so guided them towards becoming larger units. Thus the lower end of the banking system in Japan was considerably strengthened.

At the other end of the scale, the Big Five, who were gaining strength by attracting depositors who used to be satisfied with the smaller banks, were causing a stir. Initially, in the early 1920s, Yasuda Bank set off a shock wave, astonishing every banker by its scale of amalgamations, but this was brought to an abrupt halt by the disruption caused by the earthquake on 1 September 1923. However, from April 1927 onwards, in the wake of the promulgation of the Bank Act, big banks came forward to effect mergers notwithstanding the instability of the system. Daiichi Bank absorbed, in April 1927 and August 1931, two Tokyo-based big banks with capital of ¥21 and ¥10 million respectively. Sumitomo took over a Kyushu bank (¥0.3 million capital) in March 1928, a Tokyo bank (¥0.1 million capital) in November 1930 and a Wakayama bank (¥0.5 million capital) in September 1931. Yasuda and Mitsubishi absorbed a Kyushu bank (¥0.1 million capital) in July 1928 and a Tokyo bank (¥5 million capital) in April 1929 respectively. This final phase of amalgamation culminated in a merger of Konoike, Yamaguchi and Sanjushi, all Osaka based, and which had themselves absorbed one, three and three banks respectively by 1932. The three banks amalgamated on an equal basis to form Sanwa Bank in August 1933. The emergence of Sanwa meant the formation of the Big Six as Sanwa jumped up to the top of rankings in terms of both deposits and advances by the end of 1933.[6] The tremendous surge of amalgamations ceased by 1932, though there were still of course some small-scale mergers. Thanks to the amalgamations, the average paid-in capital of ordinary banking was raised from ¥1.1 million in 1927 to ¥2.8 million in 1937.

The emergence of the Big Six in 1933 enhanced their shares of deposits to more than a half of total ordinary bank deposits, of paid-in capital to exactly one-third and of advances to more than 40 per cent. However, there was a particular aspect of the Big Six banks which did not correspond with their scale and strength, that is, the size of their branch networks. In 1933 the Big Six had some 610 branches against some 4,500 branches of 601 ordinary and savings banks. The Big Six's share in branch offices was only a little more than 13 per cent, even though individually their number of branches was ten times larger than the average. A more striking contrast, however, was that between the Japanese Big Six and the English Big Five which had more than 8,500 branch offices in 1933, more than 1,700 branches per bank on average.[7]

There were probably three main causes of the backwardness of the Big Six branch banking development. First, the Big Six were based stubbornly upon Tokyo and Osaka and tended to ignore business in other financial centres. This was partly due to the fact that their *ryogae* ancestors used to operate mainly there. The continuance of their headquarters at the same places might form a sharp contrast to several of the English Big Five which gained access from different localities through amalgamations to the sole financial centre, London. From the two financial centres and big cities, the Big Six extended their branch networks to the satellite localities to conduct financing of Japanese heavy and chemical industries in those areas. For example, in the case of the Yasuda amalgamation in 1923, of ten banks taken over by Yasuda, six were based in Tokyo, Kanagawa, Osaka, Kyoto and Hyogo, and the rest were in Hokkaido, Fukushima, Nagano and Okayama, but the aggregate capital of the banks in the former areas accounted for more than three-quarters. Another example is that of Mitsui Bank, with only twenty-three branches in 1933, which never participated in the amalgamation movement and therefore concentrated their business solely in the big cities. Later, in the post-Pacific War Period, big banks came to be called 'city banks' while smaller banks were known as 'regional banks'. The origin of this division can certainly be traced to the pattern of the Big Six's branch network.

The second cause of the small branch network was that provincial business was still at this stage considered by urban-based big banks to be less profitable and more risky. Their distrust in provincial business was unfortunately confirmed through the 1927 banking crash which primarily affected the provincial branch network. Indeed, the cautious Mitsui house closed their branches in Nagasaki and Shimonoseki, remote in the west of Japan, transferring business there to Osaka and Nagoya branches.[8]

Lastly, mergers among regional banks were especially encouraged by the Ministry of Finance which was afraid that take-overs of regional banks by big urban banks would cause money flows from those provinces to big city money eaters through the big bank branch network, and as we have seen city banks were not willing to reciprocate by making advances to provinces.[9] Indeed, in September 1936, the National Association of Regional Banks was founded by 272 members to protect the regional banking business.[10] However, the Association before long would also have to face difficulties.

Concentration of big bank businesses, especially those of the Big Six, upon big cities and their environs resulted partly from the needs of heavy and chemical industries, which required big bank financing. Most of the Big Six acted as the house bank to their own *zaibatsu* industries. Therefore, by the mid-1930s, the relationships between big banks and heavy and chemical industries were firmly established, but there was emerging a certain change in big bank portfolios. Advances as percentages of deposits of the Big Six were 55 per cent on average between 1927 and 1937 as against 73 per cent for ordinary banking as a whole. The Big Six's figure was substantially lower than the 81 per cent of the Big Five in the previous decade. The prolonged depression following the two successive crises of 1927 and 1929 and the rapid heavy and chemical industrialisation joined force to increase the Big

Six's assets portfolio securities holdings, which indeed stood at 41 per cent of deposits on average from 1933 to 1937.[11] The changing bank assets management was a reflection of the increasing importance of the securities market.

Non-banking institutions, 1931–1937

The prolonged depression following the spectacular banking collapse gave an impetus to non-banking institutions to increase their business. Post offices, the oldest non-banking institution, enlarged their savings from ¥2,664 million in 1931 to ¥4,013 million in 1937, both figures being equivalent to nearly two-thirds of ordinary bank deposits. Post office savings were deposited in the trust fund department of the Ministry of Finance, constituting a little more than 70 per cent of the total funds in the department in these years. In insurance sectors[12] operating funds increased from ¥1,997 million in 1931 to ¥3,659 million in 1937, which accounted for 24 per cent and 29 per cent of ordinary bank deposits respectively. Between life and non-life sub-sectors, the former was dominant, holding a more than 85 per cent share of the aggregate operating funds as the depression damped the non-life business greatly.[13] Trust business, the leaders of which were four companies which were offshoots of Mitsui, Yasuda, Sumitomo and Mitsubishi Banks,[14] was also progressing, though less speedily than the above two sectors. The total liabilities, mainly money in trust, grew from ¥1,642 million in 1931 to ¥2,397 million in 1937, equivalent to 20 per cent and 19 per cent of the ordinary deposits each year. All in all, the aggregate resources of the three non-banking sectors exceeded 80 per cent of ordinary bank deposits between 1931 and 1937.

The increased resources of non-banking sectors found their way naturally on to the securities market. In absolute terms, the insurance and post office sectors continued to increase securities holdings from 1931 to 1937. Even the new trust sector increased its holdings except in 1932. Insurance increased its retention from ¥1,020 million in 1931 to ¥2,320 million in 1937, 56 per cent on average of the operating funds. The trust fund department of the Finance Ministry augmented its holding from ¥2,492 million in 1931 to ¥4,600 million in 1937, 79 per cent on average of the assets. Trust companies decreased their holdings from ¥501 million in 1931 to ¥466 million in 1932 but then increased them to ¥1,155 million in 1937, 41 per cent on average of the total assets.[15] All figures were far larger than the average of all banks taken together which stood at 24 per cent.[16] Those of insurance and the Finance Ministry trust fund department far exceeded even the Big Six's. These three non-banking sectors were indeed emerging as strong securities-holding institutions.

The securities market grew by more than 50 per cent in listed-value terms from ¥24,155 million in 1931 to ¥37,381 million in 1937.[17] Equities, national, municipal, financial and industrial bonds were five constituents of the listed securities. Proportionately, equities and municipal bonds were stable, accounting for 42 per cent and 10 per cent respectively on average of the total listed value. National bonds were gradually rising, standing at 32 per cent on average, while financial and industrial bonds were diminishing, being 7 per cent and 9 per cent respectively. It was therefore equities and national bonds that the Big Six and non-banking institutions were hoarding in their portfolios.

A survey executed later in the post-Pacific War period by the Bank of Japan reveals that net supply of industrial funds between 1931 and 1937 amounted to ¥15,163 million, that is, more than 15 per cent of the aggregate national income.[18] Among various industrial financing methods, only equity financing continued its growth. It could therefore be argued that the heavy and chemical industrialisation, thereto dependent chiefly upon bank lending, urgently needed another resource at the time of war preparations, that is, equity financing substantially involving non-bank institutions. The increasing proportion of national bonds also symbolised the years in which Japan was deepening its military commitments on the Chinese mainland. Indeed, total military expenditures accounted for 36 per cent of the aggregate government debts in 1937 compared to 20 per cent in 1931. Between Liutiaohu outside Mukden and Marco Polo Bridge outside Peking there were critical developments which would eventually dominate Japanese banking and the Japanese economy.

24 The challenge of militarism, and a change of roles for *Nichigin* and *Shokin*, 1929–1937

The lengthy debates on when and how to resume specie exports or to return to the full working of the gold standard resulted in a library of monetary literature, which, because of its bulk, the bank historian can only dip into.[1] The Minister of Finance, Junnosuke Inoue, in addressing the Diet, argued that lifting the specie embargo and returning to the gold standard with the old par value of yen to pound sterling and dollar would have deflationary effects upon the economy and would lower the price level, thus enhancing Japan's international competitiveness and eventually giving strength to the economy.[2] This unjustified ministerial optimism proved to be very damaging.

The specie embargo was lifted in January 1930 but had to be reimposed in December 1931. During these two years, the specie outflow was the worst in history, amounting to ¥417 million in 1931. All this was aggravated by rampant speculation as some banks were buying in dollars and pounds sterling especially in the autumn of 1931 when it was clear that the embargo would have to be reimposed. The specie reserve, at ¥1,343 million at the end of 1929, was reduced to ¥557 million at the end of 1931. The decrease of ¥786 million was larger than the total specie reserve in 1916. The Finance Minister, Inoue, was replaced by Korekiyo Takahashi on the very day of the reimposition of the specie embargo, which marked the final Japanese departure from the gold standard.

By the end of 1931, the new cabinet, with veteran Takahashi as the Finance Minister, ordered the Bank of Japan to collect bullion domestically by buying in dollars in New York and pounds sterling in London in an attempt to strengthen the reserve position.[3] Foreign exchange rates continued to deteriorate from $0.49 and 2s 2d per ¥1 on average in 1931 to $0.28 and 1s 7d in 1932[4], and the government thus in June 1932 hastened to legislate the Capital Flight Protection Act, which was soon in effect and became a definite step towards tighter exchange control. However, the Protection Act stabilised the market only for a short while and foreign exchange rates continued to fall against key currencies. To prevent further deterioration, the government legislated the Foreign Exchange Control Act in March 1933 to be effective in May that year, and this finally put the foreign exchange market under the strict direction of the Finance Ministry.[5]

Successive legislation on foreign exchange control was naturally of some help in recovering the share in the business of the Yokohama Specie Bank which had long been in severe competition with the larger ordinary banks. The buying exchange business, a symbol of overseas banking and of the power of the Specie Bank, which had been in retreat until 1931, visibly revived, gaining strength from 1933 onwards.[6] But the Specie Bank was gradually losing its old vitality: it was no longer the aggressive 'front runner'. The financial collapses of 1927 in Japan and 1929 world-wide had fatally weakened it. Its relationships with two international financial centres, London and New York, were less strong.

During the First World War boom days, the Specie Bank took in money on a short-term basis on western markets, mainly London, amounting to one-quarter of their deposits each year. This kind of western money accounted for a little more than one-fifth of total interbank borrowing on average in the five years of 1933 to 1937.[7] Of course the overseas branch network expansion could not continue during the decade after the 1927 banking collapse. During the first half of the 1930s, the Specie Bank opened only five overseas branches – in Paris, Berlin and three in Manchukuo – and it opened only two offices domestically. The offices in Manchukuo represented the Yokohama Specie Bank's disastrous, and ultimately fatal, alignment with Japanese imperialism. Also alarming was the position of specie abroad, which was kept in the vaults of the Specie Bank London and New York offices. The amount dropped from ¥255 million in 1929 to only ¥28 million in 1937, 3 per cent of the Japanese total. The Yokohama Specie Bank, original guardian of the Japanese currency base, was losing its role. Instead, the Specie Bank became the cash office in eastern Asia and on the Chinese mainland for the Japanese military. The evidence of this was the proliferation of branches in those areas specially instructed by the militaristic government.[8]

The departure from the gold standard in effect gave the Bank of Japan a free hand in issuing notes of any amount, though of course it had to keep a close watch on price indices and foreign exchange rates. However, the deliberate issuing of banknotes not backed by gold became essential as the costs of Japanese military aggression on the Chinese mainland, particularly in Manchuria, grew. In March 1932, within three months of the specie embargo, Manchukuo, the Japanese puppet state, was established under the control of Japan's Kwantung army. Manchuria, the puppet state of Manchukuo, was considered essential by the Japanese, being rich in raw materials and able to absorb the ever-increasing unemployed population.[9]

These factors had long given the radical military men an excuse to invade the area. Indeed, military expenditure, which had been increasing since the Shantung expedition of 1927, jumped nearly a third from ¥1,477 million in 1931 to ¥1,950 million in 1932.

Three months later, in June 1932, the Convertible Bank Note Regulations were revised so that the fiduciary note issue ceiling was raised from ¥120 to ¥1,000 million, the sum which was the average amount of total note issue in the past decade. This revision, though potentially dangerous, was a step towards the managed currency system in Japan. Simultaneous with the note issue revision, the government legislated the Revenue Deficit National Bond Act in June 1932. Traditionally, syndicates organised by city banks were responsible for underwriting national bonds. The emergence of revenue deficit bond issuing accordingly changed the tradition. Eigo Fukai, then deputy governor of the Bank and a prolific economic writer, expounded:

Changes in the international situation and in our state management, resulting from the Manchurian Incidents, greatly increased national expenditures and necessitated national bond issues. However, on account of economic depression and monetary pressure, the present method of national bond issue became difficult . . . In 1932, it has proved that most of the syndicate members saw inconveniences in accepting their underwriting lot in advance. Issuing the bonds directly to the general public was unthinkable . . . Instead, it was thought more appropriate to issue the whole sum to the Bank of Japan which would then sell them to would-be buyers . . . This device of issuing the national bonds may be a last resort, but it would help relieve monetary pressure as the Bank of Japan transfers money to the government in exchange for the national bonds which are then sold in the market.[10]

According to the deputy governor of the Bank, the idea came from Korekiyo Takahashi, the Finance Minister, and was known as 'the open market operation'; however, it was something quite different from the money operations conducted in western markets.

Between 1932 and 1937 the total amount of revenue deficit bonds reached ¥2,720 million. The joint use of both methods of Bank of Japan note issue and underwriting of national bonds by the Bank was certainly tremendously efficient in exploiting resources hoarded in private sectors. For instance, in the three years between 1932 and 1935, national bonds including revenue deficit bonds amounted to ¥3,379 million, more than three times the total governmental debts in 1935, of which 82 per cent was bought by the Bank of Japan. It then resold 82 per cent of the sum, of which 65 per cent was bought by banks, 5 per cent by trust companies, 4 per cent by insurance companies, 9 per cent by securities companies and 10 per cent by ministries, mainly the trust fund department in the Finance Ministry.[11] Revenue deficit bonds continued to play an indispensable part in governmental financing until 1945, though in the aftermath of 'the 1937 incident' they became war bonds.

Bank of Japan rates were kept low during these years, being reduced to an unprecedented 3.29 per cent, so that national bonds could be kept on the market through the Bank of Japan. From the summer of 1932 to the autumn of 1937, national debts grew twofold, reaching ¥13,335 million, nearly two-thirds of national income in 1937.[12] This rapid increase was of course supported by Bank of Japan note issue which grew from ¥1,426 million in 1932 to ¥2,305 million in 1937, of which more than 21 per cent was, in fact, excessive issue.

There were two tragic incidents. Four months before the Revenue Deficit Bond Act, Junnosuke Inoue, at the age of sixty-two and by then an ex-Finance Minister, was assassinated by a right-wing activist. A year and a half before the Marco Polo Bridge Incident of 1937, the beginning of the war against China, Korekiyo Takahashi was assassinated in the 1936 abortive coup at the age of eighty-one. The elimination of these two banking leaders, who were not necessarily opposed to militarism and pursued very different financial policies, marked the end of an era in which the Japanese banking system could maintain its independence from military intervention.

Historical background, 1937–1945

In June 1937, Prince Konoe was handed an imperial edict and ordered to form a cabinet. Exactly a month later, the Marco Polo Bridge Incident occurred, engineered by elements of the Japanese army, and it developed into the Sino-Japanese War. More than two years before the German invasion of Poland, Japan was effectively at war. In July 1940, the second Konoe cabinet prepared Japanese invasion plans for South East Asia, a direct response to the German success in Europe. Two months afterwards the Tripartite Pact between Japan, Germany and Italy was concluded. In June 1941 the Japanese army and navy invaded French Indo-China, an action which was fatal for the American–Japanese negotiations in which the second Konoe cabinet was desperately, if incompetently, engaged. It was, however, the Tojo cabinet in October 1941 which determined the surprise attack on Pearl Harbor on 8 December 1941 (Japan Time) initiating all-out war against the rest of the world in the Pacific area. Despite the spectacular advance of the Japanese forces south-eastwards into Asia, within six months, in June 1942, Japan lost the Battle of Midway. This was indeed, in military and in economic terms, the crucial turning point of the Pacific War. In spite of her achievement, Japan was never in a position to win this war. As early as 1942 Japanese industrial production was in the doldrums and her economic resources were, despite the National General Mobilisation policies, exhausted. Japanese banking, well integrated into the national economy, was in the same boat which ultimately sank in August 1945.

25 War budgets and the mobilisation of national resources, 1937–1943

On 7 July 1937, the Japanese troops of Kwantung army engineered a clash with the Chinese garrison at Marco Polo Bridge, near Peking. Although a ceasefire was soon negotiated, the Japanese army used the incident as an excuse to invade deep into the Chinese heartland. Nanking, General Chang Kai Shek's capital, was invaded in December 1937 when a terrible vengeance was taken by the Japanese army against local people. The escalation of the war and the behaviour of the Japanese military forces shocked the world community. Thereafter Japan and her obedient people were committed to military aggression.

Emergency financial and monetary measures were taken on 10 September 1937. The significance of these decisions remained hidden from the Western Powers. They took the form of an Extraordinary War Expenditures Special Account, the fourth in modern Japanese history, similar to those for the Sino-Japanese and Russo-Japanese Wars and the 1919 Siberian Expedition. The Japanese government did not declare war, nor indeed were they to do so, even after the Pearl Harbor attack of December 1941, but their intentions were clear. The special war account increased from ¥2,034 million in 1937 to ¥9,487 million in 1941, covering about 70 per cent of the total war expenditure for this period, which was on average 77 per cent of the total government expenditure in the same years.[1] The details of the government expenditure were kept secret even from the Bank of Japan. Possibly more than 80 per cent of the income was earmarked for munitions, some 15 per cent for personnel expenses and the rest for transportation. This money was spent in Japan; rather less than 20 per cent was used on the Chinese mainland while the rest was dispersed on the Korean peninsula, in Taiwan and in South East Asia.[2]

The Temporary Fund Adjustment Act, which aimed at ensuring strict regulatory control of new investments, specially favoured investments in munitions industries. The Industrial Bank of Japan was ordered to issue its own debentures in a bid to attract further hidden resources. The Act also stipulated that savings bonds and patriotic bonds could be newly issued to

174

draw in funds hoarded by the general public. Under this Act, the government was given extraordinary powers to examine every aspect of the nation's finance in order to put pressure on all the financial institutions to find additional funds to supply wartime needs.[3] Between September 1937 and March 1942 the Act raised ¥18,454 million new money, equivalent to more than 60 per cent of the aggregate lending outstanding of all banks, trust companies and the trust fund department of the Finance Ministry. Of this, 36 per cent was contributed by the banks. In terms of sectors, manufacturing industry accounted for 64 per cent and mining and transportation 13 per cent each. Successive revisions of the Act were made, widening its application and encouraging further government impositions.[4]

Elsewhere, the Japanese army was pinned down by determined Chinese military resistance. In April 1938 the National General Mobilisation Act, which superseded the Munitions Industry Mobilisation Act of 1918, came into force and put Japan *de facto* upon an extraordinary wartime basis. The Act symbolised Japanese preparedness for war, a year prior to the outbreak of the Second World War when the German troops invaded Poland in September 1939. On 22 September 1940, following the overthrow of the French by the Germans in Europe, the Japanese army occupied French Indo-China and within the same week the Tripartite Pact was concluded by Japan, Germany and Italy. In Japan, the government continued to pursue ever harsher economic measures.

In October 1940, the Ordinance for the Funds Management Bank and Other Institutions, which sought to bring financial authorities, ordinary banking and institutional advances under control, was introduced.[5] But these piecemeal measures were unsatisfactory. Towards the end of 1940, the cabinet still led by Prince Fumimaro Konoe projected a more comprehensive plan, which was called 'Outlines of Basic Financial and Monetary Policies' and which finally became effective in July 1941 and superseded all other measures.

In February 1942, a new Bank of Japan Act replaced all the legislation which had earlier regulated it, including the Regulations first promulgated in 1882. The new Act had three special aspects. First, the Bank became solely a servant of the government in power (Articles 1 and 2): even the notional idea that the Bank was independent was abandoned. The Bank was required to lend to the government without security (Article 22). Secondly, the business the Bank was required to do was so extended that it was requested to make advances when eligible securities were available, lend to overseas institutions and generally support the Japanese system as a whole (Articles 20, 24, 25 and 28). Thirdly, the Bank was in effect granted the freedom to issue any amount of banknotes as it judged proper (Articles 29, 30, 31 and 32). The Bank of Japan was thus empowered to work solely for national purposes and this structure was to remain the basic framework even in the post-war period.[6]

Three further institutions were also set up in March and April 1942. Two were war-related institutions, the War Cash Office and the Southern District Cash Office. The former was put under direct control of the government to supply funds to strategically crucial manufacturing industries, which included munitions, water power, shipbuilding, petroleum, substitute energy, light metal and chemicals, all to be geared to wartime demands. The War Cash Office was also authorised to support securities markets. The Southern District Cash Office was commissioned to do the same job in the southern areas outside Japan where the Japanese troops were advancing and occupying.[7] The third institution, the National Financial Control Association, was organised through the Financial Control Association Ordinance which was based on the National Mobilisation Act and was promulgated in April 1942.[8] Under the Control Association the whole system was literally put under control, including the Bank of Japan, Yokohama Specie Bank, Industrial Bank of Japan, Hokkaido Development Bank, Bank of Taiwan, Bank of Korea, all ordinary and savings banks, Korean Development Bank, War Cash Office and Central Cash Office for Industrial Associations.[9] Later the Central Cash Office for Small Commercial and Industrial Associations, Pension Cash Office and People's Cash Office, all founded around the 'China Incident' and intent on financing small business and those who were having increasing difficulties in borrowing, were forced to be put under the Control Association.[10] The framework for wartime mobilisation of the entire funds in Japan was thus completed.

26 Extraordinary banking business during the national emergency, 1941–1945

At the time of the Pearl Harbor attack, there were 194 ordinary banks: in fact, with government encouragement, 230 banks had disappeared since the beginning of the war in July 1937, mainly due to amalgamations and take-overs. The larger banks were considered to be more efficient in making bigger loans, and in supporting market prices of national bonds, the proceeds of which were transferred quickly to the money-hungry munitions industries.[1] Indeed, total amounts of financing for plant investments and for working capital grew in the five years from 1940 to 1945 more than fourfold and sixfold respectively. The most active borrowers were of course machine-tool industries: their investments in plant and working capital financing grew during the same period more than sixfold and twelvefold respectively. More than 70 per cent of these demands was met by ordinary banking[2] which found itself deeply involved in war-related financing.

Ordinary banks were organised as members of the Ordinary Bank Control Association, a section of the Sectoral Control Association. While this was going on, another Ordinance for Financial Business Consolidation, promulgated in May 1942, sought to encourage banks either to merge with each other or to absorb the smaller units. By 1945 there were only sixty-one ordinary banks. There were two notable features in this remarkable amalgamation movement.

At the top level, Mitsui and Daiichi joined together, forming in 1943 Imperial, or Teikoku, Bank. Mitsubishi and Yasuda were also active. As a result, by the end of 1945, there were eight gigantic banks, that is, Yasuda, Imperial, Sanwa, Sumitomo, Mitsubishi, Tokai, Nomura and Kobe Banks. Tokai Bank, based on Nagoya, was an amalgamation of three big regional banks in Aichi prefecture in 1941. Nomura of Osaka, which had acquired the business of seven banks before 1940, carried out another two absorptions before the end of the Pacific War. Kobe Bank, an amalgamated version of seven Hyogo prefecture banks in 1936, took over another five banks by the end of the war.[3] The aggregate amount of the nominal capital of these top eight banks accounted for well over two-thirds of the total. The emergence of these banks was in effect the formation of city bank groups which would dominate the post-war period and become the engines for growth later in the 1960s.

Another notable aspect was amalgamations effected in regions other than Tokyo, Osaka, Nagoya, Kobe and their satellite areas. The remaining fifty-three banks resulted from regional mergers, giving an important, but strictly limited geographically, provincial banking structure. Despite the importance of the regional banks they were never anything but subordinate to the big city banks. Towards the end of the Pacific War, therefore, the city banks and the regional banks were replacing the traditional ordinary and savings structure, greatly to the satisfaction of the financial authorities who, ultimately, favoured the idea of 'one bank in one prefecture'.[4]

The new pattern of city and competing regional banks affected the fate of the savings banks. In 1940 there were still seventy-one savings banks operating, but by 1944 the number had dropped to twenty as fifty-one banks were absorbed in the course of amalgamations. Bank Act revisions encouraged the ordinary banks to undertake savings business. The last and most important large-scale amalgamation, which was a kind of self-protection, was carried out among the savings banks themselves (May 1945) when nine banks joined together to set up *Nihon Chochiku Ginko*, or Japan Savings Bank. When the Pacific War was over in August 1945, there remained only four tiny savings banks in remote areas and the Japan Savings Bank with ¥27.46 million paid-in capital and 366 branches, well ranking with the big city banks.[5] Indeed, the Savings Bank later joined the city bank group. This meant that the customers of the savings bank could be served either by the city banks or by the regional banks. Savings banking had effectively disappeared before the end of the Pacific War.

It was the Industrial Bank of Japan that was most severely exploited domestically by the wartime government. The Industrial Bank was commissioned to issue bonds to gather funds and to lend them together with Bank of Japan money to munitions industries. Overseas the Yokohama Specie Bank was ordered to follow closely in the steps of the Japanese army and navy, and their offices opened everywhere in occupied Asia. The Specie Bank was indeed a cash and remittance office for the Japanese troops. Domestically, the Hypothec Bank, which had by the 'China Incident' absorbed most of its Agri-Industrial counterparts, and the Hokkaido Development Bank were placed in the same situation as the Industrial Bank. The two colonial banks, the Bank of Taiwan and Bank of Korea, were anxiously doing their job. But special banking, the brainchild of Masayoshi Matsukata, was effectively ended in the Pacific War.

Special banking did not quite disappear. In March 1945 *Kyodoyushi Ginko*, or Joint Finance Bank, was set up conjointly by seventy-seven regional banks to employ their resources in munitions demands. In May 1945, *Shikintogo Ginko*, or Fund Consolidation Bank, was established by the Bank of Japan, which held 80 per cent of the capital, and other main banks and financial institutions. The Consolidation Bank absorbed the Joint Finance Bank on 10 August 1945 when negotiations for Japan's surrender were already being considered. Funds to be absorbed by the Fund Consolidation Bank were to be used through the Industrial Bank to supply munitions industries. Special banking efforts at this stage can only appear in the tragic circumstances to be absurd.[6]

27 Crisis, 1945

Between the Marco Polo Bridge Incident of 1937 and the Japanese defeat in the Pacific War in August 1945, the total liabilities/assets of all the banks increased sevenfold to ¥188,600 million, those of trust companies, three-fold to ¥6,700 million, insurance companies, fourfold to ¥14,700 million and post offices twelvefold to ¥47,200 million. Monetary assets of the main institutions, of which banking occupied nearly three-quarters, totalled ¥257,200 million, more than twelve times the national income in 1937 when the economy was put on to a war footing. However, their figures were deceptive: there was in fact a great deal of illiquidity. First, more than one-third of these assets were in national bonds.[1] Second, lending was often of 'dead loans' locked up in munitions industries. In fact two-thirds of them proved to be unsecured by the end of 1943 when the Japanese forces were fighting the Americans desperately in south-eastern seas, losing one battle after another.[2] Nobody could believe that the loans would be reimbursed.

What sustained such a large amount of national bond holdings of banks and other institutions and such a tremendous sum of unsecured advances to munitions industries was Bank of Japan notes. In 1937, the Bank of Japan notes outstanding were ¥2,305 million, of which ¥504 million were in excess of the fiduciary limit. The fiduciary limit was extended twice before 1940 to ¥2,200 million. The new Bank of Japan Act of 1942 allowed the Bank to abandon the concept of the fiduciary issue and gave the Bank outright control of the note issue. A limit was set at ¥6,000 million but the Minister of Finance was authorised to go beyond this if necessary. Indeed, at the end of 1945, the outstanding circulation of Bank of Japan notes was ¥55,441 million, twenty-four times larger than the 1937 circulation, of which ¥49,441 million had been issued by special permission. Whether the Bank of Japan had been obliged by the government to overissue or whether it was merely patriotic is a matter of opinion. Perhaps the Bank had no choice but to follow the path paved by the military. By 1945 prices in Japan were three times those in 1937. The end of the Pacific War therefore brought not only defeat and humiliation but also the prospect of unprecedented economic misery as the banking system faced loss and disaster.

It was calculated that the total costs of wars beginning in 1937 and ending in the defeat of 1945 amounted to ¥755,889 million, a figure which was thirty-seven times larger than the 1937 national income, and twelve times larger than the estimated Japanese war casualties in money terms excluding human losses.[3] This figure, reflecting financial loss, takes no account of the incalculable loss of life whether in Japan or in other Asian countries subjected to Japanese governance.

Part VIII

American 'democratisation' and the search for growth, 1945–1959 (twentieth year of Showa to thirty-fourth year of Showa)

Historical Background, 1945–1959

The saturation bombing of Japanese cities, which started in February 1945, and the two atomic bombs dropped on Hiroshima and Nagasaki on 6 and 9 August that year, brought Japan to her knees. Upon the Emperor's insistence, Japan unconditionally accepted the Potsdam Declaration on 15 August 1945 and the Japanese people found themselves in an extraordinary situation. The Americans occupied Japan and there followed an avalanche of major decisions. Supreme war leaders were put on trial, and many officials were purged from their appointments. The Emperor himself renounced his divinity. Women's suffrage was introduced and trade union activities became legal. In November 1946, under American guidance, the new constitution was promulgated, becoming effective in May 1947. 'Democratisation', which the Americans used to redirect the Japanese, became a slogan lingering on far beyond the following decade. By 1950 American foreign policy had changed rapidly due to the cold war against the rising tide of communism. Japan was rapidly transformed from enemy to ally. The American concentration on Japanese 'democratisation' had passed, a relief for the Japanese. The cold war erupted with the Korean War in 1950, which created a tremendous amount of demands for Japanese products. As a result of the Korean War, Japan recovered her sovereignty in 1952 and the Japanese economy resumed its growth. The Japanese banks, never penetrated by American 'democratisation', had by 1950 recovered from the disaster of war and were ready for take-off.

28 MacArthur's directives, 1945–1948

On 30 August 1945, that is, fifteen days after the Emperor's radio broadcast on 15 August 1945, General Douglas MacArthur, the commander-in-chief of US forces, who had a day before the Japanese surrender been appointed the Supreme Commander for the Allied Powers (SCAP), landed at Atsugi air base near Tokyo. The Allied Powers' General Headquarters, known inevitably as GHQ, which became one of the most popular western words in post-war Japan, was accommodated appropriately in the magnificent building of Daiichi Seimei, or First Life Insurance, facing the palace, the seat of the Emperor, just beyond the moat.

On 2 September, the Japanese ambassador plenipotentiary, Mamoru Shigemitsu, on board the US battleship *Missouri*, signed the surrender document accepting the terms of the Potsdam Declaration of 26 July 1945. From then on a series of directives started to stream out from the office of SCAP at GHQ, which, in spite of its title, in effect represented and consulted only the Washington government. As John Foster Dulles later recalled, the Japanese were unexpectedly complacent as directions poured out of MacArthur's office.[1] The Japanese banking system was also subjected to directives from the Americans although, as will be seen, without real understanding. They could readily be outmanoeuvred.

It became a priority for the Americans to destroy the war-related monetary and banking system. On 30 September 1945, MacArthur issued the first directive on banking, stating:

1. You will immediately close and not allow to reopen, except at the direction of this headquarters, the head offices, branches and agencies in Japan of the banks and other financial institutions enumerated in Inclosure, attached thereto.
. . .
7. You will discharge and summarily remove from office the chairman of the board of directors, the president, the managing directors and advisors of all institutions listed in Inclosure 1, and all other persons holding comparable posts in such institutions; and you will forbid them to enter into or to act for institutions with which they were associated. You will cancel the authority of all persons holding

powers of attorney or signing authority and will not permit any authority or power to act on behalf of such institutions to be given to any other persons without authorisation of this headquarters. All the officers, directors and other officials of such institutions will remain available and will not change address without authorisation of this headquarters.[2]

The directives were a serious attempt by the Americans to eliminate those bankers who had collaborated with the wartime military dictatorship. The difficulty was that effectively everyone had supported the government war effort. Many bankers were dismissed at this time, when, in total, some 200,000 Japanese were purged from various offices.

The institutions so specified as part of the 'war machinery' included the War Cash Office, Funds Consolidation Bank, Bank of Korea, Bank of Taiwan, Southern District Cash Office, National Financial Control Association and other minor colonial financial and development institutions. Later, in July 1946, the Yokohama Specie Bank was also instructed to liquidate itself. The Bank was later reorganised under the name of the Bank of Tokyo, restarting the business from the end of 1946, but the time-honoured title of the Yokohama Specie Bank disappeared from the banking world.[3]

The Americans then turned their attention to the *zaibatsu*, issuing a memorandum on 31 October 1945 which prohibited the sales and transfers of securities of fifteen firms, including Mitsui *Honsha* (parent company), Mitsubishi *Honsha*, Sumitomo *Honsha*, Yasuda *Hozensha*, Nissan & Co. and Nomura & Co.,[4] which were considered to be the really important *zaibatsu*. Although the Japanese, representing the influential *zaibatsu* group of Mitsui, Yasuda, Sumitomo and Mitsubishi, had had informal conversations with SCAP on 1 November, the 'principles for the dissolution of *zaibatsu* industrial and commercial organisations' were formulated immediately on 4 November 1945. The Finance Minister, Keizo Shibusawa, son of Eiichi Shibusawa, referred to *zaibatsu* firms, or *honsha*, as 'holding companies'. SCAP issued on 6 November 1945 a directive that the Japanese government be requested to create a viable plan to dissolve *zaibatsu* to the satisfaction of the Allied Powers.[5]

On 24 November 1945, the Ordinance for the Liquidations and Restrictions of Companies was promulgated, and eighty-three holding companies, including fifteen *zaibatsu honsha*, and some 4,500 firms subordinate to the former, were listed. On 20 April 1946, the Ordinance of the Holding Company Liquidation Commission was accepted. The Ordinance defined the character, function and purposes of the Commission. Finally, the 'Memorandum: Ordinances and Regulations Affecting the Holding Company Liquidation Commission' issued on 23 July 1946 gave a go-ahead to the Commission which on 27 August first opened its proceedings.[6]

In the mean time, SCAP placed on the table the whole of the Japanese banking system. The memorandum, dated 5 April 1946, read:

The system of designating financial institutions to finance munitions companies inaugurated in May 1942 with the establishment of the National Financial Control Association. At the beginning, a munitions company was technically free to select one of several designated banks, but in April 1944 even this privilege was eliminated and one bank was designated for each munitions company. With the end of the war, the designated bank system was diverted to the financing of war industries converting or planning to convert to peacetime production.[7]

The conversion to peacetime banking was partly dependent on the critical question, were munitions industry borrowings, that is *de facto* governmental borrowings from the banks, redeemable at all? Replying to the Ministry of Finance queries, SCAP flatly countered in the memorandum on 'Elimination of War Profits and Reorganisation of National Finance', dated 24 November 1945, that all such liabilities arising from war industrial financing would be irredeemable in order to emphasise that 'war is financially profitless'.[8]

Eventually in 1946 the Japanese government accepted the inevitable, that all wartime liabilities would not be paid. On 31 March 1946, the outstanding war loans by banks amounted to ¥835 million: this was the three-quarters of the total bank lending. Indeed 84 per cent of the advances due to the Big Five banks, that is, Imperial (or Teikoku, the amalgamated version of Mitsui and Daiichi Banks), Mitsubishi, Yasuda, Sumitomo and Sanwa Banks, and the Industrial Bank of Japan was in fact war financing.[9] The banks were to be subjected to great losses, a situation never previously experienced.

Anticipating this terrible result, the Ministry of Finance had reached the conclusion that a 'moratorium' would be unavoidable for a successful rescue operation of banking as a whole. On this basis, the Ministry further elaborated their plan using two major devices, proclaimed simultaneously in February 1946. The appropriately termed Emergency Financial Measures Ordinance was promulgated so that the strictest ever moratorium came into being for all financial institutions including the trust fund department in the Finance Ministry. This was far more severe than the measures which had followed the Great Kanto Earthquake of 1923 and the 1927 banking collapse. Facing the SCAP prohibition of war loan repayment, the Finance Ministry reinforced the Ordinance in August 1946 so that the locked-up deposits were divided into two classes, that is, the large-scale corporate deposits and the rest. Then in October the Ministry further legislated the Financial Institution Reconstruction Act. The Act ordered the banks to divide their accounts into two, that is the old and the new, upon the latter of which they would base their business reconstruction. It allowed the banks to revalue their profits so that they would be applicable to fill the losses. It also ordered the banks to use their large-scale corporate deposits and 90 per cent of their capital stocks to cover the losses. These operations took nearly a year to complete.[10]

Simultaneous with the emergency measures in February 1946, another Ordinance specified the withdrawal of the old Bank of Japan notes, which would cease to be legal tender after 3 March 1946. New Bank of Japan notes were to be issued thereafter and were to be exchanged through deposits in financial institutions between 25 February and 7 March 1946; only a very limited amount of the new notes was allowed to be withdrawn from the institutions as the moratorium was strictly in effect.[11]

The combined operation of the two emergency Ordinances was indeed an extraordinary development in Japanese monetary history: nothing like this had happened before. The measures were, however, salutary and did reverse the dangerous decline in banking deposits which had been steadily draining away from the autumn of 1945 to early 1946. By February 1948, deposits exceeded the level of 1941. Inflation was also a serious threat which soon began to become a hindrance to recovery. During the first half of 1946, the wholesale price index (January 1948 = 100) doubled and further soared from 19.19 in June 1946 to 98.1 in December 1947.[12] How could the ailing Japanese economy fight back against dangerous hyper-inflation?

In the spring of 1946, after directing the enactment of the Ordinance of Holding Company Liquidation, which was relevant only to the dissolution of *zaibatsu*, SCAP started preparing draft procedures on preventing the emergence of monopolistic concerns in future. Responding to the SCAP directive, the Japanese government set to work on a bill aimed at 'preventing the private monopoly and preserving the fair trade', which became law in April 1947 and was known as the 'Anti-Trust Act'.

In the mean time, the Washington administration, with the consent of MacArthur, organised the State War Mission of Japanese Combines to prepare a report which would recommend measures to remove the *zaibatsu* infrastructure. The Mission was headed by Corwin D. Edwards, economics professor at Northwestern University and consultant of the State Department, and consisted of seven other members from various departments in Washington. The Edwards Mission, after the nine-week investigation tour in Japan in early 1946, laid their report before the Washington administration. It was then transmitted through the State Department to the Far Eastern Commission (comprised of the US, Britain, China, the Soviet Union and seven other member countries) for adoption as Allied policy. At this stage the report was designated *FEC–230*.[13] It was during this process that SCAP issued 'Memorandum: Dissolution of Trading

Companies' on 3 July 1947, by which Mitsui Bussan (Trading Co.) and Mitsubishi Shoji (Trading Co.) were dissolved into 223 and 139 companies respectively.[14] The dissolution of these two gigantic trading companies, symbols of the pre-war Japanese economy, sent shock waves throughout Japan.

The report, *FEC–230*, was based upon the thesis that 'dissolution of excessive private concentrations of economic power'[15] was essential to democratisation of Japanese economic and political life. Such excessive concentrations were thus defined:

Any private enterprise or combination operated for profit is an excessive concentration of economic power if its asset value is very large; or if its working force ... is very large; or if, though somewhat smaller in assets or working force, it is engaged in business in various unrelated fields, or if it controls substantial financial institutions and/or substantial industrial or commercial ones.[16]

Two weeks after the dissolution of Mitsui and Mitsubishi Trading Companies, SCAP directed the Japanese government to consider enactment of a 'bill of dissolution of excessive private concentrations of economic power'. The Act was promulgated and became effective in December 1947. In February 1948, 257 firms in the mining and manufacturing sector and 68 in the service sector were designated as institutions which were required to be dissolved under this Act. Japanese banks faced a grave situation, though the list of those to be dissolved was not actually published. SCAP was not basically opposed to the dissolutions, but commented that: 'the practical execution of such a program ... is quite beyond the size and organisation of the Occupation Forces'.[17] Just before the dissolutions could be carried out strong objections were raised by some Americans.

First came a further criticism from James L. Kauffman, a New York lawyer, who, as a young man, had been professor of law in the Imperial University of Tokyo between 1913 and 1919 and who had visited Japan in the summer of 1947 on behalf of Dillon, Read & Co.:

Demilitarisation was deemed to have been accomplished when the conquered country was physically disarmed. In Japan, however, it was decided that demilitarisation included the complete reformation of the nation's ideology ... SCAP proposes to create in Japan what it terms a 'democratic Japanese economy' ... There is no definition in writing, as far as I have been able to learn, of what is meant by a 'democratic Japanese economy'.[18]

Then W. H. Draper, under-secretary of the US Army (a partner of Dillon, Read & Co., who had visited Japan in September 1947) warned the State Department that the Dissolution Act, if really carried out, would virtually destroy the Japanese economy.

Quoting Draper and Kauffman, *Newsweek* magazine concluded:

The Troublesome FEC–230
One of the basic objectives of the American occupation of Japan has been to break up the *zaibatsu*, the great family monopolies that controlled most of the country's economic life and were used to finance Japanese aggression. However, it has never been the purpose of the American Government to weaken the Japanese economy to the point where the maintenance of Japan would become a continual charge on the American taxpayer.[19]

These objections indeed 'put the cat among the pigeons'. Implementation of the Act for the Dissolution of Excessive Private Concentrations of Economic Power, which was well in hand, suddenly came to a standstill. The American objectors had performed a useful function. The Truman Doctrine, addressed by the US President on 12 March 1947, marked the beginning of the US policies to contain communist expansion. Indeed, on the European continent, the Russian blockade of Berlin began in April 1948. Further, and more seriously for the Japanese, communist military advances on the Chinese mainland were remarkable during the first half of 1948. This led to confrontation on the Korean peninsula, where the Republic of Korea declared independence in July 1948, which was countered by the declaration of the People's Democratic Republic of Korea in August that year. With the emergence of the cold war, tension spread world-wide. The Americans realised that they needed a thriving Japan and a flourishing economy. The changes in the American world strategy were the decisive factor affecting their attitude towards the Japanese economy and banking. The number of firms subject to the Act was reduced dramatically to only eighteen by July 1948. On 2 July 1948, it was resolved that the Act would not be applicable to banking.[20] Japanese banking narrowly escaped devastating dissolution.

Although they escaped dissolution, the *zaibatsu* banks were prohibited to use *zaibatsu* firm names. Daiichi Bank became independent from Imperial Bank on 1 October 1948, and Mitsui remained known as Imperial as the title 'Mitsui' was forbidden. On the same day, Mitsubishi, Sumitomo, Yasuda and Nomura were obliged to abandon their *zaibatsu* titles and became Chiyoda, Osaka, Fuji and Daiwa respectively. The rest of the big banks, Sanwa and Tokai, together with Daiichi, which were not regarded as part of *zaibatsu*, were allowed to retain their names.

Later, in May 1952 when the restrictions ended, the traditional titles of Mitsui, Mitsubishi and Sumitomo were reinstated, but Fuji (formerly Yasuda) and Daiwa (formerly Nomura) remained. In sharp contrast to the German experience, the Japanese banks recovered their institutional identity within a decade of 1945. Moreover, independence from the former *zaibatsu honsha* and therefore *zaibatsu* families enabled the big banks to claim the pivotal positions of former *zaibatsu* industrial groups. Furthermore, it could be argued that the liquidation of *zaibatsu honsha* gave the 'house' banks greater freedom and thus put them in a position from which they could easily finance the recovering industries.

29 Remaking the banking system: the Japanese versus the Americans, 1946–1952

Towards the end of 1945, after the American operations to clear the war machinery and tackle the grave situation that faced the banks had begun, the Finance Ministry started to work out reconstruction plans. In October 1945, a Preparatory Committee for Revisions of the Bank of Japan Act was appointed, and in December that year it produced a report for the Ministry of Finance. The outgoing Preparatory Committee was immediately succeeded in December 1945 by a Commission on the Financial System, a post-war version of the 1926 Commission[1] and the first of those Commissions which later became an authoritative counselling organ for the Finance Ministry whenever crucial questions arose. This first post-war Commission promptly drafted a report on the overall plan for remaking the Japanese banking system, including the revisions in the Bank of Japan Act, based upon one prepared earlier by the Preparatory Committee.

The report included a plan for a 'Finance Agency'. According to this, the Agency, headed by the Finance Minister assisted by the Bank of Japan governor and the chief of the finance department of the Ministry, was supposed to ensure the supervision of management of national funds and adjustment of interests between industry and finance. The Agency would, according to the plan, be placed in the Ministry of Finance, but the secretarial office would be installed in the Bank of Japan.[2] The 'Finance Agency' was to become a focus of Japanese banking as will shortly be disclosed.

The Finance Ministry appointed the second Commission on the Financial System in December 1946 to work out a more detailed plan for the future. By March 1947 the Commission had produced three recommendations entitled 'Draft Plan for Temporary Regulations for Currency Issue', 'Draft Temporary Outlines for Reconstruction and Adjustment of Financial Institutions' and 'Draft Outlines for Revisions of the Act of Commercial and Industrial Association Central Cash Office'. From the draft plans, the Finance Ministry prepared a comprehensive Financial Business Bill which was completed by December 1947.

The bill was said to be based upon the principles of 'democratisation', rationalisation and adjustment of the system to take account of post-war circumstances.[3] The term 'democratisation', in American eyes the panacea for all Japan's ills, remained popular as a slogan among the Japanese for many years. Nevertheless, despite its frequent use, no one knew what it really meant, especially with regard to banking, as Kauffman, an American lawyer, rightly pointed out in *Newsweek* magazine. There was controversy over the bill at the beginning of 1948.

SCAP eventually, in April 1948, promised to make a proposal on banking, and in August made public a memorandum entitled 'Overall Revision of the Banking Structure through Enactment of New Legislation' which was handed over to the Ministry of Finance, Bank of Japan and Economic Stabilisation Board, which had been set up exactly two years ago and which was a predecessor of the Economic Planning Agency. The memorandum was illuminated by the proposal of a 'banking board':

A strong, well balanced, non-political board, independent of the Ministry of Finance; the chairman to be of Cabinet rank and the terms of the member to be sufficiently long and definite and the expiration of the terms to be staggered in such manner as to provide for continuity with gradual turnover; to be the governmental agency responsible for the formulation and enforcement of the nation's monetary and credit policies, in coordination with the government's treasury policies and operations under the Ministry of Finance; to administer the new banking and financial law and within sufficiently comprehensive and definite limits fixed by the law, regulate and supervise all banks and all other credit and financial institutions, including the Bank of Japan, to further insure that all such institutions are maintained in sound condition and operated in accordance with the provisions and purposes of the law and sound and fair practices.[4]

This 'bank board' was the SCAP equivalent of a 'Financial Agency'. Both plans had some common ground – both would provide independent institutions – but were fundamentally different from each other in the fact that the banking board would be independent of the government and the finance agency would be the government agent. The banking board proposal, therefore, became a hotly argued issue between SCAP and the Japanese financial authorities.[5]

In the mean time, in Washington, a compromise proposal was emerging as Joseph Dodge, adviser to SCAP, negotiated with the Truman administration. Dodge thought the 'Overall Revision' unrealistic, particularly as the cold war was gaining strength.[6] This necessitated a change in American attitudes. When these changes were disclosed to the Japanese government, it became clear that the title 'banking board' had been changed to 'policy board', which was to be installed in the Bank of Japan. Its members were to be appointed by the cabinet, including the Bank of Japan governor, Finance Minister and representatives from various financial institutions, and they were to be responsible for overall policy making.[7] The proposal was acceptable to the Japanese and after some minor revisions, for example regarding membership on the board,[8] the Bank of Japan Act was revised in June 1949 so that the policy board could be set up.

The Americans, however, did not forget to remind the Japanese financial authorities that the Americans were still in a position of supervising the Japanese:

The primary objectives of the Policy Board of the Bank of Japan are to formulate as well as direct, supervise, and publish monetary and credit policy for the Central Bank so as to harmonise the interests of all agencies of the Government and the entire banking system in such a way as to serve the best interest of the national economy. To accomplish this task, it will be necessary for the Board to organise itself into an operating body in compliance with the law, by issuing rules of organisation and procedure for the purpose of creating a structure within the bank which will operate smoothly and efficiently. Before these are adopted it will be necessary to submit them to this Headquarters for coordination.

Once this has been accomplished there are many problems now pending, the solution of which falls within the jurisdiction of this body. In view of the number, only a few outstanding ones will be discussed at this time.

The Board will have to keep under view the loan and rediscount policies of the Central Bank . . . In this connection also, the Board will have to turn its attention to developing a sound and equitable relationship between the Central Bank and its client banks, looking forward to the establishment of a reserve system . . .

Furthermore, their renewed efforts to develop a more active bill market for liquid short-term commodity and commercial bills and the seasonal rediscounting and purchasing of such bills by the Central Bank, places emphasis upon such a method of financing rather than the present method of extensive use of direct loans to financial institutions by the Central Bank . . .

While the Ministry of Finance is actively preparing a revision of the Banking Law, the Policy Board should be advised of developments by the representatives from the Ministry, and the Board should likewise assume the responsibility of making recommendations so that the new legislation will be coordinated with the policies of the Board. The Policy Board, being composed of outstanding leaders selected from all segments of the Japanese economy, will have the opportunity to fill a much needed function of coordinating the various interests . . .

When the Board becomes operative it will be expected to keep the public informed of its activities, problems, and decisions through the publication of monthly bulletins, the issuance of which should be prescribed in the rules of organisation and procedure.[9]

Careful examination of the SCAP statements discloses that the recommendations were scarcely new to the Japanese financial system except for 'democratisation' of the management. It should be noted that 'the publication of monthly bulletins', which had been launched by the Bank of Japan in

1908, had appeared in America in the form of the *Federal Reserve Bulletin* from 1915. 'Rediscounting policies' and 'a more active bill market' were longstanding problems for the Japanese financial authorities who had them under consideration since the 1926 Commission on the Financial System or even before it. Although it was not yet to be incorporated in central banking, 'a reserve system' had long been operated in Japanese banking and was an integrated part of time-honoured *ryogae* business. It should also be added that even the 'policy board' itself might not be peculiar to the Japanese as it was originally put forward as a countermeasure against the 'Finance Agency' and the composition of the board was very similar to the Temporary Rate Regulation Committee, a Japanese invention, as will shortly be discussed.

It was felt in Japan that the intervention of the Americans, through SCAP, demonstrated a lack of understanding of the sophisticated banking system which had evolved in Japan prior to the war and that the Japanese needed no outside advice in the management of their financial system. It was, indeed, true that the Americans at their earlier stages were 'more richly endowed with enthusiasm and self-confidence than with political or economic expertise'.[10] However, as Edwin Reischauer recollects, there was an absolute shortage in the American staff of Japanese experts. This shortage perhaps explains the remarkable shift of their policies from the 'abortive' dissolution of the big banks to taking the line advocated by Dodge.[11] In fact this marked the end of American interference in Japanese banking. The encroachment of communism on mainland Asia was soon to force the Americans to consider problems other than those of Japan.

Now that the United States policy shifted away from 'punishment' towards encouraging an economic self-reliance for Japan,[12] the principal problem was how to overcome hyper-inflation which had been rampant since the middle of 1946.[13] During the course of 1948, prices rose constantly, soaring from an index of 100 in January to 220.1 in December.

Hyper-inflation was stimulated by the financial operations carried out by *Fukko Kinyu Kinko*, or the Reconstruction Finance Cash Office, set up first inside the Finance Ministry in June 1946, at the recommendation of the first Commission on the Financial System, and then independently in January 1947. From then on the Reconstruction Finance Cash Office undertook large-scale industrial financing to encourage production measures which had been adopted in August 1946 under the first Yoshida administration and rigorously pursued by the succeeding coalition administration of the socialists and the democrats. These measures aimed at strengthening infrastructural industries such as energy, iron and steel, and fertiliser. The Reconstruction Finance Cash Office financing showed strong increases from the middle of 1947 and reached ¥131,965 million in March 1949, equivalent to 32 per cent of total bank lending. Two-thirds of the Reconstruction Office money came from the Bank of Japan and the rest from other banks.[14] The increase in this lending, which went hand in hand with increases in the note issue, resulted in runaway inflation. Although it was undeniable that basic Japanese industries urgently needed investment, the over-enthusiastic provision was largely responsible for the hyper-inflation.

In December 1948 SCAP prepared a programme of nine articles for the Japanese government to carry into effect as soon as possible.[15] These were to achieve a balanced budget, introduce an efficient taxation system, restrict credit, stabilise wages, impose price controls, strengthen trade and exchange control, expand exports, increase the production of essential raw materials and improve the provision of food supplies. Between February and May 1949, American advisers, including Joseph M. Dodge and Carl S. Shoup, Columbia University professor and director of the Tax Mission to Japan, rushed to Japan. Dodge was responsible for the 'Dodge Line', the overall policy, and was particularly competent in persuading the Japanese government to put an end to the Reconstruction Finance Cash Office lending and pushing for a balanced budget. He set the Japanese foreign exchange rate as $1 = ¥360 and installed a special account in the budget to utilise the counterpart funds of the United States 'Government Appropriations for Relief in Occupied Areas' and 'Economic Rehabilitation of Occupied Areas', widely known as GARIOA and EROA.

Although the objectives of the Japanese and the Americans were not necessarily the same, between them they produced a splendid result. Prices steadied by early 1951 and even began to fall by nearly seven points in the course of the year.[16] Hyper-inflation was at last routed. In the mean time, in January 1952, the Reconstruction Finance Cash Office was discontinued, handing over part of the business to a newly founded governmental bank.

30 The rise of governmental banking and the search for stability: Japanese initiatives, 1949–1958

The Americans felt that the colonial banks and the Yokohama Specie Bank had been part of the Japanese war economy and they therefore insisted that they close down and that the Specie Bank convert itself into a small harmless Bank of Tokyo. The three remaining industrial banks, the Industrial Bank of Japan, Hypothec Bank and Hokkaido Development Bank, although still in existence, were vulnerable. SCAP first required the special banks to decide their own future by opting to become ordinary banks or debenture-issuing institutions. Two months later, in August 1948, SCAP issued a memorandum on 'Overall Revision of Banking Structure',[1] which was designed to erase any traces of special banks reregistered themselves as ordinary banks, though the Industrial Bank did in fact soon discover a way to resume its old business. The prohibition of new advances by the Reconstruction Finance Cash Office, in addition to the suspension of special banking, was particularly unfortunate because demand for long-term borrowing strengthened as tension on the Korean peninsula was developing in early 1950. In these circumstances the government, with American consent, promulgated the Act of Issuing Bank Debentures in March 1950. The Industrial Bank was included. This heralded the start of the recovery. What was the government to do?

The government's approach to the problem was hesitant as, fearful of American disapproval, they laid down two moderate financial schemes to encourage the setting up of small businesses and consumer finance corporations. Small industries had been severely hit during the war and consumer goods were in very short supply. In any case the government only had the resources to remake smaller institutions. The result was two corporations, that is, the People's Finance Corporation in 1949, an amalgamated version of the Common People's Cash Office and the Pension Cash Office, and the Housing Finance Corporation in 1950. The capital of both corporations was totally dependent on the government.

However, internationally the situation was changing and American anxieties deepened as Communist China became more powerful and an opportunity for the Japanese to set up a substantial governmental financial institution was emerging. Yen counterpart funds of GARIOA/EROA, or American assistance funds, were advanced to Japan, and it became possible for the Japanese to submit more radical proposals. Accordingly, in April 1950, premier Shigeru Yoshida, heading his third cabinet, dispatched Finance Minister Hayato Ikeda with Jiro Shirasu, a Cambridge graduate and the ex-deputy chief of the Economic Stabilisation Board, as special adviser, and Kiichi Miyazawa, later premier in the early 1990s, as secretary, to Washington to discuss with the American administration overall economic recovery policies, including a possible Export Import Finance Bank. This marked the start of a six-month negotiation. As Kiichi Miyazawa, secretary and interpreter, recollects:

We originally had an idea of setting up 'an Export Import Finance Bank'. But Mr Dodge, I have yet been unable to understand why, strongly objected to the term 'bank' being used. Mr Dodge's policies were entirely involved in pumping up money – the policies with which to turn off the tap on the one hand and to pump up extra liquid on the other hand – and therefore it was taboo to supply money. Furthermore he also strenuously disapproved of conducting 'import finance'. He stuck to the idea that it would be exports and not imports which were essential to Japan at that time. That was why we drafted a plan for the 'Export Finance Corporation'.[2]

In addition Dodge insisted that the institution projected should be, despite being owned by the government, independent. The argument was that if the proposed institution carried the title of bank and conducted a full range of foreign business then it would be the same as the special banks which the Americans were determined to dissolve. The Americans eventually conceded the use of the title of bank, but were resolute on their other two points.

In the autumn of 1950, when Dodge paid his third visit to Tokyo, a final agreement was reached along guidelines he had already laid down in his memorandum dated 9 November 1950:

It has been agreed that the following principles will control these final decisions:

1. The Export Finance Bank will be established with the simplest possible structure and operating organisation and with a maximum of independence from any direct government control.
. . .
3. The constitutional responsibility of the Bank to the Diet will be discharged through the Minister of Finance and an operating budget will be submitted annually by the Bank to the Finance Minister for administrative approval.
4. The Bank will have an outstanding individual head as President, appointed by the Prime Minister with approval of the Cabinet, for a term of years, whose function will be to give the business a responsible, effective, and independent management.
. . .

7. The Bank will not compete with the Japanese Commercial Banks and will only handle business referred to it on a discount or participation basis, at appropriate current rates of interest.

8. The principal function and first responsibility of the Bank will be to grant credits for financing the production of capital goods in Japan for export. However, if sufficient funds are made available and it appears advisable, a limited amount of resources may be used for financing foreign imports from Japan where the Japanese and the importers' foreign exchange restrictions permit such transactions and firm, financially responsible, and acceptable contracts have been made.

9. The Bank will have no access to the Bank of Japan, the private banking system or the private capital market for operating funds.[3]

Nobody knows how, in Japan, this kind of bank could be independent from the government, as Dodge strongly insisted shortly before. However, in December 1950, the Japan Export Finance Bank Act became law. The Bank opened its doors in February 1951 with a paid-in capital of ¥5,000 million, for which the Japanese general budget account and the counterpart funds account were equally responsible.

To meet further industrial demands for finance, which were becoming clamant, from the middle of 1950 another scheme for a government bank was floated. This was the Development Bank, and arrangements, thanks to the earlier work on the Export Bank, went smoothly. As the Japan Development Bank was to succeed to the business of the earlier Reconstruction Finance Cash Office, it was carefully stressed by SCAP that 'the keynote of the economic policy in and after JFY [American abbreviation of Japanese Financial Year] 1951 when the Japan Development Bank is in operation is to build up the firm groundwork of Japan's self-supporting economy in future without disturbing the basis of the stabilised economy established in and after the JFY 1949'.[4] On this basic understanding, the Development Bank was to be allowed to finance equipment funds to industries for a period longer than one year. In the light of the excessive issues of Reconstruction Cash Office debentures contributing to hyper-inflation, the Development Bank was prohibited to issue debentures. However, it was to be sanctioned, as a long-term finance institution, to 're-finance the long-term loan made by city banks, which re-financing is soon to be put into effect',[5] but the Bank was warned not to compete with those city banks. The Japan Development Bank Act was legally established in March 1951 and the Bank opened for business in May that year with paid-in capital of ¥2,500 million, which was provided by GARIOA/EROA.

These two important financial institutions came into existence despite tough negotiations during the last phase of the occupation period. They were in effect the establishment of a post-war version of special banking which SCAP had earlier attacked. Were these moves part of a silent

Japanese 'fight-back'? Months later, on 28 April 1952, the San Francisco
Peace Treaty, together with the US–Japan Security Treaty, became effective,
bringing to an end the Allied Powers' occupation of Japan.

Anticipation of the end of the occupation gave a fresh impetus to banking
initiative. First, in April 1952, the regulations which controlled the Japan
Export Finance Bank Act were amended so that the Bank could expand its
business to enable it to conduct import financing together with guarantee
business and borrowing of foreign currency in addition to Bank of Japan
money. The title was naturally changed to Japan Export Import Finance
Bank. Then, in July of the same year, the Japan Development Bank Act was
revised so that the Bank would be allowed to issue debentures together with
conducting guarantee business, floating foreign loans and borrowing
foreign currency and government money. 'Special banking' *de facto* revived.
During the mid-1950s five more corporations were added, all with specific
banking tasks. In 1953 the Agriculture and Fishery Finance Corporation
and Small Business Finance Corporation were founded, with roles in their
respective fields. In 1956, the Hokkaido Development Corporation was set
up to replace the Hokkaido Development Bank, which American intervention had now forced into ordinary banking. The Corporation was reorganised the next year as Hokkaido Tohoku Development Corporation
responsible for the whole area of north-eastern Japan. For supplementary
supports, the Public Firm Finance Corporation and Small Business Credit
Insurance Corporation were set to work in 1957 and 1958 respectively. By
the late 1950s there was an enormous government banking workforce ready
and waiting to finance new demands.

31 The post-war system, 1946–1959

Integration, 1946–1954

By the end of March 1948, under the Financial Institution Reconstruction Act of October 1946, the disastrous losses of all wartime bank advances were liquidated. The amount thus eliminated totalled ¥24,800 million, of which nearly two-thirds belonged to ordinary banking.[1] A series of antitrust measures and enactments by the end of 1947, which dissolved the *zaibatsu*, nullified the bank agreements on interest rates. Urgent action was needed and, with the aid of advice from SCAP, the Temporary Rate Regulation Act was promulgated in December 1947. Under the Act, any rates of interest, from Bank of Japan Rates to call market and mutual loan rates, were to be subject to the directive of the Bank of Japan governor in consultation with a Rate Regulation Committee.[2]

A comprehensive Financial Business Bill, together with a Financial Institution Accountancy Bill, proved, by the middle of 1949, to be abortive. They were overtaken by a surge of policy changes brought about by the Dodge Line. Before the breaking apart of the two bills, the Finance Ministry tried hard to put the system together and base it on a more sound foundation. In the autumn of 1946, the government started surveying and reviewing the branch network of banking and other financial institutions. By the spring of 1952, due to the designation of all offices, other than the head office, as 'branches', the number of branches increased by more than 1,000.[3]

Looking at the American examples, the government had earlier, in the autumn of 1947, presented an outline of deposit insurance, which developed into the 'Outlines for Deposit Insurance Act' in October 1949. However, 'the Act' too was abortive, perhaps on account of the Japanese authorities being still unaware of its importance. The Act would only be realised later in 1971.[4] In May 1948 SCAP issued a memorandum on bank audits, though unofficially, to the Ministry of Finance. Quickly responding to this directive, the Ministry of Finance in July 1948 reinforced the audit section in the banking bureau. The instalment of the audit section enabled the Ministry for the first time to initiate bank inspections without notice. This was very different from previous Bank of Japan auditing which could cover only ordinary banking and was always undertaken with due notice.[5]

In the wake of the abortive attempts for a Financial Business Bill, the Finance Ministry abandoned its efforts to produce comprehensive financial legislation. Between October 1949 and October 1950 the Finance Ministry prepared various drafts of a Bank Act which would cover ordinary banking. The Ministry's scheme for a new Bank Act provoked strong objections from the National Federation of Bank Associations, founded in October 1945, which represented sixty-nine local bank associations from both city and regional banks. What made the Federation most anxious about the draft Act was its intention to nullify the policy board at the Bank of Japan and thus to strengthen further the governmental control.[6] The Ministry of Finance had to wait until 1981 before a new Bank Act came into existence.

While the Americans left intact less important financial institutions,[7] trust companies were, first among non-bank institutions, given a new legal status in 1948 by the Trust Bank Act. Thereafter they became trust banks, of which by January 1950[8] there were seventeen. Small-scale ordinary banks, regional banks, were also encouraged by SCAP and increased to twelve between October 1950 and February 1954.[9] On the contrary, savings banks were finally discontinued in March 1949. The biggest, Japan Savings Bank, had reregistered as Kyowa Bank in 1948. The disappearance of savings banking was not required by SCAP but followed the disaster of hyper-inflation.

The 1950s brought a transformation in Japan's economic expectations as she was no longer an enemy, but a vital friend for America, off the coast of mainland China. Thus in the first half decade of the 1950s a spate of banking legislation was dispatched from the office of the Finance Ministry. In June 1951, preceding the governmental institutions for financing small businesses, two financial institutions for small business obtained new legal bases. Mutual loan companies, which had long been doing near-banking business, were given the title of mutual banks under the Mutual Bank Act of 1951. In the same year, numerous credit associations were registered under the Credit Cash Office Act. The rest of the associations remained in the category of credit cooperatives under the Small Business Cooperative Act of 1949.[10]

Responding to the rapid increase of long-term financing, the government, with continued support of Joseph Dodge, reorganised the trust funds department at the Finance Ministry between December 1950 and March

1951 to form the funds management department which was sanctioned to use funds in sectors other than the governmental. But demand for industrial financing was never ending. Between 1950 and 1951 the increase in bank advances was ¥523,100 million, representing 152 per cent growth in only one year. This was the beginning of the so-called 'over-loans' by city banks to industries, which were ultimately relying on Bank of Japan money. The Bank of Japan was being put in a very difficult position in that it had to steer the economy between disinflation and supplying money for growth. Indeed, the Bank made a prodigious effort from June 1950 to November 1951.[11] The early 1950s thus witnessed remarkable economic progress and by 1954 industrial production had recovered to the pre-war level.

From these critical circumstances emerged a scheme of non-governmental long-term credit banking. The scheme, carefully prepared by the Finance Ministry from the end of 1951 to the spring of 1952, resulted in legislation of the Long-term Credit Bank Act in June 1952, effective in December that year. The Act was to authorise the Japan Longterm Credit Bank registered under it to receive the privilege of issuing bank debentures instead of deposit taking, which ordinary banking was not allowed. The Industrial Bank of Japan was immediately willing to register itself under the Act. This was sanctioned. But the other former special banks, the Hypothec Bank and the Hokkaido Development Bank, did not prefer long-term credit banking as they had already been deeply involved in deposit-taking business. However, heavy demands which could not be met by the established Industrial Bank were expected. Against this background, another long-term credit bank was projected, with the support of the Hypothec Bank, the Hokkaido Development Bank and regional banks. Later, in 1957, the Japan Realty Finance Bank, partly succeeding to the assets of the liquidating Bank of Korea, joined the two, later being renamed as Japan Credit Bank.

In the wake of the achievement of complete independence in April 1952, Japan could consider the possibilities for international banking. In May, Japan was admitted to the International Monetary Fund and International Bank for Reconstruction and Development, or the so-called World Bank. Simultaneously Japanese overseas banking, thereto totally under SCAP control and supervision, resumed independent business. In April 1952, the government encouraged the Bank of Tokyo, the reincarnation of the Yokohama Specie Bank, to open offices in New York and London, Mitsui (still Imperial) reappeared in London, Mitsubishi in New York, Fuji in London and Sumitomo in New York.[12] Two years later, by the Foreign Exchange Bank Act of 1954, the Bank of Tokyo was given the privilege of being the sole specialist bank. The other banks could of course be engaged in foreign business, albeit on the more restricted basis stipulated by the Foreign Exchange Regulation Act of 1949.

Japanese resumption of overseas business was certainly stimulated by the increasing presence of foreign banking in Japan which had earlier, in the middle of 1946, started coming back. By April 1954, there were thirteen foreign banks with thirty-four offices in Tokyo, Yokohama, Osaka, Kobe and Nagoya. These included the Hongkong and Shanghai Bank, Chartered Bank of India, Australia and China, Mercantile Bank of India, Bank of America and Chase National Bank.[13] Thus, by the middle of the 1950s, all elements of revived Japanese banking were integrated into the world system. The stage was set for recovery and expansion.

Growth potential, 1954–1959

By 1954, in terms of all industries, the production index had recovered to the level of 1936, which had been the peak of the pre-war economy. The economic recovery was about to turn itself into a net economic growth. The indexation of industrial production, taking the year 1960 as the basis of 100, shows, indeed, that production recovered from 44.1 in 1954 to 80.3 in 1959, a 182 per cent increase compared to 174 per cent between 1960 and 1965 when the high-speed era began.[14] Even a glimpse at the demand side of resources during this proto-high-speed growth period reveals that on average 81 per cent of monetary needs was met through advances made either by banks or by other financial institutions. Equities and debenture financing were 15 per cent and 4 per cent respectively.[15] This was certainly due in part to the fact that recovery of securities markets was retarded on account of various factors, for example, company assets revaluation according to the tax reform, 'democratisation' of the markets for access by the common people, legislation of the new Securities Transaction Act on the American model and so on, all of which had to be fitted in a new post-war system.[16]

On the supply side, four categories of banks provided industries with 90 per cent on average of their borrowings. Of the four, the non-governmental, or ordinary and long-term, banks were responsible for 57 per cent of the total lending, the governmental for 23 per cent, mutual banking for 6 per cent and trust banking for 4 per cent. The rest was supplied by the various financial institutions lining up just behind the banks.[17] Of the four categories, ordinary, long-term and governmental banks accounted for 80 per cent of the total. In the post-war Japanese banking system, the governmental and the long-term banks quickly took the position that special banking had long occupied until 1945. Perhaps this speed contributed to a remarkable development of advances, deposits and bank debentures in the years from 1954 to 1959. The growth rate of advances was only second to that recorded in the First World War boom of 1915 to 1919. Deposits became a little less than two and a half times larger, compared to more than three times in 1915 to 1919, but the growth of debentures far exceeded that of the First World War boom. This 'troika' of the ordinary, the long-term and the governmental banks was indeed the machinery that was essential to the recovery of the economy and was to bring life to the growth potential in the coming decade of the 1960s.

An extraordinary century, 1859–1959

Japanese banking has travelled a long way since 1 July 1859 when a group of foreign merchants ruthlessly drained away her irreplaceable gold reserves because the exchange of gold with silver had been fixed at too low a rate. At that time Japanese currency was full of debased coins and local paper money, and the Japanese had no knowledge of the gold–silver ratio dominant in the rest of the world. Japan's first harsh lesson in international finance was one which she has never forgotten.

The Yokohama Specie Bank was set up in 1880 to do Japanese business overseas and to collect specie worldwide to bring back to Japan. Did bankers, other than the Japanese, know the primary aim of the Specie Bank? Did John Robertson, the manager of the Oriental Bank in Yokohama, which had previously done business for the Japanese government, know the real aim of the Specie Bank? Certainly he was horrified when the Specie Bank opened, because the Specie Bank eventually deprived him of Japanese business. The Oriental Bank closed its doors in 1884.

Then, during the sixteen years from 1881, when Matsukata was dreaming of going on to the gold standard, did anyone, other than the Japanese, know of the Japanese ambitions? Even in Japan only a handful of persons knew Matsukata's intention. When, in 1902, the Industrial Bank of Japan was set up, not only to provide capital for industries, but also to scour the world for specie collection, was this known outside Japan? In fact, one of the greatest assets which the Japanese had was the language, which virtually closed the country to the world outside. This meant that however interested the westerners were about the Japanese, in banking or in anything else, they were excluded. Information on banking is still flowing, in general, from outside to inside Japan. The Japanese are perhaps still conscious of themselves as 'insiders' and see everyone else as 'outsiders'. This reinforces the tendency to reticence and secrecy which is still powerful in Japanese society.

The 'insider–outsider' theory could be put in a wider context. The Japanese have good reason to be fearful of foreigners whom they do not readily understand and by whom they are easily offended. Therefore it was, or still is, inevitable that in banking, as in everything else, they should seek to be independent of, or even isolated from, foreigners. They have been assisted in this determination by their impenetrable language and by the West's easy assumption of superiority. There have also been some racist attitudes on both sides.

Was Japan then a case of 'economic backwardness', a theory which has interested economists and historians since the days of John Stuart Mill in the 1850s? As Alexander Gerschenkron developed the theme (1952), there were a number of characteristics which might be thought to be relevant in any one country as indicators of relative backwardness.

There is no doubt that the Japanese state played a commanding part in Japanese economic development, encouraging many initiatives which would have remained the preserve of self-motivated entrepreneurs in other countries. It can also be argued that there was a remarkable release of energy once the shackles which had bound Japanese society had been broken. This does suggest the validity of some 'backwardness' theory in this case. But what of the quasi-banking system already in operation in Japan?

Internally within Japan, the existence of a network of *ryogae*, merchant bankers, who had operated in Edo, Osaka and other urban areas in pre-Meiji Japan and who knew a good deal about credit facilities, lending and borrowing, was of great importance. The *ryogae* tradition was based on an instrument called the *soroban*, or the abacus, which was universally used in Japan from the fourteenth century, both in *ryogae* houses and modern banking premises until their replacement by the electronic calculator and macro-computer in the 1970s. The *ryogae* houses, especially in Edo and Osaka, were so closely integrated into the pre-Meiji Japanese economy, as well as aided by the 'insider–outsider' outlook which prevailed in Japan, that western banking could never hope to break through and penetrate into Japan. It should also be noted that there was always strong government intervention with the *ryogae* business both before and in the early Meiji years. However attractive their monetary resources and techniques might appear to the Meiji government, it was not easy for the financial oligarchs in those days to persuade Japanese merchant bankers to support government banking experiments. *Ryogae* had never co-operated with others in financial business and remained opposed to it. Nevertheless the Meiji financial oligarchs did succeed in organising the *ryogae* into national banks or into private banks, both of which eventually became ordinary banks after 1896.

The reorganisation of *ryogae* into modern banks *de facto* only underlined the strong government control over the making of the Japanese banking system as a whole. Despite the successful opening of the imperial mint in 1871, the early Meiji financial authorities had to struggle to find a successful system in which currency would not be devalued. Hyper-inflation, further fuelled by the demands caused by financing the civil war in 1877, made their struggle more urgent. The beginnings of a solution came in 1880 when the Ministry of Finance initiated the Yokohama Specie Bank. Two years later, in 1882, Matsukata confidently established the Bank of Japan and in 1885 it triumphantly launched the issuing of silver-convertible notes. Twelve years afterwards, in 1897, the Japanese currency was officially based on the gold standard, in line with British banking, then the world's most developed system. By then, with the firm control of the Finance Ministry, the Japanese banking system, led by the Bank of Japan and the Yokohama Specie Bank, was well established. However difficult these years proved for the making of Japanese banking, the decisive factors that brought success to the Japanese were the tight government control and the skill with which foreign bankers were corralled within the treaty ports. By the time foreign privileges in the treaty ports had gone, it was too late for foreign banking to make any progress within Japan.

The Japanese banking system, however, posed two formidable questions for the financial authorities. Despite the enormous amount of the Chinese indemnity, the Ministry of Finance and the Bank of Japan could never get rid of a chronic specie shortage, due primarily to the necessary importation of engineering, shipbuilding and chemical products essential to the building up of Japanese economic strength, particularly during and after the Russo-Japanese War. The Japanese did make full use of the Yokohama Specie Bank and the Industrial Bank of Japan, which, following the conclusion of the Anglo-Japanese Alliance, could rely heavily upon the London money market.

The First World War was for the Japanese a bonanza, from which the Japanese economy gained greatly. Because the war was primarily fought in Europe, by great powers all focusing their production on war materials, there was a huge demand for Japanese products. This prosperous war, however, overstretched the Japanese economy and delayed the inevitable elimination, in Japan, of small and weak banks. The post-war depression was therefore a reaction not only to the war boom, but also to the weakness of some sectors of Japanese banking.

It seems obvious that (from the beginning in the 1850s) there was rivalry between the British and the Americans over Japan. (If you read the American accounts of Perry *et al.* you would not know that the British ever existed.) The Americans had always resented the Anglo-Japanese Alliance, blaming the British for the Russo-Japanese War, which gave the Japanese freedom to operate in the Far East. Therefore, as the price for rescuing the British in the First World War, the Americans demanded that the British abandon the Japanese. As Winston Churchill noted, in his *The Second World War*, 'The annulment [of the Anglo-Japanese Alliance] had caused a profound impression in Japan and was viewed as the spurning of an Asiatic Power by the Western World'.[1]

The Washington conferences of the early 1920s, which reimposed a naval agreement on the 5–5–3 principle on the Japanese, entirely changed the circumstances in which the system would work. In America, then in Australia, stringent acts against further Japanese immigration were passed. Internally, in Japan rising militarism played on Japan's isolation. Japanese banking, because of its isolation, was necessarily cautious, recognising that in time of crisis specie and resources would become increasingly difficult to obtain. In the uneasy atmosphere in Japan, leading financial figures became targets for assassination by military and right-wing extremists. The Great Kanto Earthquake of 1 September 1923 worsened the situation and precipitated Japanese banking into a major financial crisis in the spring of 1927, which was followed immediately by the Wall Street Crash in 1929. This sense of crisis encouraged the aggression of the Japanese military in Manchuria. The puppet regime in Manchukuo was set up in 1932, for the Japanese believed that they must have colonies to obtain vital raw materials which would provide jobs for the unemployed Japanese. The outbreak of the war against China in 1937 and against the United States and Britain in 1941 inevitably put the system on course to disaster. Ironically it was in these devastating circumstances that the Japanese banking system could finally squeeze out the small weak banks. This meant that after the war the Japanese could rebuild successfully to support the recovery of the economy and sustain firm economic growth.

The Ministry of Finance, or *Okurasho*, one of the oldest ministries, is undoubtedly one of the most powerful institutions in the Japanese system. During more than three-quarters of a century from 1868 to 1945, some fifty men occupied the seat of power in the Ministry of Finance, from which they directed overall banking policy. Of these men, fewer than half a dozen left their mark on banking history.

Before 1900, Toshimichi Okubo, Shigenobu Okuma and Masayoshi Matsukata were the distinguished figures, but it is to Matsukata that Japanese banking success in the nineteenth century owed the greatest debt. Okubo occupied the office of the Finance Ministry for more than two of the early Meiji years, but although he was a formidable political leader, the times were too chaotic, and he left no remarkable accomplishment in banking. Okuma's tenure of the Finance Ministership for more than six years was hamstrung because of internal confusion in monetary terms in Japan and in addition he did not understand that the actions of overseas bankers determined some banking matters in Japan. He was overwhelmed by galloping inflation and abortive bank experimentation. Therefore Matsukata, who came to power in the last phase of the inflation, was in a sense fortunate, but it may be that only he knew what modern banking meant and what, in Japan, would have to be done. Matsukata retained the Finance Ministership for two decades until 1900 with only a few brief intermissions.

As the ageing Meiji oligarchs were gradually being replaced, so were the financial authorities, although the Ministry of Finance, which recruited primarily from the Imperial University of Tokyo, maintained and increased its tight grip on financial and banking affairs. Against this background, however, it is still possible to distinguish two men from amongst the officials who, after Matsukata, exerted great influence on banking development. These men, Korekiyo Takahashi and Junnosuke Inoue, very different from the elder statesmen (*genro*) of the Meiji financial authorities who were all of *samurai* stock, were bankers turned Finance Minister with substantial experience in western money and banking. Although Takahashi belonged to the *Seiyukai* (Society of Political Friends) and Inoue, in opposition, to *Kenseikai* (Constitutional Party of Democratic Politics), both had similar careers and both experienced the management of the Siamese twins, *Nichigin* and *Shokin*. Both became targets of assassins and were killed, shortly before the Sino-Japanese and Pacific Wars.

The defeat of Japan in the Second World War and its aftermath was a period which can only be compared with the opening of the ports in 1859 and the subsequent turbulence leading to the Meiji Restoration. Once again, as during their early encounter with the westerners, the Japanese were well protected by the Japanese language. Japanese deference was also invaluable in easing relations between former enemies. The Americans, in their turn, despite their enthusiasm for introducing democracy to all things Japanese, failed to penetrate Japanese banking. When the Americans rebuked them for the failure of the Bank of Japan to provide statistics, which would be available to the public, the Japanese bowed their heads. In fact the Bank of Japan had been publishing a monthly statistical bulletin from 1908. Similar material was available in the USA from 1915.

Within five years of the American take-over in Japan, there was a major change of policy as the Americans, alarmed by what they perceived as the rising communist threat in Asia, transformed the Japanese into allies, removing restrictions on banking and everything else. When Japanese banking was effectively left to its own devices, the search for growth started and indeed accelerated mightily as the outbreak of the Korean War in 1950 enormously increased demands in Japan. The Korean War gave a great impetus to the recovery of the Japanese economy, stimulated Japanese banking and brought renewed prosperity. The tremendous growth of the economy, which started from the early 1960s, sustained itself for more than two decades with few intermissions.

As the dark-suited Japanese bankers hurried about their business in Marunouchi, the financial area of Tokyo, a century after their kimono-clad grandfathers had first encountered the foreign 'barbarians' they had reason to congratulate themselves. The momentous century had transformed Japan; that this was possible owed much to the steadiness of purpose of the Japanese bankers.

Appendices

Appendix I

Glossary of Japanese terms

Ansei	Japanese era name for the years 1854 to 1859, followed by Manen 1860, Bunkyu 1861–3, Ganji 1864, Keio 1865–7, Meiji 1868–1912, Taisho 1912–26 and Showa 1926–89
bakufu	The Shogun's administration during the *samurai* era
boki	bookkeeping
chochiku	savings
Choshu	clan or *han*, now Yamaguchi Prefecture in the extreme south-west of Honshu Island, headed by the Mori family. Like Satsuma most influential group in government after 1868
daiichi	first
daimyo	feudal lord
dajokan	the name given to the administrative body, on the model of the ancient regime of the seventh century, of the Meiji Restoration government between 1868 and 1885
dajokansatsu	paper currency issued throughout Japan by the *dajokan*
Deshima	artificial small island specially built for foreigners, effectively for the Dutch consulate in Nagasaki, to isolate them from contact with the Japanese
doso	merchants conducting business in the rice and brewing trades and financing, concurrently before 1600. They were so called as they kept their treasure in storehouses built of thick dried mud termed *doso*
Edo, or Yedo	Old name for Tokyo, renamed in 1869
ginko	bank
gomei kaisha	unlimited liability company
goshi kaisha	company whose partners have limited or unlimited liabilities
goyogaikokunigawase	authorised foreign exchange business for promoting direct exports, or *jikiyushitsu*
gumi, or *kumi*	co-operative body, the term being still used for business
han	domain held in fief by *daimyo*

hansatsu	paper currency issued locally by *han*
honsha	head office, or parent company
jikiyushitsu	direct exports by the Japanese
junin ryogae	the prestigious ten houses of *ryogae* in Osaka policing the *ryogae* community
kabushki kaisha	joint-stock company with limited liabilities
kaisha	company
kaisho	official trading office and market authorised by the Tokugawa *bakufu*
kangyo	encouragement of industry, or setting up the Hypothec Bank and thus mobilising capital for that purpose
kinsatsu	*dajokansatsu* convertible into gold coins
kokuritsu	state establishment
Meiji	Japanese era name for the years 1868 to 1912, meaning 'enlightenment'. From this era on, one Emperor was to have one era name. Mutsuhito became Emperor Meiji after death
mujin	mutual loan association, the origins of which go back to the thirteenth century
Nihon, or Nippon	Japan
Okurasho	Ministry of Finance founded in 1869
ryo	counting unit of gold coin consisting of four *bu*, which consisted of four *shu*; gave way to yen (¥) in 1871
ryogae	merchant who also undertook banking functions before the Meiji Restoration period (the nearest equivalent in England being goldsmiths in the seventeenth century)
Saga	now Sage Prefecture and name for *Hizen han* situated in western Kyushu, near Nagasaki and headed by the Nabeshima family
samurai, or *bushi*	feudal retainer
Satsuma	now Kagoshima Prefecture situated to the south of Kyushu headed by the Shimazu family. Like Choshu, the most influential group in government after 1868
sen	counting unit of copper coin, or one-hundredth of a yen
Shogun	Japan's ruler during the Edo era, though the title was formally given by the Emperor to a nominee selected among the members of the Tokugawa family. The origin of the title goes far back to ancient times
shogyo	commerce
shoji	trading company
shokai	trading company
shoten	trading company
Showa	Japanese era name for the years 1926 to 1989, the reign of Hirohito, who after his death became Emperor Showa
sogo	mutual

soroban	abacus indispensable for *ryogae* daily business and still in wide use in Japan
Taisho	Japanese era name for the years 1912 to 1926, the reign of Yoshihito, who after death became Emperor Taisho
takushoku	development and colonisation
tegata	bill of exchange, or promissory note
teikoku	empire, or imperial
Tokugawa	family name adopted in 1566 by Iyeyasu who formerly addressed himself as Iyeyasu Matsudaira
yen, or ¥	Japanese money counting unit adopted in 1871
zaibatsu	concern, or interest group of gigantic firms dominant in the Japanese economy. Originated in pre- and early-Meiji era and transformed, chiefly between 1900 and the First World War boom, into the modern organisation with *honsha* as the headquarters. Temporarily dissolved in the wake of the defeat in the Pacific War
zeni ryogae	small-scale *ryogae* usually dealing in copper coins

Appendix II

Directory of Japanese bankers

Hara, Rokuro
(1844–1923)
Hyogo farmer turned *samurai*, studied money and banking in the US and in London 1871–7, returned to Japan setting up national banks in Tokyo and Chugoku district, recruited by Matsukata in 1883 to be president of the Yokohama Specie Bank, carrying out Matsukata's policies for the Bank until 1890 when he left the Bank to embark upon various other enterprises

Ikeda, Hayato
(1899–1965)
Kyoto University graduate, elected to the Diet in 1949, becoming Finance Minister 1949–52 and 1956–7, and premier 1960–4, being a main planner of high speed economic growth policies in the 1960s

Inoue, Junnosuke
(1869–1932)
Tokyo University graduate, entered Bank of Japan, studied banking in London 1897–9, became president of the Yokohama Specie Bank 1913–19, governor of the Bank of Japan 1919–23 and Finance Minister 1923–4, again assumed governorship of the Bank 1927–8 and Finance Ministership 1929–31, and assassinated by a right-wing activist in 1932, aged sixty-three

Inoue, Kaoru
(1835–1915)
Choshu *samurai*, one of the 'Choshu Five' in Britain in the 1860s to learn things western, undertook various offices in the Meiji administration: secretary to Finance Ministry, public works minister, foreign minister, agriculture and commerce minister, interior minister and Finance Minister 1898, being closely involved in Mitsui business

Ito, Hirobumi
(1841–1909)
Choshu *samurai*, one of 'Choshu Five' in Britain in the 1860s, travelled world-wide on the Iwakura mission (1871–3), was one of the most prominent Meiji oligarchs and as such the supreme political leader; preferred German method of government, became first premier of Japan's modern cabinet system and was assassinated by a Korean patriot in 1909, aged sixty-eight

Iwakura, Tomomi
(1825–83)

Court noble who, unusually, played a vital role at the imperial court in Kyoto of organising a coup in early 1868 which led to the collapse of the Shogunate. He led a great mission to America and Europe 1871–3 to negotiate the treaties and investigate things western. Despite an early death, he was one of the most influential oligarchs

Iwasaki, Yataro
(1835–85)

Tosa (southern Shikoku) *samurai*, was active in Nagasaki as agent of Tosa domain, from which he created a shipping company around the Restoration period. The company was renamed as Mitsubishi in 1873, from which various businesses grew into *zaibatsu*

Kataoka, Naoharu
(1859–1934)

Son of Tosa farmer, encouraged by Hirobumi Ito, was attached to interior ministry 1884–9 and conjointly founded in 1903 Japan Life Insurance of which he became vice-president. In the Diet from 1892 to 1927, he became Finance Minister in 1926 but his slip of the tongue, suggesting collapse of Watanabe Bank, precipitated the banking crisis

Kato, Wataru
(?–1889)

Satsuma *samurai*, entered Finance Ministry, was part of the Japanese delegation to the Paris exhibition (1878) led by Matsukata. He was left to examine closely the banking system in mainland Europe including that of Belgium, returned to Japan in 1880, was appointed chief of the banking department at the Finance Ministry and led a task force, under Matsukata, drafting the Regulations of the Bank of Japan

Konoike, Zenemon

The house of Konoike (founded 1580s), was a most celebrated Osaka rice merchant and *ryogae*. Konoike was said to have invented modern *sake*. As such they were proud of a long tradition in the Osaka commercial world, but they were severely disadvantaged by the huge loans demanded by the *bakufu* government and so were left behind by Mitsui and Sumitomo. Zenemon is the first name given successively to the head of the house

Maeda, Masana
(1850–1921)

Satsuma *samurai*, who studied in Paris as an official at Japan's legation 1869–75 and joined the Matsukata delegation to the Paris exhibition of 1878. He recognised the importance of financing direct exports and proposed the idea to the Finance Ministry which he served, and later joined the agriculture and commerce ministry, leaving the officialdom in 1885 to engage himself in promoting various industrial schemes

Matsukata, Masayoshi
(1835–1924)

Satsuma *samurai*, having experience as accountant in clan office, was in the Meiji administration engaged in tax reform and the delegation to the Paris exhibition in the 1870s, started to build his ideas of modern banking on the western model, took over from Shigenobu Okuma as Finance Minister and presided over the whole matters of money and banking from 1881. He was the maker of the Japanese banking system and also assumed premiership twice in the 1890s

Mitsui, Hachiroemon
The house of Mitsui (founded 1630s) was a leading merchant house of *ryogae* and the silk trade, with offices in Edo, Osaka and Kyoto, and became a leading *zaibatsu* after the Meiji Restoration. Hachiroemon is the first name given successively to the head of the house

Nakai, Yoshigusu (1853–1903)
Wakayama *samurai*, graduated from Keio College, entered the Yokohama Specie Bank in 1880, became specialised in foreign exchange operation and was appointed London manager 1891–1903 where he played a crucial part in receiving and remitting the Chinese indemnity money, which became a basis for Japan's adoption of the gold standard in 1897

Nomura, Tokushichi (1878–1945)
Son of Osaka *ryogae*, inherited business of long standing in 1896 from his father's name Tokushichi and the firm Nomura Tokushichi Shoten, which developed into Nomura Bank and Nomura Securities Co. He also extended his business concern to foreign trade, gasworks and cotton spinning, which became *zaibatsu*

Okubo, Toshimichi (1830–78)
Satsuma *samurai*, one of the most prominent leaders in overthrowing the Shogunate and opening the Meiji era, was also most responsible for Matsukata's successful start as financial authority, but was unfortunately assassinated at the age of forty-eight in the aftermath of the Satsuma rebellion by a discontented ex-*samurai*

Okuma, Shigenobu (1838–1922)
Saga *samurai*, and so not part of the 'Satsuma–Choshu clique', was Finance Minister during the greater part of the 1870s and initiated various banking experiments which did nothing to halt runaway inflation. Following the assassination of Toshimichi Okubo (1878), he increasingly became a target of the Satsuma–Choshu clique who ousted him in 1881. Although he later became premier, he never had any further influence on finance. He was founder of Waseda University

Saigo, Takamori (1828–77)
Satsuma *samurai*, an outstanding leader, commanding the imperial anti-*bakufu* troops in 1868, and after the Restoration became the commander-in-chief of the imperial guard. He, with no experience outside Japan, could not fit into the new regime. He resigned as a result of a split over the Korean invasion and in 1877 led the last disastrous Satsuma rebellion, the expenses of which

	plunged the Meiji government into ever deeper financial crisis
Sakatani, Yoshio (1863–1941)	Son of Okayama (middle Chugoku) scholar, graduated from Tokyo University, entered the Finance Ministry, was commissioned to draft a budget law, assisted Matsukata in the adoption of the gold standard, became secretary to the Finance Minister during the Russo-Japanese War and Finance Minister 1906–8. He was strongly opposed to militarism
Shibusawa, Eiichi (1841–1931)	Saitama (north of Tokyo) farmer turned *bakufu-samurai*, under the new regime joined the Finance Ministry and was particularly competent in setting up the First National Bank (Daiichi Bank), of which he soon became president. His wide business interests reflected his great skills and helped to promote more than 250 enterprises and he also pioneered bank associations
Sonoda, Kokichi (1847–1923)	Satsuma *samurai*, after serving education and foreign ministries, became official at the Japanese legation in London 1873–9 and again the senior officer in London 1881–90 when he was appointed president of the Yokohama Specie Bank. Resigning as president, he was engaged in various business appointments including president of the Fifteen Bank. He was killed in the Great Kanto Earthquake of 1923
Soyeda, Juichi (1864–1929)	Son of Fukuoka farmer, graduated from Tokyo University and entered the Finance Ministry, but was soon commissioned to study in Cambridge 1884–7. On his return to the Finance Ministry he assisted Matsukata in the adoption of the gold standard and played a vital role in setting up the Bank of Taiwan and the Industrial Bank of Japan, of both of which he became the first president. He seems to have aroused jealousy in some of his colleagues and left banking in 1912
Sumitomo, Kichizaemon	The house of Sumitomo (founded 1590s) has a long tradition of copper mining and refining, from which they developed into *ryogae*. They suffered greatly around the Restoration period, but successfully converted themselves into a modern bank with a substantial industrial basis. Kichizaemon is the first name given successively to the head of the house
Takahashi, Korekiyo (1854–1936)	Sendai (eastern Tohoku) *samurai*, born in Tokyo, serving as house boy in the US 1867–9, returned to Japan to engage himself in various jobs until 1892 when he joined the Bank of Japan and was quickly promoted: vice-president of the Yokohama Specie Bank 1897,

concurrently deputy governor of the Bank of Japan 1899, president of the Specie Bank 1906, governor of the Bank of Japan 1911. He served as Finance Minister 1913–14, 1918–22, 1931–4 and 1934–6, and also assumed premiership 1921–2. He was the most prominent financial authority after Matsukata and was assassinated in an abortive coup in 1936, aged eighty-two

Tanaka, Giichi
(1863–1929)

Choshu *samurai*, graduated from the Military Academy, assumed war ministership 1918–21 and 1923–4, became premier in 1927, in the midst of the banking crisis, but was ignorant of, and resistant to, any knowledge of economics, being strongly in favour of a Japanese rice economy, and initiated militaristic policies including the Shangtoung expeditions

Wakatsuki, Reijiro
(1866–1949)

Shimane (northern Chugoku) *samurai*, Tokyo University graduate, entered Finance Ministry, rose to be secretary, and joined Soyeda in setting up special banks. He was Finance Minister from 1912–13 and 1914–15 and became premier in 1926, resigning from the office in the middle of the banking crisis of 1927

Yamamoto, Tatsuo
(1856–1947)

Oita *samurai*, graduated from Keio College, was recruited from Nihon Yusen to enter the Bank of Japan in 1890 and became the governor 1898–1903. Assuming presidency of Hypothec Bank and Finance Ministership in 1913, he spent later years in politics

Yasuda, Zenjiro
(1838–1921)

Native of Toyama (northern Chubu), started a small *ryogae* business in Edo in 1864, joined the foundation of Third National Bank of Tokyo and also successfully launched his own Yasuda Bank in 1880, from which financial *zaibatsu* emerged. He was assassinated in 1921 by an insane man

Yoshida, Kiyonari
(1845–91)

Satsuma *samurai*, who spent several years in London and the US before entering the Finance Ministry in 1871, was engaged in fierce debates against Hirobumi Ito, but soon lost enthusiasm for banking and became a diplomat. In 1874 he became Japan's minister in the US and in 1888 a member of the privy council

Yoshida, Shigeru
(1878–1967)

Tokyo University graduate, entered foreign ministry. As ambassador to the Court of St James's 1936–8, he much regretted the unrelenting deterioration of Japan's relationships with Britain and the US. As a known anti-militarist he became an important leader in the post-Pacific War period

Appendix III

Statistics

The statistics are abstracted mainly from BOJ (1966) as the source given at the bottom of each table indicates. BOJ have compiled the figures either from MF materials or from their own. For the figures before its establishment, BOJ built up the statistics from materials collected by MF. It is not known how accurate the early figures are.

Principal accounts of all banks, 1873–1941[1]

Year	Number of banks	Advances	Debentures issued	Deposits	Paid-in capital
1873	2	3,352	—[3]	2,867	2,440
1874	4	3,572	—	3,491	3,432
1875	4	2,136	—	1,470	3,450
1876	6	. . .[2]	—	. . .	4,350
1877	27	. . .	—	. . .	24,986
1878	96	. . .	—	. . .	35,596
1879	161	. . .	—	. . .	43,906
1880	191	. . .	—	. . .	52,321
1881	239	. . .	—	. . .	57,333
1882	320	. . .	—	. . .	64,358
1883	349	. . .	—	. . .	67,873
1884	355	. . .	—	. . .	66,957
1885	358	. . .	—	. . .	66,214
1886	357	. . .	—	. . .	65,375
1887	358	. . .	—	. . .	69,234
1888	347	147,618	—	65,579	68,138
1889	353	183,410	—	68,476	69,653
1890	352	204,231	—	62,724	72,120
1891	387	202,839	—	66,171	72,997
1892	404	228,098	—	85,204	75,681
1893	702	309,417	—	111,825	84,005

223

Principal accounts of all banks, 1873–1941 (cont.)

Year	Number of banks	Advances	Debentures issued	Deposits	Paid-in capital
1894	864	333,712	—	133,947	91,319
1895	1,012	387,499	—	184,411	104,922
1896	1,276	460,390	—	234,549	141,548
1897	1,504	396,642	—	304,616	179,488
1898	1,751	514,719	4,997	371,464	219,938
1899	1,942	687,336	7,948	535,575	252,582
1900	2,271	809,724	10,384	575,812	300,332
1901	2,358	776,127	14,545	579,085	318,731
1902	2,323	858,271	19,429	692,110	330,112
1903	2,274	923,258	29,150	758,514	333,859
1904	2,226	943,236	36,492	811,018	332,846
1905	2,229	1,048,332	47,275	973,666	341,988
1906	2,209	1,419	61	1,395	359
1907	2,193	1,479	74	1,325	402
1908	2,171	1,466	92	1,304	417
1909	2,152	1,527	112	1,506	438
1910	2,144	1,737	149	1,649	449
1911	2,143	2,029	220	1,776	480
1912	2,151	2,304	288	1,941	534
1913	2,155	2,568	315	2,110	574
1914	2,153	2,683	353	2,212	608
1915	2,149	2,872	396	2,569	622
1916	2,140	3,574	424	3,464	648
1917	2,110	4,795	427	5,146	751
1918	2,086	6,819	592	7,236	888
1919	2,049	9,161	714	8,734	1,207
1920	2,036	9,521	899	8,829	1,639
1921	2,012	10,239	1,071	9,494	1,747
1922	1,976	10,492	1,143	9,551	1,875
1923	1,871	11,212	1,291	9,692	1,929
1924	1,796	11,568	1,450	10,232	1,953
1925	1,701	12,214	1,569	10,821	1,918
1926	1,575	12,702	1,636	11,272	1,924
1927	1,425	11,801	1,744	11,247	1,886
1928	1,160	11,145	1,835	11,691	1,792
1929	1,004	11,059	1,912	11,972	1,801
1930	895	10,844	2,080	11,546	1,714
1931	794	10,747	2,153	11,093	1,668
1932	651	10,589	2,290	11,445	1,644
1933	627	10,106	2,126	12,049	1,617

Principal accounts of all banks, 1873–1941 (cont.)

Year	Number of banks	Advances	Debentures issued	Deposits	Paid-in capital
1934	587	9,969	1,972	12,775	1,593
1935	569	10,096	1,916	13,626	1,565
1936	521	10,754	1,838	14,726	1,527
1937	462	12,328	2,302	16,405	1,455
1938	429	13,839	2,575	20,716	1,424
1939	401	17,559	2,773	27,626	1,451
1940	369	21,692	3,829	34,284	1,456
1941	267	24,272	5,212	41,518	1,436

Notes:
(1873–1905 figures are thousands of yen; 1906–1941 figures are millions of yen)
[1] National banks, private banks, special banks (except BOJ) included
[2] ... Figures not available
[3] – Not issued
Source: BOJ (1966)

Principal accounts of all banks, 1942–1959[1]

Year	Number of banks	Cash	Securities	Advances	Debentures issued	Deposits	Borrowed money	Call money	Capital
1942	226	3,251	26,354	26,710	6,356	50,041	1,703	137	1,938
1943	150	2,048	33,415	32,354	...[2]	56,328	4,159	...	...
1944	113	2,481	42,945	51,154	...	77,926	20,153	...	...
1945	69	4,210	55,228	97,620	12,973	119,829	37,706	518	2,029
1946	69	109	588	1,464	138	1,448	436	9	20
1947	69	241	836	1,682	149	2,343	305	5	21
1948	75	726	1,170	3,813	87	5,053	558	35	147
1949	74	1,211	1,061	6,790	229	7,920	907	48	161
1950	76	1,588	1,345	9,947	488	10,485	1,471	42	191
1951	80	1,821	1,759	15,178	948	15,063	2,201	128	257
1952	85	3,352	2,360	21,280	1,422	22,238	2,386	324	295
1953	86	3,459	3,282	26,712	2,028	27,076	3,203	474	466
1954	87	3,734	4,040	29,119	2,427	30,366	2,563	633	485
1955	86	4,770	5,187	31,958	2,861	37,243	859	837	512
1956	86	7,440	6,590	40,661	3,334	47,642	2,130	1,200	892
1957	87	9,741	7,958	50,244	3,975	55,048	5,829	1,813	915
1958	86	10,412	9,720	58,129	5,306	64,840	4,223	2,359	1,002
1959	87	9,385	12,090	68,028	6,855	74,136	4,684	2,691	1,462

Notes:

(1942–1945 figures are millions of yen; 1946–1959 figures are 100 millions of yen)

[1] Savings banks and special banks (except BOJ) included

[2] ... Figures not available

Source: BOJ (1966).

Principal accounts of national banks, 1873–1898

Year	Number of banks	Number of branches	Advances	Deposits	Paid-in capital	Reserves
1873	2	5	3,352	2,867	2,440	. . .[1]
1874	4	8	3,572	3,491	3,432	29
1875	4	10	2,136	1,470	3,450	62
1876	5	10	6,017	2,502	2,350	81
1877	26	19	18,155	4,506	22,986	137
1878	95	39	34,537	8,067	33,596	378
1879	151	82	51,355	16,226	40,616	971
1880	151	103	58,158	14,915	43,041	1,665
1881	148	110	78,123	19,583	43,886	2,716
1882	143	121	70,368	19,714	44,206	3,830
1883	141	122	62,832	24,223	44,386	4,259
1884	140	124	75,993	20,370	44,536	4,677
1885	139	119	64,938	27,476	44,456	5,130
1886	136	122	86,845	32,359	44,416	5,488
1887	136	134	105,347	33,439	45,838	6,019
1888	135	149	117,015	35,585	46,877	7,750
1889	134	149	141,384	36,429	47,681	9,609
1890	134	149	157,931	33,598	48,644	12,461
1891	134	145	162,789	40,214	48,701	13,730
1892	133	140	187,649	49,976	48,325	15,278
1893	133	153	250,957	59,833	48,416	16,071
1894	133	175	266,056	66,977	48,816	17,634
1895	133	180	286,925	74,999	48,951	19,209
1896	121	165	280,372	61,825	44,761	34,196
1897	58	66	116,782	27,766	13,630	6,057
1898	4	1	813	867	390	91

Notes:
(thousands of yen)
[1] . . . Figures not available
Source: BOJ (1966)

Principal accounts of private/ordinary banks, 1876–1945[1]

Year	Number of banks	Number of branches	Advances	Deposits	Paid-in capital	Reserves
1876	1	. . .[2]	. . .	. . .	2,000	. . .
1877	1	. . .	. . .	. . .	2,000	. . .
1878	1	. . .	. . .	. . .	2,000	. . .
1879	10	. . .	. . .	. . .	3,290	. . .
1880	39	. . .	. . .	. . .	6,280	. . .
1881	90	. . .	. . .	. . .	10,447	. . .
1882	176	. . .	. . .	. . .	17,152	. . .
1883	207	. . .	. . .	. . .	20,487	. . .
1884	214	. . .	. . .	. . .	19,421	. . .
1885	218	. . .	. . .	. . .	18,758	. . .
1886	220	. . .	. . .	. . .	17,959	. . .
1887	221	. . .	. . .	. . .	18,896	. . .
1888	211	. . .	25,169	14,527	16,761	. . .
1889	218	. . .	36,698	24,904	17,472	. . .
1890	217	. . .	39,532	24,690	18,976	. . .
1891	252	. . .	33,067	20,590	19,796	. . .
1892	270	. . .	33,736	32,523	22,856	. . .
1893	545	165	49,083	38,426	30,583	2,826
1894	700	196	59,178	49,196	37,380	4,141
1895	792	277	89,165	84,252	49,807	5,692
1896	1,005	428	157,200	141,937	87,899	8,947
1897	1,223	651	241,899	207,741	147,812	13,407
1898	1,444	912	438,099	287,045	189,439	20,214
1899	1,561	1,069	581,036	392,256	209,973	27,762
1900	1,802	1,374	661,973	436,779	239,364	33,032
1901	1,867	1,457	635,106	450,186	251,700	38,868
1902	1,841	1,470	697,551	536,702	258,111	45,679
1903	1,754	1,441	725,355	566,227	253,033	50,503
1904	1,708	1,404	733,145	605,316	248,776	54,477
1905	1,697	1,415	796,432	692,520	252,697	59,000
1906	1,670	1,476	1,111	1,033	256	68
1907	1,658	1,611	1,113	944	286	84
1908	1,635	1,648	1,098	938	295	93
1909	1,617	1,645	1,123	1,054	311	92
1910	1,618	1,700	1,249	1,185	315	101
1911	1,613	1,784	1,393	1,256	327	111
1912	1,621	1,946	1,522	1,357	369	111
1913	1,614	2,099	1,670	1,443	391	122
1914	1,593	2,175	1,726	1,519	401	132
1915	1,440	1,940	1,728	1,699	357	127

Principal accounts of private/ordinary banks, 1876–1945[1] (cont.)

Year	Number of banks	Number of branches	Advances	Deposits	Paid-in capital	Reserves
1916	1,424	2,158	2,232	2,256	373	134
1917	1,395	2,216	2,978	3,233	436	141
1918	1,372	2,367	4,146	4,639	511	161
1919	1,340	2,540	5,666	5,744	707	171
1920	1,322	2,772	5,902	5,826	948	263
1921	1,327	3,129	6,242	6,444	1,029	335
1922	1,794	5,122	7,848	7,801	1,430	488
1923	1,698	5,239	8,059	7,805	1,471	540
1924	1,626	5,288	8,289	8,095	1,488	583
1925	1,534	6,320	8,842	8,726	1,488	626
1926	1,417	5,297	9,219	9,178	1,484	662
1927	1,280	5,218	8,180	9,027	1,469	628
1928	1,028	5,044	7,545	9,330	1,371	592
1929	878	4,917	7,246	9,292	1,373	603
1930	779	4,763	6,818	8,738	1,289	589
1931	680	4,542	6,594	8,269	1,241	535
1932	538	4,311	6,343	8,319	1,217	530
1933	516	4,021	6,085	8,815	1,186	515
1934	484	3,893	5,987	9,438	1,162	540
1935	466	3,708	6,193	9,950	1,134	564
1936	424	3,654	6,765	11,077	1,099	586
1937	377	3,621	7,793	12,434	1,047	597
1938	346	3,600	8,848	15,191	1,018	628
1939	318	3,600	11,350	19,966	1,000	664
1940	286	3,658	13,838	24,671	979	701
1941	186	3,694	15,142	29,406	944	722
1942	148	3,712	17,657	35,737	912	781
1943	86	3,413	22,466	43,131	848	895
1944	72	3,337	34,797	60,962	875	967
1945	61	3,144	72,053	102,349	543	773

Notes:
(1876–1905 figures are thousands of yen; 1906–1945 figures are millions of yen)
[1] From 1899 on, ordinary banks only
[2] ... Figures not available
Source: BOJ (1966)

Principal accounts of savings banks, 1893–1948

Year	Number of banks	Number of branches	Advances	Deposits	Paid-in capital	Reserves
1893	23	12	1,066	6,035	506	25
1894	30	30	675	6,871	623	63
1895	86	107	2,728	12,178	1,664	104
1896	149	224	8,088	20,673	2,888	303
1897	221	270	22,360	33,044	6,546	812
1898	260	453	31,485	42,707	8,311	1,371
1899	333	631	48,184	67,641	10,879	2,188
1900	419	814	63,714	78,881	15,245	2,907
1901	441	542	60,880	74,210	17,131	3,462
1902	431	536	62,962	84,965	15,994	3,548
1903	469	586	82,229	106,707	24,136	5,403
1904	467	585	87,118	120,759	27,031	6,489
1905	481	636	101,047	153,818	29,284	7,771
1906	488	673	126,311	200,661	32,721	9,876
1907	484	711	148,770	218,743	36,948	11,421
1908	485	746	147,241	214,974	40,304	13,126
1909	483	777	153,793	248,679	41,780	15,023
1910	474	785	171,872	277,683	43,722	16,865
1911	478	836	202,451	311,983	46,342	18,752
1912	478	886	232,096	333,928	49,602	20,584
1913	489	983	261,865	356,078	58,728	23,423
1914	508	1,098	293,155	376,066	68,444	26,400
1915	657	1,401	437,670	528,938	120,944	42,432
1916	664	1,480	514,230	687,539	126,139	45,706
1917	663	1,569	669,774	932,948	143,331	51,848
1918	661	1,684	952,500	1,288,529	165,337	58,873
1919	656	1,897	1,466,819	1,777,547	221,186	68,671
1920	661	2,128	1,597,592	1,843,000	320,308	92,658
1921	636	2,111	1,618,758	1,945,989	325,728	99,747
1922	146	545	186,372	651,245	33,659	15,549
1923	139	553	202,448	693,560	34,023	18,637
1924	136	565	188,050	793,512	36,397	21,309
1925	133	597	191,881	904,605	37,647	23,962
1926	124	594	264	1,067	41	27
1927	113	576	297	1,101	42	31
1928	100	479	348	1,249	40	33
1929	95	463	406	1,421	40	34
1930	90	479	477	1,539	41	33
1931	88	473	467	1,635	43	36
1932	87	475	405	1,687	43	38

Principal accounts of savings banks, 1893–1948 (cont.)

Year	Number of banks	Number of branches	Advances	Deposits	Paid-in capital	Reserves
1933	85	465	349	1,821	47	43
1934	79	450	335	1,879	47	47
1935	79	447	329	2,039	47	53
1936	74	379	238	1,842	42	49
1937	72	387	253	2,116	42	53
1938	71	424	253	2,571	41	57
1939	71	444	275	3,362	42	62
1940	71	462	321	4,452	45	67
1941	69	489	360	5,541	45	73
1942	69	505	400	7,477	45	81
1943	27	448	569	8,905	33	87
1944	20	425	786	10,022	30	82
1945	4	278	772	7,432	66	20
1946	4	310	764	8,377	66	20
1947	4	. . .[1]	1,989	10,290	66	. . .
1948	2	. . .	81	172	5	. . .

Notes:
(1893–1925 figures are thousands of yen; 1926–1948 figures are millions of yen)
[1] . . . Figures not available
Source: BOJ (1966)

Principal accounts of special banks, 1880–1949[1]

Year	Number of banks	Advances	Debentures issued	Deposits	Paid-in capital
1880	1	2,577	—[2]	2,588	3,000
1881	1	4,877	—	4,495	3,000
1882	1	3,225	—	3,660	3,000
1883	1	4,935	—	13,104	3,000
1884	1	7,855	—	19,534	3,000
1885	1	6,476	—	16,439	3,000
1886	1	6,879	—	17,472	3,000
1887	1	7,570	—	12,758	4,500
1888	1	5,434	—	15,467	4,500
1889	1	5,328	—	7,143	4,500
1890	1	6,768	—	4,436	4,500
1891	1	6,983	—	5,367	4,500
1892	1	6,713	—	2,705	4,500
1893	1	8,311	—	7,531	4,500
1894	1	7,803	—	10,903	4,500
1895	1	8,681	—	12,982	4,500
1896	1	14,730	—	10,114	6,000
1897	2	15,601	—	36,065	11,500
1898	43	44,322	4,997	40,845	21,798
1899	48	58,116	7,948	75,678	31,730
1900	50	84,037	10,384	60,152	45,723
1901	50	80,141	14,545	54,689	49,900
1902	51	97,758	19,429	70,443	56,007
1903	51	115,674	29,150	85,580	56,720
1904	51	122,973	36,492	84,943	57,057
1905	51	150,853	47,275	127,328	60,007
1906	51	182,458	61,317	162,686	71,794
1907	51	218,091	74,474	163,025	80,370
1908	51	221,140	92,680	152,900	82,754
1909	52	251,004	112,864	204,086	86,869
1910	52	317,635	149,442	187,180	91,869
1911	52	434,855	220,418	209,619	107,520
1912	52	550,905	288,430	251,357	116,758
1913	52	637,712	315,880	311,178	125,243
1914	52	664,045	353,890	317,376	139,182
1915	52	707,301	396,904	342,348	145,095
1916	52	828,169	424,723	521,096	149,395
1917	52	1,148,785	427,902	981,562	172,942
1918	53	1,721,225	592,074	1,309,268	212,123
1919	53	2,029,374	714,458	1,213,149	279,201

Principal accounts of special banks, 1880–1949[1] (cont.)

Year	Number of banks	Advances	Debentures issued	Deposits	Paid-in capital
1920	53	2,022,444	899,620	1,160,303	371,497
1921	49	2,379,041	1,071,940	1,105,821	393,664
1922	36	2,458,106	1,143,549	1,099,478	412,330
1923	34	2,951,915	1,291,345	1,094,320	424,901
1924	34	3,091,224	1,450,417	1,346,037	429,301
1925	34	3,181,131	1,569,739	1,191,211	393,924
1926	34	3,219	1,636	1,027	399
1927	32	3,324	1,744	1,119	375
1928	32	3,252	1,835	1,112	381
1929	31	3,407	1,912	1,259	388
1930	26	3,549	2,080	1,269	384
1931	26	3,686	2,153	1,189	384
1932	26	3,841	2,290	1,439	384
1933	26	3,672	2,126	1,413	384
1934	24	3,647	1,972	1,458	384
1935	24	3,574	1,916	1,637	384
1936	23	3,751	1,838	1,877	386
1937	13	4,282	2,302	1,855	366
1938	12	4,738	2,575	2,954	365
1939	12	5,934	2,773	4,298	409
1940	12	7,533	3,829	5,161	432
1941	12	8,770	5,212	6,571	447
1942	12	8,434	6,413	8,444	374
1943	12	16,393	8,296	15,298	374
1944	7	67,618	10,482	46,330	400
1945	4	129,019	13,273	271,080	369
1946	3	31,650	13,479	7,771	251
1947	3	30,540	15,162	15,198	415
1948	3	50,627	9,575	50,285	2,000
1949	3	102,096	25,904	83,529	2,500

Notes:
(1880–1925 figures are thousands of yen; 1926–1949 figures are millions of yen)
[1] Special and colonial banks
[2] – Not issued
Source: BOJ (1966)

Bank of Japan note issues, 1885–1940

Year	Total	Issues covered by specie reserve	Specie[1] abroad	Fiduciary issues	Limit of fiduciary issues	Issues exceeding the limit
1885	3,956	3,311	—[2]	645	—	—
1886	39,761	24,066	—	15,695	—	—
1887	53,469	31,594	—	21,875	—	—
1888	65,822	45,074	—	20,748	70,700	—
1889	79,109	57,410	—	21,699	70,000	—
1890	102,932	44,623	—	58,309	85,000	—
1891	115,735	63,178	—	52,557	85,000	—
1892	125,843	81,158	—	44,685	85,000	—
1893	148,663	85,929	—	62,734	85,000	—
1894	149,814	81,718	—	68,096	85,000	4,198
1895	180,337	60,371	—	119,966	85,000	55,083
1896	198,314	132,730	51,840	65,584	85,000	—
1897	226,229	98,261	—	127,968	85,000	47,313
1898	197,400	89,570	—	107,830	85,000	24,017
1899	250,562	110,142	—	140,420	120,000	20,722
1900	228,570	67,349	—	161,221	120,000	41,221
1901	214,097	71,358	—	142,739	120,000	22,739
1902	232,094	109,119	—	122,975	120,000	2,975
1903	232,921	116,962	—	115,959	120,000	—
1904	286,626	83,581	53,502	203,045	120,000	83,045
1905	312,791	115,595	78,892	197,196	120,000	77,196
1906	341,766	147,202	123,134	194,564	120,000	74,564
1907	369,984	161,742	124,767	208,242	120,000	88,242
1908	352,734	169,505	107,733	183,229	120,000	63,229
1909	352,763	217,843	101,681	134,920	120,000	14,920
1910	401,625	222,382	87,463	179,243	120,000	59,243
1911	433,399	229,154	98,311	204,245	120,000	84,245
1912	448,922	247,023	111,086	201,899	120,000	81,899
1913	426,389	224,366	94,413	202,023	120,000	82,023
1914	385,589	218,237	90,285	167,352	120,000	47,352
1915	430,138	248,418	111,750	181,720	120,000	61,720
1916	601,224	410,519	183,053	190,705	120,000	70,705
1917	831,372	649,618	188,280	181,754	120,000	61,754
1918	1,144,739	712,925	260,338	431,814	120,000	311,814
1919	1,555,101	951,976	249,960	603,125	120,000	483,125
1920	1,439,241	1,246,689	133,411	192,552	120,000	72,552
1921	1,546,546	1,245,574	106,391	300,972	120,000	180,972
1922	1,558,402	1,063,887	—	494,515	120,000	374,515
1923	1,703,597	1,057,472	—	646,125	120,000	526,125

Bank of Japan note issues, 1885–1940 (cont.)

Year	Total	Issues covered by specie reserve	Specie[1] abroad	Fiduciary issues	Limit of fiduciary issues	Issues exceeding the limit
1924	1,662,315	1,059,024	—	603,291	120,000	483,291
1925	1,631,784	1,056,999	—	574,785	120,000	454,785
1926	1,569,708	1,058,132	—	511,576	120,000	391,576
1927	1,682,390	1,062,737	—	619,653	120,000	499,653
1928	1,739,096	1,061,636	—	677,460	120,000	557,460
1929	1,641,852	1,072,273	—	569,579	120,000	449,579
1930	1,436,296	825,998	—	610,298	120,000	490,298
1931	1,330,575	469,549	—	861,026	120,000	741,026
1932	1,426,159	425,068	—	1,001,091	1,000,000	1,091
1933	1,544,798	425,069	—	1,119,729	1,000,000	119,729
1934	1,627,349	466,338	—	1,161,011	1,000,000	161,011
1935	1,766,555	504,065	—	1,262,490	1,000,000	262,490
1936	1,865,703	548,342	—	1,317,361	1,000,000	317,361
1937	2,305,071	801,003	—	1,504,068	1,000,000	504,068
1938	2,754,923	501,287	—	2,253,636	1,700,000	553,636
1939	3,679,031	501,287	—	3,177,744	2,200,000	977,744
1940	4,777,429	501,287	—	4,276,142	2,200,000	2,076,142

Notes:
(figures are thousands of yen)
[1] This is included in the total specie reserve
[2] Not existent
Source: **BOJ** (1982/86) Materials vol.

Bank of Japan note issues, 1941–1959

Year	Total	Limit of fiduciary issues	Issues exceeding the limit
1941	5,979	4,700	1,279
1942	7,149	6,000	1,149
1943	10,266	6,000	4,266
1944	17,746	6,000	11,746
1945	55,441	6,000	49,441
1946	93,398	6,000	87,398
1947	219,142	6,000	213,142
1948	355,280	330,000	25,280
1949	355,312	350,000	5,312
1950	422,063	390,000	32,063
1951	506,386	470,000	36,386
1952	576,431	510,000	66,431
1953	629,892	510,000	119,892
1954	622,061	510,000	112,061
1955	673,891	510,000	163,891
1956	784,862	650,000	134,862
1957	837,115	650,000	187,115
1958	891,043	650,000	241,043
1959	1,029,467	800,000	229,467

Note:
(figures are millions of yen)
Source: BOJ (1982/86) Materials vol.

Notes

Part I. A bankrupt Shogunate, 1859–1868

1. Japanese merchant bankers: ryogae, *1859–1868*

1. E. H. Norman (1940), p. 58 n.
2. Anon. (1913). The records were thought to be prepared and edited in the early seventeenth century probably by some Mitsui people. *Daimyo* business done by *ryogae* is briefly explained in C. D. Sheldon (1958), pp. 76–7.
3. For further information, see Y. Sakudo, 'Japan's business history general review', and Matao Miyamoto, 'Japan's business history, Edo era', both in Japan Business History Society (1985).
4. R. Mikami (1987), chapter 4. Originally *doso* was a warehouse built of mud in which valuable goods were stored. *Doso* became the title of a business which sold *sake* and also operated as pawnbroker. For the western reader, a useful and helpful account of *doso* is found in D. M. Brown (1951), pp. 46–51.
5. 'Shogyo kanrei shirabe' (Reports on custom in commerce), H. Kuroha, ed. (1934/40), vol. 2, p. 238.
6. Z. Yasuda (1911). A rare copy of this interesting book is held in the Diet Library, Tokyo. 1 sen equals 10 rin; 1 sen also stands for 1 per cent.
7. H. Kuroha, ed. (1934/40), vol. 4, pp. 19–20.
8. *Ibid.*, vol. 1, p. 86.
9. *Ibid.*, vol. 1, p. 88. 1 *ryo* is approximately 1 yen.
10. Iwasaki Yataro Denki Hensankai, ed. (1967), vol. 2, pp. 346–73. See also W. D. Wray (1984).
11. See pp. 134–6.

2. A bankrupt regime, 1859–1866

1. University of Tokyo (1937/43), vol. 2, pp. 596–7. See also S. G. Checkland (1988).
2. P. A. G. Basle, the Dutch consul, strongly advised that Japan should not cause any war against the western powers, especially the British. See Kaishu Katsu, 'Kaikoku kigen' (Origins of the opening of the country) II, in K. Katsu (1972/83), vol. 2, pp. 314–15, 317–21.

238   **Notes to pages 10–17**

3. University of Tokyo (1937/43), vol. 2, p. 301. The *bakufu*'s official report gave some details on the gift to the ruler of Japan that Lord Elgin brought with him, but it did not mention anything about Lord Elgin himself. See K. Katsu, 'Kaikoku kigen' in K. Katsu (1972/83), vol. 4, p. 271.
4. See E. O. A. Checkland (1989), p. 213.
5. See S. G. Checkland (1988), pp. 157–8.
6. Three main branches, the three Houses, of the Tokugawa family were instituted by Iyeyasu Tokugawa, the founder of the Tokugawa Shogunate regime in 1603. Newly selected Iyemochi was the *daimyo* of Wakayama, one of the three, situated to the south of Osaka, an important location keeping close eyes on the court in Kyoto and powerful western domains.
7. 'Keiki' must formally be pronounced as Yoshinobu.
8. The port Kanagawa was named in the treaty, but the government deliberately changed the place to Yokohama, just off Kanagawa.
9. See E. O. A. Checkland (1989), pp. 17–18, *passim*.

3. Ryogae struggling for survival, 1859–1868

1. T. Ishii (1987), p. 69.
2. *Ibid.*, pp. 28–41.
3. R. Alcock (1863), chapter XVII. For the western reader, P. Frost (1970) provides a fuller account of the problem the *bakufu* was facing.
4. T. Ishii (1987), p. 121.
5. See 'Document 28. Treaty between the United States and Japan signed on 29 July 1858' in W. G. Beasley (1955), p. 184.
6. BOJ (1972/76), vol. 6, pp. 219–20.
7. S. Osborn (1859), pp. 43–4.
8. Yokohamashi (1958/76), vol. 2, pp. 679–84.
9. 1 Mexican dollar = 0.75 *ryo*.
10. Mitsui Ginko (1957), pp. 27–8.
11. Y. Oguchi (1981).
12. Y. Yamamoto (1988/90), pp. 114–19.
13. A. Hayami and Matao Miyamoto (1988/90).
14. Mitsui Bunko (1971/80), vol. 1, pp. 649–50; Y. Oguchi (1988), p. 163.
15. Y. Yamamoto (1988/90), p. 117.
16. Mitsui Bunko (1971/80), vol. 1, p. 650.
17. *Ibid.*, pp. 649–50.
18. H. Kuroha, ed. (1934/40), vol. 3, pp. 131–3.

4. The arrival of western banking, 1863–1868

1. K. Ishii (1984), p. 148.
2. *Ibid.*, pp. 148–9.
3. *BM* (1863), p. 455.
4. K. Ishii (1984), p. 151; K. Tatewaki (1987), pp. 28–9; S. Sugiyama (1988), p. 40; E. O. A. Checkland (1989), p. 36.

5. US $1 = 5.85 *ryo*. £1 = US $4.48 (S. Marriner (1961), p. 163).
6. *BM* (1863), p. 621.
7. *Ibid.*, p. 621.
8. *Ibid.*, 1864, pp. 894–5.
9. K. Tatewaki (1987), pp. 12–13. From the West, C. Mackenzie (1954), p. 94, and G. Fox (1969), give clear, though sketchy, accounts of western banking in Japan.
10. *Japan Gazette*, 1875.

Part II. The Meiji Restoration: monetary confusion and banking experiments, 1868–1881

5. The first banking experiment, 1868–1872

1. University of Tokyo (1937/43), vol. 8, p. 523; S. Lane-Poole and F.V. Dickens (1894), vol. 2, pp. 96–7.
2. As a later investigation revealed: 'There is much variety in the kind of coins and the standard value, so that there is no uniformity in the system. For instance among the gold coins there are the *Keicho*, the *Kioho*, the *Monji*, the *Oban* and *Koban*, the *Ichibu*, the *Nibu*, the *Nishu*, while among the silver coins there are the *Ichibu*, the *Ichishu*; besides these there are also the *Tohiyaku* sen and other copper coins of various descriptions. There are also some coins which circulated only for a limited period, but which circulate now no longer. Again there are other coins which are limited in circulation to one province or even one district. Added to these is the fact that the coins of same denomination do not always possess the same quality and size, being no legal standard of weight and fineness. All this confusion is increased yet more by the presence of numerous counterfeits' (M. Matsukata (1899), p. 6).
3. MF (1931/36), vol. 13, pp. 22–37; BOJ (1972/76), vol. 7, pp. 152–3.
4. *North China Herald*, 22 August 1868. *Boo*, or *bu*, was one-quarter of a *ryo*.
5. MF (1880), in MF (1931/36), vol. 2, pp. 139–42; M. Matsukata (1899), p. 2; T. Hamashita (1983), pp. 323–4; E. O. A. Checkland (1989), pp. 33–4.
6. *North China Herald*, 21 April 1871.
7. T. Hamashita (1983), p. 323; E. O. A. Checkland (1989), pp. 33–4.
8. R. Mikami (1989), chapter 2. Professor Mikami discloses that the title of 'yen' was being used among the intellectuals from as early as the 1840s.
9. J. J. Gerson (1972), p. 202.
10. For this interpretation, E. O. A. Checkland (1989), chapter 15, 'A Copartnery: on Japanese terms?' is very suggestive. See also *ibid.*, p. 38; J. J. Gerson (1972), p. 202; and Kiyonari Yoshida's letter to Hirobumi Ito, 23 March 1869 (Ito Hirobumi Kankeimonjo Kenkyukai (1973/1981), vol. 8, pp. 218–21). Yoshida was the chief negotiator for Japan.
11. M. Matsukata (1899), p. 5.
12. MF (1925/28), vol. 12, pp. 8–13.
13. *Ibid.*, pp. 44–89.
14. *Ibid.*, pp. 330–4.
15. H. Shinbo (1968), pp. 116–17.

16. MF (1925/28), vol. 12, pp. 351–6, 399–414.
17. H. Shinbo (1968), pp. 116–17.
18. *Ibid.*, pp. 200–1.
19. A. Sawada, ed. (1921), p. 158. 'Segaiko' was Kaoru Inoue, from Choshu, later the Finance Minister and intimate friend of Hirobumi Ito.
20. See pp. 4–9.

6. The national bank system: the American influence, 1870–1881

1. MF (1925/28), vol. 12. pp. 500–1. The term *gumi* roughly stands for 'the company'.
2. *Ibid.*, pp. 502–21.
3. *Ibid.*, pp. 501, 524–5.
4. Chronological, full accounts of the Mission are given in K. Kume (1878). See also T. Okubo (1976) and E. O. A. Checkland (1989).
5. A. Sawada, ed. (1921), pp. 324–5.
6. MF (1925/28), vol. 13, p. 18.
7. *Ibid.*, p. 18.
8. For more on Okuma, see Ijichi (1940) and below, pp. 46–54. Domain Saga was situated near Nagasaki and was third in importance during the Restoration Campaign ranking only next to Satsuma and Choshu.
9. When Okubo joined Okuma in October 1873, the first serious political change in the Meiji government occurred on the Korean question and Saigo and his followers were ousted from power. At the same time Okuma even succeeded as Finance Minister Okubo, who thereafter concentrated upon the overall policies including finance. Okubo was assassinated later in 1878 in the aftermath of the Satsuma Rebellion, but Okuma survived him, occupying office in the *dajokan* until October 1881 when the second, and most serious, political change deprived him of power (see pp. 49–54). In November 1871, Okubo, together with Hirobumi Ito and other notable members of the government, left Japan in the Iwakura Mission and were abroad for more than two years. Okuma, therefore, took strong initiative in banking controversy, assisted by Kaoru Inoue and Eiichi Shibusawa.
10. MF (1825/28), vol. 3, p. 30.
11. *Ibid.*, pp. 25–57.
12. *Ibid.*, pp. 39–41, 46. Clause 6 of Article 11 reads as follows: 'the national bank must put in its safe 25%, or 25 hundredths, of the total amount deposited by its customers as the reserves for casual withdrawals. – The reserves should not be confounded with those for the conversion'. (*Ibid.*, p. 46.)
13. Daiichi Ginko (1957/58), vol. 1, pp. 76–7.
14. *Ibid.*, p.77.
15. *Ibid.*, pp. 77–8.
16. BOJ (1956/61), vol. 3, pp. 97–144; S. Teruoka (1963), pp. 97–103.
17. For Ono's failure, see M. Miyamoto (1970), vol. 4, chapter 16.
18. MF (1925/28), vol. 13. pp. 420–1.
19. *Ibid.*, p. 297.

20. Fukuchi was born the son of a townsman and brought up in Nagasaki. He became an official interpreter in the Foreign Office at Yokohama. He went abroad four times in official suites of attendants. His first two experiences were on the mission during the last days of the ancient regime. In the autumn of 1870 he was on the team organised by Hirobumi Ito. He was also in a suite of attendants in the Iwakura Mission. Leaving the service of the government, Fukuchi later became well known as a journalist.

21. BOJ (1956/61), vol. 5, pp. 3–6.

22. For Shand, see E. O. A. Checkland (1989), pp. 37, 250.

23. The complete volumes are reproduced in Japanese in BOJ (1956/61), vol. 5, pp. 705–893. Shand was said to have based his drafts on Charles Hutton's *A Complete Treatise on Practical Arithmetic and Book-Keeping*. Hutton was a well-known mathematician and prolific writer on the subject. This was, however, preceded by Yukichi Fukuzawa's translation of *Bryant and Stratton's Common School Book-Keeping*.

24. In August 1873, Shand lost his baby boy. To come to terms with the tragedy, he and his wife returned to Britain in October 1873. A year off gave him energy to resume the duties for the Finance Ministry. See T. Tsuchiya (1976), p. 24.

25. MF (1925/28), vol. 13, pp. 626–8; T. Tsuchiya (1956/61), p. 702; T. Tsuchiya (1976), pp. 25–7.

26. Daiichi Ginko (1957/58), vol. 1, p. 217.

27. *Ibid.*, p. 219.

28. A. Crum entered the Bank of England, aged eighteen, and left there, aged thirty-eight, to become the Stockholm branch manager of an English bank. Returning to London, he obtained the city editorship of *The Times* after experience as correspondent for *The Economist* and the *Pall Mall Gazette*. In 1897 the book was revised and enlarged as *The English Manual of Banking*.

29. The story is fully explained by Ukichi Taguchi in his editorial of the inaugural issue of his own journal *Tokyo Keizaizasshi* dated January 1897. See also pp. 43–5.

30. MF (1925/28), vol. 13, pp. 113–41.

31. MF (1936/40), vol. 8, pp. 590–601.

32. For the political turbulence, see W. G. Beasley (1972), chapter XV.

33. MF (1925/28), vol. 13, pp. 102–13.

34. *Ibid.*, pp. 221–34, 260–73.

35. M. Matsukata (1899), pp. 29–33.

36. MF (1925/28), vol. 13, pp. 603–14.

37. K. Asakura (1961), p. 122.

38. M. Takezawa (1968), p. 76.

7. The origins of ordinary banking: another bank mania, 1875–1881

1. See pp. 30–3.

2. 'Opinions regarding the treatments of the First National Bank and Mitsui Gumi', in BOJ (1956/61), vol. 4, p. 1178. The letter is dated only as '25 December', but it was undoubtedly 1875.

3. Mitsui Ginko (1957), p. 83.
4. *Ibid.*, pp. 84–5.
5. *Ibid.*, p. 85.
6. Tokeiin (1882/1941), vol. 2, pp. 321–2.
7. K. Asakura (1988), p. 18.
8. Tokeiin (1882/1941), vol. 1. p. 282.
9. *Ibid.*, vol. 2, pp. 322–3.
10. K. Asakura (1988), pp. 18–21. Professor Asakura details the cases in his earlier work: see Asakura (1961), chapters 5, 6 and 7.
11. *Takuzenkai gijiroku*, in BOJ (1956/61), vol. 12, p. 5.
12. T. Tamura (1963), pp. 35–6.
13. N. Tamaki (1988), pp. 225–8. In launching the journal, Taguchi, economist and great supporter of free trade principles, was immensely stimulated by A. A. Shand who insisted that Japanese businessmen would not be well represented without their own newspaper like *The Economist* in London. For the Finance Ministry's journals, see pp. 33–6.
14. T. Tamura (1963), p. 327. Tamura even doubts whether the friendly society did exist. He poses that the friendly society might have been the result of inner conflicts within *Takuzenkai*.
15. BOJ (1956/61), vol. 12, pp. 101, 115–16.
16. See pp. 4–9.
17. BOJ (1956/61), vol. 7, p. 177.

8. The search for stability: the last bank controversy, 1879–1881

1. Perhaps under Okuma's directive, the issuing arrangements were negotiated with the Banque de Paris et des Pays Bas, as *The Times*, London, 20 April 1880, reported.
2. Two schemes were joined at the suggestion of Yukichi Fukuzawa, educator and founder of Keio Gijuku, later Keio University, and intimate friend of Okuma, founder of Waseda University. See Fukuzawa's letters to Okuma, 2 August 1879, 12 September 1879, 5 and 13 October 1879 (Y. Fukuzawa (1958/71), vol. 17).
3. Letter from J. Robertson to Okuma, 2 March 1880, in Waseda University (1952), C. 655. Hennessy was a maverick who hated Henry Parkes (E. O. A. Checkland (1989), pp. 11, 241).
4. YSB (1920), Appendices vol. 1, p. 65.
5. Maeda's scheme is detailed in M. Maeda (1881), which was originally written in the autumn of 1879 as a proposal to the Finance Ministry. His renewed proposal is in his letter to Okuma dated 21 July 1880, Waseda University (1952), B. 130.
6. Anon. (W. H. Talbot) (1882), p. 56. Okuma's *General View* was originally published in Japanese as *Okumakun zaiseiyoran*, but the English version soon appeared in *Japan Gazette* (Talbot was the editor).
7. Anon. (W. H. Talbot) (1882), p. 82.
8. *Ibid.*, p. 82.

9. *Ibid.*, p. 111.
10. N. Nakamura (1961), an analytical account of the whole career of Okuma, does not mention the point.
11. *The Times*, London, 7 February 1888. See also J. C. Lebra (1973), pp. 35–6.
12. Shand to Okuma, 16 December 1881, in Waseda University (1952), C. 728. Shand accepted the invitation, but Okuma's downfall made his transfer impossible. See pp. 92–4.
13. Robertson to Okuma, 25 September 1882, in Waseda University (1952), C. 660. For Okuma's foreign connections, see N. Nakamura (1968), pp. 199–201 and Mineo Matsukata (1979/93), vol. 10, p. 10.
14. H. M. Reischauer (1986), pp. 21–41. Haru Reischauer's account of Masayoshi Matsukata is a very useful inside story of the formidable Finance Minister.
15. T. Tokutomi (1935), vol. 1, p. 701.
16. BOJ (1982/86), vol. 1, p. 119.
17. C. A. Conant (1910), p. 5.
18. *Ibid.*, p. 5.
19. O. Soda (1973), pp. 63–9.
20. See pp. 82–5.
21. This document is reproduced in BOJ (1956/61), vol. 4, pp. 979–82.
22. BOJ (1956/61), vol. 4, pp. 979–82.
23. *Ibid.*, pp. 983–8.
24. *Ibid.*, p. 984.
25. The best account of the political change in Japan is given in T. Okubo (1957). T. Okubo is the grandson of Toshimichi Okubo.

Part III. Matsukata, the wizard of Japanese banking, 1881–1897; the Yokohama Specie Bank (1880) and the Bank of Japan (1882)

9. The Bank of Japan, or Nichigin, 1881–1897

1. These passages were written by Matsukata in retrospect of his appointment address reproduced in his 'Shiheiseirigaiyo', or 'Outline of Note Redemption', in BOJ (1956/61), vol. 16, p. 154.
2. *Ibid.*, p. 154.
3. BOJ (1966), p. 170; M. Matsukata (1899), pp. 127–8.
4. I. Tokutomi (1935), vol. 1, p. 851.
5. MF (1936/40), vol. 12, pp. 248–9; Tokeiin (1882/1941), vol. 16, pp. 155–6.
6. Toyo Keizai Shinposha (1926), pp. 2–3; BOJ (1966), p. 76; MF (1969), pp. 126–7.
7. J. Teranishi (1983), pp. 171–2.
8. M. Kobayashi (1977).
9. M. Matsukata (1899), pp. 129–30.
10. *Ibid.*, p. 130.
11. *Ibid.*, p. 132.
12. *Ibid.*, p. 135.
13. *Ibid.*, pp. 132–5.

14. BOJ (1982/86), Materials vol. pp. 340–1. The figures in BOJ (1982/86) are slightly smaller than those shown in M. Matsukata (1899), pp. 104–5.
15. M. Matsukata (1899), p. 99.
16. For other members of the 'think-tank', see pp. 82–5.
17. M. Matsukata (1899), p. 43.
18. *Ibid.*, p. 44.
19. *Ibid.*, p.43.
20. *Ibid.*, p.44.
21. *Ibid.*, p.44.
22. *Ibid.*, p. 45.
23. *Ibid.*, p. 45.
24. *Ibid.*, p. 45.
25. *Ibid.*, p. 60.
26. BOJ (1982/86), vol. 1, p. 181; M. Matsukata (1899), p. 70.
27. C. A. Conant (1910), pp. 210–11.
28. BOJ (1982/86), vol. 1, p. 178. For the Belgian counterpart, see C. A. Conant (1910), p. 207.
29. BOJ (1956/61), vol. 16, p. 51.
30. BOJ (1966), p. 166; BOJ (1982/86), Materials vol., p. 332.
31. *Ibid.*, vol. 1, pp. 317–18.
32. *Ibid.*, vol. 1, pp. 273–9, 464–8.
33. *Ibid.*, Materials vol., pp. 272–3.
34. See W. Bagehot (1873), pp. 187–207; R. G. Hawtrey (1932), pp. 116–19; R. S. Sayers (1967), pp. 101–11; S. G. Checkland (1975), p. 549.
35. See pp. 30–3.
36. M. Takezawa (1968), pp. 123–4.
37. BOJ (1982/86), vol. 1, p. 432.
38. *Ibid.*, vol. 1, p. 448.
39. *Ibid.*, vol. 1, p. 439.
40. *Ibid.*, Materials vol., pp, 274–7.
41. *Ibid.*, Materials vol., pp. 450–2; BOJ *Eigyohokokusho* (Business reports), in BOJ (1956/61), vol. 10, pp. 87–91, 345–54.
42. BOJ (1982/86), vol. 2, pp. 15–27.

10. The Yokohama Specie Bank, or Shokin, *1882–1897*

1. For severe effects of the Matsukata deflationary policy, see G. C. Allen (1962), pp. 50–2.
2. MF (1936/40), vol. 15, p. 6.
3. Originally, in *On Finance*, Matsukata thought that the Yokohama Specie Bank should be absorbed by the Bank of Japan as one of the latter's departments. The legislation of the Yokohama Specie Bank Decree might suggest abandonment of this initial intention. But it may also be argued that the exchange clause involving cession of both banks made unnecessary the absorption of the Specie Bank into the Bank of Japan.
4. YSB (1920), Materials, vol. 4.

5. *BM* (1884), pp. 613–16.
6. YSB (1920), Appendices, vol. 1, p. 477.
7. *Ibid.,* Appendices, vol. 1, pp. 194–5.
8. K. Takahashi (1976), vol. 2, pp. 82–4.
9. Thanks to half-yearly business reports of the Specie Bank during ten years from 1887 to 1898, we are provided with a rough picture of the Bank's customers, including foreigners. During this period, more than 40 per cent of the Bank's money was given at the head office and at Kobe branch, both at the busiest ports of Japan. Although merchants were favoured in terms of the number of advances, banks were given much larger sums than the merchants.

11. Consolidation and expansion, 1883–1897

1. MF (1925/28), vol. 13, p. 236.
2. Tokeiin (1882/1941), vol. 4, p. 395, vol. 17, pp. 702–3.
3. *Ibid.,* vol. 4, p. 395.
4. Professor K. Asakura's discussions support the leadership of merchants in the national banks (K. Asakura (1961), pp. 163–70).
5. MF (1925/28), vol. 12, pp. 538–88.
6. *Ibid.,* vol. 12, p. 594.
7. *Ibid.,* vol. 12, p. 603.
8. The Japanese post office savings business originated on the model of Britain, where savings banks first appeared in Scotland in 1810 (S. G. Checkland (1975), p. 316).
9. K. Shirai (1939), pp. 72–4.
10. MF (1925/28), vol. 12, pp. 845–6.
11. BOJ (1982/86), Materials vol., p. 424.
12. MF (1925/28), vol. 12, p. 889.
13. *Ibid.,* pp. 889–90.
14. *Ibid.,* p. 907.
15. See pp. 64–8 and 70–3.
16. N. Takizawa (1912), pp. 206–10.
17. *Ibid.,* pp. 283–4.
18. The works edited by Professor K. Yamaguchi, ed. (1966), (1970), (1974), and S. Watanabe and D. Kitahara, eds. (1966), give some detailed accounts of sectoral lending.
19. Mitsubishi Bank formally adopted this title in 1919. Before then Mitsubishi banking business was conducted by the banking department in Mitsubishi & Co. Limited partnership.
20. S. Goto (1970), pp. 76–7, 117–19.

12. The adoption of the gold standard, 1893–1897

1. Soyeda and Sakatani were certainly a new generation of Matsukata's select circle. See pp. 61–3. For Soyeda, see E. O. A. Checkland (1994). He was the Japanese correspondent for *Economic Journal*, Cambridge.

2. I. Tokutomi (1935), vol. 2, p. 673.
3. *Tokyo Keizaizasshi*, 7 May 1887.
4. K. Ono (1963), pp. 72–9.
5. Sakatani's arguments were ingenious. He stressed, 'I should like to make one point. Those who argued for the silver and against the gold are those who are in the gold standard countries. They uniformly say that the gold standard is not good and that one should stick to the silver but they remain gold standard countries. The remaining silver countries are China, Korea, Malaya and Japan. If silver is good, why do the European and American people desert the silver standard?' (Sakatanishishaku Kinenjigyokai, ed. (1951), pp. 188–9.)
6. BOJ (1956/61), vol. 17, p. 658.
7. In the wake of the settlement of the metallic question, Matsukata resigned from the office of Finance Minister on account of differences in policies concerning the colonies.
8. MF (1925/28), vol. 2, p. 307. See pp. 92–4.
9. See pp. 92–4.
10. *BM* (1896), I, p. 46, II, p. 719.
11. *BM* (1896), I, p. 46.
12. *BM* (1897).
13. *The Times*, 26 September 1896.

Part IV. The Japanese on the London money market, 1897–1911

13. The 'Siamese twins': Nichigin *and* Shokin, *1897–1911*

1. T. Yoshino (1975/79), vol. 3, p. 517; BOJ (1982/86), Materials vol., p. 198. For *Tokyo Economist*, see pp. 43–5.
2. See pp. 64–8.
3. BOJ (1982/86), vol. 2, p. 52.
4. *Ibid.*, p. 56.
5. *Ibid.*, pp. 89–92; T. Yoshino (1975/79), vol. 1, pp. 472–3.
6. For the Bank of England figures, see J. Clapham (1944), vol. 2, Appendix A. For the Bank of Japan figures, see BOJ (1982/86), Materials vol., pp. 350–6, 374.
7. BOJ (1982/86), vol. 2, pp. 92–5.
8. *Ibid.*, p. 215.
9. For the figures on the Big Five, see S. Goto (1970), p. 90.
10. First National Bank of Tokyo, later Daiichi Bank, opened several offices on the Korean peninsula in 1898, but they served entirely the Japanese government (Daiichi Ginko (1957/58), vol. 1, pp. 633–4, 715).
11. Koizumi was one of the disciples of Yukichi Fukuzawa and also one of the original members on the board of directors of the Specie Bank at its outset in 1880. He was the man dispatched by Okuma to London in 1881 to persuade Shand to come to the Specie Bank as the head office general manager (see pp. 46–8). Resigning from the board in the aftermath of Meiji 14th Year Political Change and serving briefly as first president of Keio University in 1890, Koizumi returned to banking as an official of the Bank of Japan. His premature

death in 1894 caused another, and more important, personnel exchange as will be seen.

12. See pp. 82–5.

13. Tatsuo Yamamoto was also one of Fukuzawa's disciples and seven years younger than Koizumi. Yamamoto later became briefly Minister of Finance.

14. BOJ (1982/86), vol. 2, pp. 101–2.

15. K. Takahashi (1976), vol. 2, chapters 11, 12 and 13.

16. Kokichi Sonoda, former president of the Yokohama Specie Bank, mentioned about the relationship of the two Banks that 'Our bank and the Bank of Japan are sometimes called "Twin banks"'. (*BM*, 1896, II, p. 711.)

17. The mandatary was Yoshigusu Nakai.

18. BOJ (1925/28), vol. 2, p. 333.

19. Yoshigusu Nakai, the London manager of the Specie Bank, did this job marvellously throughout. In 1899 he was awarded a decoration. Also in 1899 he was promoted to the board of directors of the Specie Bank. Sadly Nakai died prematurely in the spring of 1903 when he had returned to Japan for final arrangements with the Ministry of Finance and Bank of Japan regarding the closing business of Chinese indemnity remittance, which came to an end shortly after his death.

20. A remote cause of the fall of Okuma was his proposal for borrowing abroad in 1880. See pp 46–8.

21. MF (1936/40), vol. 12, pp. 413, 418–23.

22. See pp. 30–3 and 46–8.

23. Tokyo Ginko (1980/84), vol. 2, pp. 88–9.

24. F. H. H. King, ed. (1987/91), vol. 2, p. 98.

25. I. H. Nish (1966), p. 219. See also *ibid.*, chapter XIV, and I. H. Nish (1985).

26. Takahashi recollected, 'it was one evening towards the end of April, 1904, that I met Mr Schiff for the first time . . . On the following day I received from Mr A. A. Shand of Parr's Bank the intimation that an American banker was inclined to take up the issue of the remaining portion of our loan. (C. Adler (1929), vol. 1, pp. 213, 215). It was, of course, Jacob Schiff of Kuhn, Loeb & Co. Schiff became a close friend of Takahashi and his family. Schiff was later conferred the Order of the Rising Sun by the Emperor (*Ibid.*, p. 235).

27. YSB (1920), pp. 341–2.

28. See pp. 70–3.

29. See pp. 118–21.

30. YSB annual reports cease to carry the list of correspondents after this date.

31. YSB (1920), Materials vols. 3 and 4.

14. Special banking, 1897–1911

1. BOJ (1956/61), vol. 4, p. 985.

2. K. Yamaguchi (1976), chapter 4 and G. C. Allen (1962), chapter V.

3. MF (1925/28), vol. 14, pp. 611–21.

4. *Ibid.*, pp. 736–43, 777–99.

5. MF (1936/40), vol. 16, p. 868.

6. MF (1925/28), vol. 14, pp. 893–8.
7. MF (1936/40), vol. 15, pp. 501–3, 906–7.
8. *Ibid.*, vol. 16, pp. 181–2, 251.
9. MF (1925/28), vol. 14, pp. 962–3.
10. *Ibid.*, pp. 943–56.
11. R. Wakatsuki (1983), p. 140.
12. See pp. 46–8.
13. As F. H. H. King writes, the Hongkong and Shanghai Banking Corporation mistook the Industrial Bank for the Specie Bank. F. H. H. King, ed. (1987/91), vol. 2, p. 143.
14. MF (1936/40), vol. 15, pp. 151–2.
15. For Japanese imperialism, W. G. Beasley gives a full account in his work (W. G. Beasley (1987)).
16. MF (1936/40), vol. 16, p. 355.
17. See pp. 144–6 and 149–54.
18. MF (1896/1943), vols. 1–17.
19. MF (1936/40), vol. 16, pp. 264–70.
20. MF (1896/1943), vol. 19. All figures for the year 1911 come from this volume.
21. Mira Wilkins discloses in her work (1989) that eight Japanese banks were operating in San Francisco between 1903 and 1910. They were banks for Japanese immigrants settling down there. Chuo Shogyo Bank, a small ordinary bank based in Tokyo and having an office in San Francisco, was probably doing business with these immigrants. Successors to Chuo Shogyo Bank are not traceable. The Bank might have transferred itself over to San Francisco.
22. Figures for the Bank of Korea include those at the time of the Bank of Khankuku.

15. Banking at the end of the Meiji era, 1900–1911

1. S. Goto (1970), pp. 56–7.
2. MF (1936/40), vol. 14, pp. 67–71.
3. *Goshi* is a partnership comprising those with limited and unlimited liabilities, while *gomei* is that constituted entirely by partners with unlimited liabilities. See also Glossary.
4. S. Goto (1970), pp. 116–19.
5. MF (1896/1943), vols. 8 and 19.
6. C. P. Kindleberger (1974).
7. See pp. 90–2.
8. Zenkoku Ginkokyokai Rengokai (1979), pp. 4–5; S. Goto (1970), pp. 263–6.
9. MF (1900/42), 1931 issue, p. 61.

16. Banking and the securities market, 1897–1911

1. Toyo Keizai Shinposha (1927), p. 263.
2. The stock of the Tokyo Stock Exchange itself long remained listed even in the post-Pacific War Years as *Heiwa Fudosan*, or Peace Estate, at the top of the

market list. 'Peace Estate' was so termed, perhaps, because every one wished 'peace' in the aftermath of the Pacific War.

3. Tokyo Kabushiki Torihikijo (1928), pp. 7–14.
4. Toyo Keizai Shinposha (1927), pp. 264–5.

Part V. War, the Japanese boom years, 1911–1919

17. Bank of Japan money supply, 1911–1919

1. BOJ (1982/86), vol. 2, p. 295. For their discussions, see *ibid.*, pp. 278–93.
2. *Ibid.*, pp. 295–6.
3. G. C. Allen (1925), p. 72.
4. K. Yamaguchi (1976), pp. 179–80.
5. BOJ (1966), pp. 28–9; BOJ (1982/86), Materials vol., p. 324.
6. BOJ (1982/86), Materials vol., pp. 332–4.
7. *Ibid.*, pp. 350–74.
8. See pp. 131–3.
9. BOJ (1982/86), vol. 2, p. 401.
10. *Ibid.*, pp. 404–5.
11. *Ibid.*, pp. 357–62, 369–71. Activities of the two Banks will shortly be more detailed.
12. *Ibid.*, pp. 367–8.
13. See pp. 118–25.

18. The expansion of special banking, 1911–1919

1. Figures are all from YSB (1920), Materials vol. 4.
2. See pp. 70–3.
3. BOJ (1914), in Kanagawaken, ed. (1971/82), vol. 16.
4. YSB (1920), Appendices vol. 2, p. 429.
5. YSB (1920), pp. 391–2, 518–19.
6. Inoue Junnosuke Ronso Henshuiinkai, ed. (1935), pp. 25–41, 888–93.
7. When Inoue returned from Britain, the governor of the Bank of Japan wrote to the branch manager of Parr's Bank (24 October 1899): 'Mr A. G. Peace, Dear sir, I take the liberty of writing to express my sincere thanks for the kindness you showed to our two friends, Hijikata and Inoue. They came back imbued with new ideas and they have begun their work with fresh energy, and they are proving themselves to be my efficient helpers. Kindly accept the lacquered box, which I send you by a relative of mine, Mr Yanagiya, as a mere token of gratitude for your kind instruction. The box is considered to be a work of art, peculiar to our country. Thank you again, I remain, yours respectfully, Tatsuo Yamamoto (Governor of the Bank of Japan)'. (*Ibid.*, pp. 40–1.) The letter is evidence of Inoue's status. Hisaakira Hijikata entered the Bank with Inoue. Later in 1911, when Inoue became vice-president of the Specie Bank, Hijikata was promoted to be a director of the Bank of Japan. In 1918 Hijikata was transferred to the presidency of the Industrial Bank, returning to the Bank of Japan

in 1926 as deputy governor. He succeeded the governorship of Inoue in 1928, who assumed Finance Ministership. Hijikata's career, which was another example of the Takahashi-type elite though on a more moderate scale, also lends credence to our assumption that the Industrial Bank was a dummy institution of the Specie Bank. For the discussion see pp. 98–101.

8. MF (1936/40), vol. 15, pp. 506–9, 511–14.
9. *Ibid.*, pp. 643–50.
10. MF (1936/40), vol. 16, pp. 150–2.
11. *Ibid.*, pp. 239–40.
12. See pp. 140–2.
13. MF (1936/40), vol. 16, pp. 248–9.
14. *Ibid.*, pp. 255–6; Nihon Kogyo Ginko (1982), pp. 40–3. The 'Nishihara Loan' was so termed as Kamezo Nishihara, private secretary of Masatake Terauchi the prime minister from 1916 to 1918, was the negotiator among the Japanese government, Chinese government and the financiers. For the 'Twenty-One Demands', see W. G. Beasley (1987), chapter 8.
15. Nihon Kogyo Ginko (1934), pp. 3–4.
16. See pp. 98–101.
17. Taiwan Ginko (1919), pp. 265–6, 272–3.
18. MF (1936/40), vol. 16, pp. 488–93.
19. See pp. 149–54. For the inspection see MF (1936/40), vol. 14, pp. 73–7.
20. Chosen Ginkoshi Kenkyukai (1987), pp. 90, 190. Figures are also available for the years 1914/16, but on account of the smallness of Japanese deposits the comparison for these three years is meaningless. Siberian figures are included in those of Manchuria.
21. *Ibid.*, pp. 850–1; MF (1936/40), vol. 16, p. 298.
22. *Ibid.*, pp. 268–351.
23. S. Watanabe and D. Kitahara, eds. (1966), pp. 166, 338–9.

19. Ordinary and savings banks, the search for strength, 1911–1919

1. MF (1936/40), vol. 14, pp. 72, 79.
2. MF (1936/40), vol. 16, pp. 539, 598–600.
3. Mutual loan associations were an example and will be further discussed in the following chapter.
4. Fifteen Bank, or *Jugo Ginko*, is again not included among the number. The Bank had a large amount of capital well ranking with the top five, but its deposits were considerably smaller, even below the top ten's. Fifteen Bank, big only in terms of capital stock, was a very peculiar institution.
5. Mitsubishi Ginko (1964), pp. 145–56.
6. S. Goto (1970), pp. 102–14.
7. Foreign banking information in this paragraph comes from MF (1896/1943), vols. 6–27.
8. F. H. H. King, ed. (1987/91), vol. 3, pp. 42, 100–1.
9. *Ibid.*, p. 41.
10. *Ibid.*, p. 41.

11. *Ibid.*, p. 82.
12. Mitsui Ginko (1901). The report detailed every aspect of western banking and even included the plans of banking premises of the National Park Bank at Broadway Street, New York, and Parr's Bank at Bartholomew Lane, London. The report was indeed the banking version of the Iwakura Mission report.
13. Mitsui Ginko (1957), pp. 190–5.
14. Sumitomo Ginko (1979), p. 149.
15. MF (1896/1943), vols. 19–20.
16. Royal Commission on Chinese and Japanese Immigration (1902), p. 389; Shinnichibei Shinbunsha (1961), p. 9.
17. Sumitomo Ginko (1979), pp. 203–14. At the time of the establishment of the Sumitomo Bank of Seattle, there were three Japanese local banks operating there: Japanese Commercial Bank, Oriental American Bank and the Specie Bank of Seattle, whereas there was no Japanese bank in Hawaii when the Sumitomo Bank of Hawaii was set up. The Sumitomo Bank of Seattle was of course a limited company, but the state law did not request the attachment of 'Ltd' to the firm name. For further information on Japanese banks, see M. Wilkins (1989).
18. Mitsubishi Ginko (1964), pp. 138–45.
19. MF (1896/1943), vols. 24–7.
20. Figures are all from MF (1896/1943).
21. MF (1900/42), 1931 issue, pp. 223–30.
22. Tanshikyokai (1966), pp. 62–72; MF (1936/40), vol. 16, pp. 912–19.
23. BOJ (1982/86), vol. 2, pp. 519–29; MF (1936/40), vol. 16, pp. 912–19.
24. The number of subscribers to telecommunication services doubled during the boom, reaching nearly 2 million in 1919, when 1,330 exchange stations were operating in Japan (Toyo Keizai Shinposha (1927), p. 673).
25. Tanshikyokai (1966), pp. 70, 75–6.
26. *Ibid.*, p. 69.
27. *Ibid.*, pp. 70–1.
28. M. Takezawa (1968), pp. 275–7; BOJ (1982/86), vol. 2, pp. 443–4.
29. *Ibid.*, pp. 447–9.
30. Tanshikyokai (1966), pp. 90–2.

20. Other financial sectors in the boom years, 1911–1919

1. BOJ (n.d.), in BOJ (1956/61), vol. 22, p. 414.
2. MF (1936/40), vol. 16, pp. 821–47.
3. Nikko Shoken Kabushikikaisha (1970), p. 10.
4. Nomura Shoken Kabushikikaisha (1976), pp. 60–2.
5. Daiwa Shoken Kabushikikaisha (1963), pp. 67–8, 112–27.
6. Yamaichi Shoken Kabushikikaisha (1958), pp. 544, 553–7. The young man was Kunizo Koike who, after the setting up of his own firm, travelled to the United States becoming interested in conducting bank business concurrently.
7. Nikko Shoken Kabushikikaisha (1970), pp. 1–7, 127–33, 177–80. Nikko is an abbreviation of Nihon Kogyo Ginko, or Industrial Bank of Japan.

Part VI. Crisis and the road to war, 1919–1937

21. Post-war collapse, 1919–1923

1. BOJ (n.d.), in BOJ (1956/61), vol. 22, pp. 502–26.
2. BOJ (1982/86), Materials vol., p. 334.
3. BOJ (n.d.), in BOJ (1956/61), vol. 22, p. 535.
4. *Ibid.*, pp. 494–502, 535.
5. *Ibid.*, pp. 536–7, 547–8; MF (1896/1943), vol. 28, pp. 427–31.
6. BOJ (1982/86), vol. 3, pp. 14–15.
7. For emergency loans to the securities market, see the following chapter.
8. BOJ (n.d.), in BOJ (1956/61), vol. 22, pp. 548–9.
9. MF (1936/40), vol. 16, pp. 600–1.
10. *Ibid.*, pp. 541–9.
11. BOJ (n.d.), in BOJ (1956/61), vol. 22, pp. 730–2.
12. Kinyukeizai Kenkyujo (1979).
13. Kinyukenkyukai (1934), pp. 60–1.
14. Fuji Ginko (1982), pp. 236–56.
15. S. Goto (1970), pp. 102–20.
16. Ginkomondai Kenkyukai, ed. (1929), chapters 4 and 7.
17. Figures are available only from T. Yui, ed. (1968/81).
18. Kinyukenkyukai (1934), pp. 150–7.
19. MF (1936/40), vol. 15, pp. 650–1.
20. *Ibid.*, vol. 16, pp. 240–2.
21. *Ibid.*, pp. 242–9. See pp. 121–3.
22. BOJ (1982/86), vol. 3, pp. 40–2.

22. The 1923 catastrophic earthquake, 1927 financial disaster and the new Bank Act, 1923–1927

1. BOJ (1956/61), vol. 22, pp. 753–6.
2. *Ibid.*, p. 756. *Daishin* was a small ordinary bank.
3. *Ibid.*, pp. 760–1.
4. *Ibid.*, pp. 762–3.
5. *Ibid.*, p. 763.
6. *Ibid.*, p. 877.
7. *Ibid.*, pp. 878–82.
8. *Ibid.*, pp. 880–2.
9. BOJ (1961/74), vol. 13, pp. 1–109.
10. *Ibid.*, vol. 25, p. 431.
11. *Ibid.*, p. 432.
12. MF (1896/1943), vol. 33.
13. R. Wakatsuki (1983), pp. 289–95.
14. BOJ (1961/74), vol. 25, pp. 750–1. Miyoji Ito was the first secretary to the first Hirobumi Ito cabinet of 1885, which replaced the *dajokan* system. When, in 1888, establishing the privy council partly on the British model to counter political pressures for opening the Diet and to prepare a constitution, Premier Ito ten-

dered his resignation and transferred himself to the chairmanship of the privy council, secretary Miyoji Ito also accompanied Hirobumi Ito to be the latter's secretary at the privy council. In 1899 Miyoji Ito himself was promoted to councillor. In 1927, when the unprecedented financial crisis occurred, *genro*, or elder statesmen who played vital roles in the Meiji Restoration, had almost all gone.

15. The reports of investigations are contained in BOJ (1961/74), vol. 24, on which our case studies have drawn heavily.
16. *Ibid.*, pp. 168–90.
17. *Ibid.*, pp. 446–58.
18. *Ibid.*, pp. 211–312.
19. *Ibid.*, pp. 478–529.
20. See pp. 140–2.
21. MF (1927), pp. 369–73.
22. MF (1928), pp. 382–7; T. Tsuchiya (1969), pp. 4–5; MF (1896/1943), vol. 35; BOJ (1982/86), vol. 3, pp. 195–202.
23. For Giichi Tanaka and his diplomacy, see N. Banba's account (N. Banba (1972), chapter 7).
24. G. Ogawa (1930). Ogawa studied in Europe for six years from 1906, on mainly public finance. He was appointed professor of public finance at the Imperial University of Kyoto in 1912 and won a seat in the Diet in 1917. Later, in 1936, he became the minister of trade and industry, predecessor of the ministry of international trade and industry (MITI). On returning from the office of High Commissioner to Japanese occupied Burma, he was killed on board a ship sunk by an American submarine in 1945. For further references, see C. Johnson (1982), pp. 127f.
25. G. Ogawa (1930), pp. 2–4.
26. See pp. 33–6.
27. Korekiyo Takahashi never failed to appreciate Shand as one of the first rate British bankers (K. Takahashi (1976), vol. 2, pp. 114–16).
28. BOJ (1961/74), vol. 35, p. 457. The volume contains a series of interviews with retired distinguished bankers.
29. *Ibid.*, pp. 273, 285.
30. G. Ogawa (1930), p. 5.
31. *Ibid.*, p. 10.
32. *Ibid.*, p. 12.
33. Records of full discussions on the bill in the Diet are reproduced in BOJ (1961/74), vol. 13, pp. 227–363.
34. G. Ogawa (1930), p. 19.
35. BOJ (1982/86), vol. 3, p. 290.
36. *Ibid.*, pp. 286–92.

23. Financing heavy industries, 1927–1937

1. BOJ (1966), pp. 76–7, 92.
2. For the figures of each special bank, see BOJ (1966). For the Industrial Bank, see also Nihon Kogyo Ginko (1982), pp. 47–53.

3. For quick comparison of securities holdings among various financial institutions, the table 'Securities Holdings by Type of Financial Institution', pp. 268–9 of BOJ (1966), is convenient.
4. Kinyukenkyukai (1934), Appendix.
5. *Ibid.*, pp. 60–1.
6. *Ibid.*, Appendix; S. Goto (1970), pp. 118–20.
7. Kinyukenkyukai (1934), pp. 192–5; S. Goto (1970), pp. 102–15.
8. Kinyukenkyukai (1934), pp. 195–6.
9. *Ibid.*, p. 196.
10. T. Tsuchiya, ed. (1961), pp. 236–9.
11. S. Goto (1970), pp. 118–20.
12. The insurance business was still in this period under the supervision of the ministry of commerce and industry, separated from the ministry of agriculture and commerce and predecessor of the ministry of international trade and industry in the post-Pacific War time, but in 1941 the supervision was transferred to the Ministry of Finance.
13. For post office and insurance figures, see BOJ (1966), pp. 239–45.
14. S. Asajima (1969), pp. 182–94.
15. BOJ (1966), pp. 217, 239–41, 243.
16. Management and Coordination Agency (1987/88), vol. 3, p. 167.
17. Statistics on the securities markets in this period are incomplete and yet to be compiled. Figures in the following discussions are calculated from BOJ (1966), p. 251 and Toyo Keizai Shinposha (1980), vol. 1, p. 561. Figures for equities include only those on the Tokyo Stock Exchange.
18. BOJ (1966), p. 248.

24. The challenge of militarism, and a change of roles for Nichigin *and* Shokin, *1929–1937*

1. A full range of contemporary literature is listed in the appendix to BOJ (1961/74), vol. 23. There is, however, a volume handsomely edited by a study group, Ginkomondai Kenkyukai, or Society for Banking Question Research. See Ginkomondai Kenkyukai, ed. (1929). The volume was originally published as a special issue of their journal *Ginkoronso*, or *Bank Review*.
2. For Inoue's address to the Diet on 21 January 1930, see BOJ (1961/74), vol. 21, pp. 98–9.
3. BOJ (1982/86), vol. 4, pp. 71–6.
4. MF (1900/42), 1942, p. 36.
5. BOJ (1982/86), vol. 4, pp. 84–94.
6. BOJ (1961/74), vol. 27, pp. 65–6.
7. Tokyo Ginko (1980/84), vol. 6, pp. 428–9.
8. *Ibid.*, vol. 4, pp. 463–4, vol. 6, pp. 212, 215–19.
9. G. C. Allen (1940) gives a full account of the Japanese economy heavily dependent upon Manchuria. Contemporary accounts from the Japanese and the western viewpoints are also found in R. Ishii (1937), chapter 9, and F. C. Jones (1949), chapter 5, respectively.

10. BOJ (1948), p. 24.
11. *Ibid.*, p. 25; Toyo Keizai Shinposha (1980), vol. 2, p. 64.
12. BOJ (1966), p. 32.

Part VII. Complete commitment, struggle and defeat, 1937–1945

25. War budgets and the mobilisation of national resources, 1937–1943

1. Toyo Keizai Shinposha (1980), vol. 2, p. 30.
2. BOJ (1948), p. 102.
3. *Ibid.*, pp. 116–17; MF (1954/65), vol. 12, pp. 3–4.
4. BOJ (1948), pp. 117–18; MF (1954/65), vol. 12, p. 4.
5. BOJ (1948), pp. 119–20; MF (1954/65), vol. 12, p. 5.
6. BOJ (1982/86), vol. 4, pp. 488–506.
7. BOJ (1948), pp. 221–3.
8. Also under the Act, the Sectoral Control Association, Control Union and Regional Financial Council were organised. However, these three were in fact placed subordinate to the National Financial Control Association.
9. For the Korean Development Bank and the Central Cash Office for Industrial Associations, see pp. 124–5 and 144–6.
10. BOJ (1948), p. 220.

26. Extraordinary banking business during the national emergency, 1941–1945

1. BOJ (1948), p. 129.
2. *Ibid.*, pp. 240–2.
3. Kobe Bank later in the post-war period effected another two mergers, joining Mitsui Bank and becoming only recently in 1992 Sakura Bank.
4. BOJ (1948), pp. 223–4; S. Goto (1981), pp. 75–6; S. Yakura and Y. Ikushima, eds. (1986).
5. Kyowa Ginko (1969), pp. 261–2; Kyowa Ginko (1969a), p. 3.
6. BOJ (1948), pp. 225–6.

27. Crisis, 1945

1. BOJ (1966), pp. 274–5.
2. MF (1976/84), vol. 12, p. 20.
3. BOJ (1966), pp. 27, 143.

Part VIII. American 'democratisation' and the search for growth, 1945–1959

28. MacArthur's directives, 1945–1948

1. BOJ (1967), p. 7. Dulles was then a member of the US Delegation to the San Francisco Conference, later special representative of the President in negotiating the Japanese peace treaty and afterwards in 1952 the secretary of state.
2. MF (1976/84), vol. 20, p. 798.

3. Tokyo Ginko (1980/84), vol. 5, part 8, details the liquidation process.
4. MF (1976/84), vol. 20, p. 333.
5. *Ibid.*, pp. 331–7; T. A. Bisson (1954), appendix one.
6. Mochikabukaisha Seiriiinkai (Holding Company Liquidation Commission) (1951), 2 vols., gives detailed accounts of *zaibatsu* and their dissolution. The report was produced after fifty-one meetings. The Commission was discharged in July 1951. For a brief account, see T. A. Bisson (1954).
7. MF (1976/84), vol. 20, p. 800.
8. BOJ (1967), p. 12.
9. *Ibid.*, p. 12.
10. *Ibid.*, pp. 12–13.
11. BOJ (1946), pp. 426–7.
12. MF (1976/84), vol. 19, pp. 38, 480–3.
13. E. M. Hadley (1970), p. 125; Y. Asai (1989), pp. 85–110. I am indebted to Professor Asai for comments on American directives.
14. BOJ (1967), pp. 16–17; J. G. Roberts (1973), p. 390.
15. E. M. Hadley (1970), p. 497.
16. *Ibid.*, p. 498.
17. *Ibid.*, p. 126.
18. *Newsweek*, 1 December 1947.
19. *Ibid.*
20. BOJ (1977a), p. 108.

29. Remaking the banking system: the Japanese versus the Americans, 1946–1952

1. BOJ (1967), pp. 53–61. For the 1926 Commission, see pp. 155–9.
2. *Ibid.*, p. 56.
3. *Ibid.*, p. 69.
4. *Ibid.*, p. 79.
5. Details of the disputes are recorded in *ibid.*, pp. 76–107, and in BOJ (1982/86), vol. 5, chapter 4(3).
6. BOJ (1977), p. 319.
7. BOJ (1967), p. 108.
8. Eventually the members were to be the governor, one representative each from the Finance Ministry and the Economic Stabilisation Board, one each from city and regional banks and one each from the manufacturing and commercial and the agricultural sectors. BOJ (1982/86), vol. 6, p. 214.
9. BOJ (1967), pp. 109–10.
10. Robert C. Christopher (1983), p. 24.
11. E. O. Reischauer (1986); W. Tsutsui (1988).
12. W. G. Beasley (1990), p. 244. See also C. Johnson (1982), pp. 194–200.
13. See p. 189.
14. BOJ (1982/86), vol. 5, pp. 92–8; BOJ (1967), p. 43.
15. The programme is based upon a report prepared by William Draper (BOJ (1967), pp. 104–5).
16. MF (1976/84), vol. 19, pp. 44–6.

30. The rise of governmental banking and the search for stability: Japanese initiatives, 1949–1958

1. See the preceding chapter.
2. Nihon Yushitsunyu Ginko (1963), p. 135.
3. MF (1976/84), vol. 20, p. 667.
4. *Ibid.*, p. 823.
5. *Ibid.*, p. 823.

31. The post-war system, 1946–1959

1. See pp. 186–92.
2. BOJ (1967), pp. 20–2. The Committee was composed of the Finance Ministry banking department chief, the deputy governor of the Bank, the finance department chief of the Economic Stabilisation Board, seven members from banks, three from manufacturing industries and two academics.
3. MF (1976/84), vol. 13, pp. 485–9.
4. *Ibid.*, pp. 474–82.
5. *Ibid.*, pp. 467–74.
6. BOJ (1967), pp. 158–86; Zenkoku Ginkokyokai Rengokai (1979), pp. 5–7.
7. They were the Central Cash Office for Agriculture and Forestry (the reorganised version of the Central Cash Office for Industrial Associations), the Agricultural Cooperative Association (successor to the Industrial Associations), the Central Cash Office for Commercial and Industrial Associations and pawnbroking firms.
8. BOJ (1967), p. 48.
9. MF (1976/84), vol. 13, pp. 483–4; BOJ (1967), pp. 150–1.
10. *Ibid.*, pp. 141–51.
11. BOJ (1982/86), vol. 5, pp. 380–96.
12. Sumitomo Ginko (1979), p. 426.
13. MF (1952/91), vol. 3, p. 236.
14. BOJ (1966), p. 92.
15. Management and Coordination Agency (1987/88), vol. 3, pp. 190–5.
16. Minoru Segawa, former president of Nomura Securities Co., expounds the situations vividly (M. Segawa (1986), chapters 2 and 3).
17. *Ibid.*

An extraordinary century, 1859–1959

1. M. D. Kennedy (1969), p. 56.

Bibliography

Place of publication given if not Tokyo.
Abbreviations are as in the text (see List of Abbreviations, p. xxi)

Adams, T. F. M. and Iwao Hoshii (1972). *A Financial History of the New Japan*
Adler, Cyrus (1929). *Jacob H. Schiff, His Life and Letters*, 2 vols. (London)
Akashi, Teruo (1957/58). *Nihon kinyushi* (History of Japan's money and banking), 3 vols
Alcock, Rutherford (1863). *The Capital of the Tycoon*, 2 vols. (London)
Allen, G. C. (1925). 'The Recent Currency Exchange Policy of Japan', *Economic Journal*
  (1937). 'The Concentration of Economic Control in Japan', *Economic Journal*
  (1940). 'Japanese Industry: its Organization and Development to 1937', in Schumpeter, ed. (1940)
  (1959). *Japan's Economic Recovery* (Oxford)
  (1962). *A Short Economic History of Modern Japan* (London)
  (1983). *Appointment in Japan* (London)
Allen, G. C. and A. G. Donnithore (1954). *Western Enterprise in Far Eastern Economic Development, China and Japan* (London)
Altman, A. A. (1966). 'Guido Verbeck and the Iwakura Mission', *Japan Quarterly*
Anburn, H. W., ed. (1960). *Comparative Banking* (Dunstale)
Anderson, B. L. and P. L. Cottrell (1974). *Money and Banking in England* (Newton Abbot)
Anon. (W. H. Talbot) (1882). *The Currency of Japan* (Yokohama)
  (1913). *Chonin kokenroku* (Records on the rise and fall of merchants)
  (1940). *Manshu chizucho* (Maps of Manchukuo)
Araki, M. (1933). *The Financial System in Japan*
Asai, Yoshio (1989). 'Senryoki no kinyuseido kaikaku to dokusenkinshi seisaku' (Reformation of the financial system and anti-trust policies during the occupation period), *Keizai kenkyu nenpo* (Seijo University)
Asajima, Shoichi (1969). *Nihonshintakugyo hattenshi* (History of development of trust business in Japan)
Asakura, Kokichi (1961). *Meijizenki Nihon kinyukozoshi* (History of Japan's financial structure in the first half of the Meiji era)
  (1988). *Shinpen Nihon kinyushi* (New monetary history of Japan)

Austin, L. (1976). *Japan: the Paradox of Progress* (New Haven)

Bagehot, W. (1873). *Lombard Street* (London)

Banba, Nobuya (1972) *Japanese Diplomacy in a Dilemma: New Light on Japan's China Policy, 1924–29* (Kyoto)

The Bank For International Settlements (1963). *Eight European Central Banks* (London)

Barker, A. J. (1979). *Japanese Army Handbook, 1939–1945* (London)

Baster, A. S. J. (1929). *Imperial Banks* (London)

   (1935). *The International Banks* (London).

Beasley, W. G. (1951). *Great Britain and the Opening of Japan 1834–1956* (London)

   (1955). *Select Documents on Japanese Foreign Policy, 1853–1868* (London)

   (1963). *The Modern History of Japan* (London)

   (1972). *The Meiji Restoration* (Stanford)

   (1987). *Japanese Imperialism* (Oxford)

   (1990). *The Rise of Modern Japan*

Beck, C. L. and A. W. Bucks, eds. (1983). *Aspects of Meiji Modernization* (New Brunswick)

Beckhart, B. H., ed. (1954). *Banking Systems* (New York)

Beckman, G. M. (1975). *The Making of the Meiji Constitution, the Oligarchs and the Constitutional Development of Japan* (Connecticut)

Bird, R. M. (1977). 'Land Taxation and Economic Development in Meiji Japan', *Journal of Development Studies*

Bisson, Thomas Arthur (1954). *Zaibatsu Dissolution in Japan* (Connecticut)

Black, C. E., ed. (1975). *The Modernization of Japan and Russia* (New York)

Black, J. R. (1880/81). *Young Japan, Yokohama and Yedo: A Narrative of the Settlement, and the City from the Signing of the Treaties in 1858 to the Close of the Year 1879*, 2 vols.

Blacker, C. (1964). *The Japanese Enlightenment* (Cambridge)

BOJ (n.d.). 'Sekaisenso shuryogo niokeru honpo zaikaidoyoshi' (History of difficulties in our economy in the post-World-War period), BOJ (1956/61), vol. 22

   (1914). 'Honpo gaikokuboeki ni taisuru kinyu no jikkyo' (Real situations of financing of foreign trade of our country), Kanagawaken, ed. (1971/82), vol. 16

   (1928). 'Sho kyugyoginko no hatangenin oyobi sono seiri' (Causes of failures of the closed banks and their liquidations), BOJ (1961/74), vol. 24

   (1933). 'Kantoshinsai yori Showa ninen kinyukyoko ni itaru waga zaikai' (Our business world during the period from the great earthquake to the financial crisis of the second year of Showa), BOJ (1956/61), vol. 22

   (1946). 'Kinyu hijosochi jisshi to sono eikyo' (Emergency financial measures and their influences), BOJ (1978/91), vol. 9

   (1948). 'Manshujihen igo no zaiseikinyushi' (Financial history after the Manchurian Incident), BOJ (1961/74), vol. 27

   (1956/61). *Nihon kinyushi shiryo Meiji Taisho hen* (Documentary collections on Japan's monetary and banking history: Meiji Taisho), 25 vols.

   (1961/74) *Nihon kinyushi shiryo Showa hen* (Documentary collections on Japan's monetary and banking history: Showa), 35 vols.

(1966). *Meijiiko honposhuyokeizaitokei* (One-hundred-year statistics of the Japanese economy)

(1967). 'Sengo wagakuni kinyuseido no saihensei' (Restructuring of the financial system of our country in the post-war period), BOJ (1978/91), vol. 10

(1972/76). *Zuroku Nihon no kahei* (Pictorial accounts of Japanese coins), 11 vols.

(1973). *Money and Banking in Japan* (trans. by S. Nishimura; ed. by L. Pressnell) (London)

(1977). 'Sengo Kinyushi' (Post-war financial history), BOJ (1978/91), vol. 9

(1977a). 'Senryoki kinyuseido no ichidanmen' (An aspect of the financial system during the occupied period), BOJ (1978/91), vol. 11

(1978/91). *Nihon kinyushi shiryo Showa zokuhen* (Documentary collections on Japan's monetary and banking history: Showa sequel edition), 23 vols.

(1982/86). *Nihon Ginko hyakunenshi* (One-hundred-year history of BOJ), 6 vols. and Materials vol.

(1986). *Wagakuni no kinyuseido* (Financial system of our country)

Bordo, M. D., ed. (1989). *Money, History and International Finance* (Chicago)

Borg, D. and Shunpei Okamoto (1973). *Pearl Harbor as History: Japanese–American Relations 1931–1941* (New York and London)

Born, Karl Erich (1983). *International Banking in the 19th and 20th Centuries* (Leamington)

Borton, Hugh (1955). *Japan's Modern Century* (New York)

(1957). *Japan between East and West* (New York)

Boulding, K. E. and T. Mukerjee, eds. (1972). *Economic Imperialism* (Ann Arbor)

Bowen, R. W. (1980). *Rebellion and Democracy in Meiji Japan* (Berkeley)

Brieda, K. (1970). *The Structure and Operation of the Japanese Economy* (Sydney)

British Government (1865). *Commercial Reports from Her Majesty's Consul in Japan 1863–64* (London)

British Intelligence Objectives Sub-Committee (1945/47). *Allied Intelligence Reports on War-time Japan, 1944, to 1947*, 20 vols. (London)

Broadbridge, S. (1968). 'The Economic Development of Japan 1870–1920', *Journal of Development Studies*

Brofenbrenner, M. (1961). 'Some Lessons of Japan's Economic Development', *Pacific Affairs*

Brown, D. M. (1951). *Money Economy in Medieval Japan* (New Haven)

Brunton, Richard Henry (1991). *Building Japan 1868–1876* (Kent)

Bryant, H. B. and H. D. Stratton (1861). *Bryant and Stratton's Common School Book-keeping* (New York and Chicago).

Buckley, R. (1985). *Japan Today* (Cambridge)

Burke, William (1964). 'Japan's Entrance into the International Financial Community', *American Journal of Economics and Sociology*

Cairncross, A. K. (1975). *Home and Foreign Investment 1870–1913* (Sussex)

Cameron, Rondo, ed. (1967). *Banking in the Early Stages of Industrialization* (Oxford)

(1972). *Banking and Economic Development* (Oxford)

Cattermole, M. J. G. and A. F. Wolfe (1987). *Horace Darwin's Shop. A History of the Cambridge Scientific Instrument Company, 1878–1968* (Bristol)

Chapman, S. (1984). *The Rise of Merchant Banking* (London)

Checkland, E. O. A. (1989). *Britain's Encounter with Meiji Japan, 1868–1912* (London)

(1944). 'Soyeda Juichi: Japanese banker', in E. O. A. Checkland, Nishimura and Tamaki, eds. (1994)

Checkland, E. O. A., Shizuya Nishimura and Norio Tamaki, eds. (1994). *Pacific Banking* (London)

Checkland, S. G. (1975). *Scottish Banking* (Glasgow and London)

(1988). *The Elgins 1766–1917* (Aberdeen)

Chosen Ginkoshi Kenkyukai (1987). *Chosen Ginkoshi* (History of the Bank of Korea)

Christopher, Robert C. (1983). *The Japanese Mind: The Goliath Explained* (New York)

Clapham, J. (1944). *Bank of England*, 2 vols. (Cambridge)

Clark, R. (1979). *The Japanese Company* (New Haven)

Cohen, J. B. (1949). *Japan's Economy in War and Reconstruction* (Minneapolis)

(1959). *Japan's Post-War Economy* (Bloomington)

Conant, Charles A. (1910). *The National Bank of Belgium* (Washington)

Connaughton, R. M. (1988). *The War of the Rising Sun and Trumbling Bear, a Military History of the Russo-Japanese War 1904–5* (London)

Cortazzi, H. (1987). *Victorians in Japan, in and around the Treaty Ports* (London)

(1990). *The Japanese Achievement* (London)

Cortazzi, H. and Gordon Daniels, eds. (1991). *Britain and Japan* (London and New York)

Cottrell, P. L. (1980). *Industrial Finance 1830–1914* (London)

Craig, A. M. (1961). *Choshu in the Meiji Restoration* (Cambridge, Mass.)

(1979). *Japan – A Comparative View* (Princeton)

Craig, A. M. and D. Shively, eds. (1970). *Personality in Japanese History* (Berkeley)

Crawcour, E. S. and Kozo Yamamura (1970). 'The Tokugawa Monetary System: 1787–1868', *Economic Development and Cultural Change*

Crick, W. F. (1965). *Commonwealth Banking Systems* (Oxford)

Crick, W. F. and J. E. Wadsworth (1936). *A Hundred Years of Joint-Stock Banking* (London)

Crump, Arthur (1866). *A Practical Treatise on Banking, Currency and the Exchanges* (London)

(1879). *The English Manual of Banking* (London)

Crump, T. (1992). *The Japanese Numbers Game: the Use and Understanding of Numbers in Modern Japan* (London)

Daiichi Ginko (1957/58). *Daiichi Ginkoshi* (History of Daiichi Bank), 2 vols.

(1969). *Daiichi Ginko gojunenshi* (Fifty-year history of Daiichi Bank) (Osaka)

Daiwa Shoken Kabushikikaisha (1963). *Daiwa Shoken rokujunenshi* (Sixty-year history of Daiwa Securities)

Dale, Peter N. (1986). *The Myth of Japanese Uniqueness* (London)

Davenport-Hines, R. P. T. and Geoffrey Jones, eds. (1989). *British Business in Asia Since 1860* (Cambridge)

Davies, S. G. (1960). *Central Banking in South and East Asia* (Hong Kong)

De Cecco, M. (1974). *Money and Empire* (Oxford)
   (1987). *Changing Money* (Oxford)
Der Wee, H. Van, ed. (1972). *The Great Depression Revisited* (The Hague)
Dore, R. P. (1959). *Land Reform in Japan* (Oxford)
   (1971). *Aspects of Social Change in Modern Japan* (Princeton)
Dower, John W. (1979). *Empire and Aftermath: Yoshida Shigeru and the Japanese* (Cambridge, Mass.)
   (1986). *War Without Mercy* (New York)
Duus, P. (1976). *The Rise of Modern Japan* (Boston)
   (1988). *The Twentieth Century,* vol. 6 of *The Cambridge History of Japan* (Cambridge)
Ehrlich, E. E. and F. M. Tamagna (1954). 'Japan', in Beckhart, ed. (1954)
Eichengreen, Barry (1990). *Elusive Stability* (Cambridge)
Far Eastern Geographical Establishment (1917). *The New Atlas and Commercial Gazetteer in China* (Shanghai)
Feavearyear, A. (1963). *The Pound Sterling* (Oxford)
Fischer, G. C. (1968). *American Banking Structure* (New York)
Fischer, W., et al., eds. (1986). *The Emergence of World Economy 1500–1914* (Stuttgart)
Fletcher, G. A. (1976). *The Discount Houses in London* (London)
Fox, G. (1969). *Britain and Japan 1858–1883* (Oxford)
Francks, P. (1984). *Technology and Agricultural Development in Prewar Japan* (New Haven)
Frost, Peter (1970). *The Bakumatsu Currency Crisis* (Massachusetts)
Fuji Bank (1980). *The Fuji Bank*
Fuji Ginko (1960). *Fuji Ginko hachijunenshi* (Eighty-year history of Fuji Bank)
   (1982). *Fuji Ginko hyakunenshi* (One-hundred-year history of Fuji Bank), 2 vols.
Fukai, Eigo (1938). *Shintei tsukachosetsuron* (New studies on the adjustment of currency)
Fukuzawa, Yukichi (1958/71). *Fukuzawa Yukichi zenshu* (Collected works of Yukichi Fukuzawa), 22 vols.
Furuya, S. (1982). *Japan's Foreign Exchange and her Balance of International Payments* (New York)
Fuse, T., ed. (1975). *Modernization and Stress in Japan* (Leiden)
Gaimusho (1938). *Gaimusho nenkan* (Yearbook of the Ministry of Foreign Affairs), 2 vols.
Gerschenkron, Alexander (1962). *Economic Backwardness in Historical Perspective* (Cambridge, Mass.)
Gerson, J. J. (1972). *Horatio Nelson Lay and Sino-British Relations 1854–1864* (Cambridge, Mass.)
Gilbart, J. W. (1922). *The History, Principles and Practice of Banking* (revised by E. Sykes: original publication 1911), 2 vols. (London)
Gillet Brothers Discount Co. (1952). *The Bill on London* (London)
Ginkomondai Kenkyukai, ed. (1929). *Kinyushitsu kinshishi* (History of prohibition of specie exports)

Goldsmith, R. W. (1983). *The Financial Development of Japan 1868–1977* (New Haven)

(1983a). *The Financial Development of India, Japan and the United States* (New Haven)

Goodhart, C. A. E. (1972). *The Business of Banking, 1891–1914* (London)

Goodhart, C. A. E. and G. Sutija, eds. (1990). *Japanese Financial Growth* (London)

Goto, Shinichi (1968). *Honop ginkogodoshi* (History of bank amalgamations in our country)

(1970). *Nihon no kinyutokei* (Banking statistics of Japan)

(1981). *Showaki ginkogodoshi* (History of bank amalgamation in Showa era)

Grew, J. C. (1944). *Ten Years in Japan* (London)

Griffis, W. E. (1876). *The Mikado's Empire* (New York) (reprint Tokyo, 1971)

Gubbins, J. H. (1911). *The Progress of Japan, 1853–1871* (Oxford)

(1922). *The Making of Modern Japan* (London)

Gulick, S. L. (1935). *Toward Understanding Japan* (New York)

Hadley, E. M. (1970). *Antitrust in Japan* (Princeton)

Hall, Ivan Parker (1973). *Mori Arinori* (Cambridge, Mass.)

Hall, J. W. (1968). *Japan from Prehistory to Modern Times* (London)

Hall, J. W. and M. B. Jansen, eds. (1968). *Studies in the Institutional History of Early Modern Japan* (Princeton)

Halliday, J. (1975). *A Political History of Japanese Capitalism* (New York)

Hamaoka, Itsuo (1902). *A Study on the Central Bank of Japan*

Hamashita, Takeshi (1983). 'A History of the Japanese Silver Yen and the Hongkong and Shanghai Banking Corporation, 1871–1913', in F. H. H. King, ed (1983)

Hanley, S. B. and K. Yamamura (1977). *Economic and Demographic Change in Pre-industrial Japan 1600–1868* (Princeton)

Hara, Kunizo, ed. (1937). *Hara Rokuro O den* (Biography of Rokuro Hara), 3 vols.

Hara, Shiro (1958/76). 'Yokohama Shokin Ginko no setsuritsu to sono seikaku' (Establishment and characteristics of YSB), Yokohamashi (1958/76), vol. 3

Hattori, Yukimasa (1904). *The Foreign Commerce of Japan Since the Restoration, 1869–1900* (Baltimore)

Hauser, W. B. (1974). *Economic Institutional Change in Tokugawa Japan* (Cambridge)

Hawtrey, R. G. (1932). *The Art of Central Banking* (London)

(1938). *A Century of Bank Rate* (London)

Hayami, Akira and Matao Miyamoto (1988/90). 'Gaisetsu 17–18 seiki' (Survey of the seventeenth to eighteenth centuries). Umemura and Nakamura, eds. (1988/90), vol. 1

Hayami, Y. (1975). *A Century of Agricultural Growth in Japan*

Hijikata, Susumu (1980). *Yokohama Shokin Ginko* (YSB)

Hirschmeier, Johannes (1964). *The Origins of Entrepreneurship in Meiji Japan* (Cambridge, Mass.)

Hirschmeier, Johannes and Tsunehiko Yui (1975). *The Development of Japanese Business* (Cambridge, Mass.)

Hishida, S. G. (1905). *The International Position of Japan as a Great Power* (New York)

(1940). *Japan among the Great Powers* (London)

Homer, S. (1977). *A History of Interest Rates* (New Brunswick)

Honjo, Eijiro (1938). 'Bakumatsu no Shanghai boeki' (Shanghai trades in the last days of the *bakufu*), *The Economic Review* (Kyoto University)

(1965). *The Social and Economic History of Japan* (New York)

Hubbard, G. E. (1935). *Eastern Industrialization and its Effect on the West, with Special Reference to Great Britain and Japan* (Oxford)

Humbert, Aime (1874). *Japan and the Japanese* (New York)

Hunter, Janet (1984). *Concise Dictionary of Modern Japanese History*

Hutton, Charles (1778). *A Complete Treatise on Practical Arithmetic and Book-Keeping* (London)

Ijichi, Sumimasa (1940). *The Life of Marquis Shigenobu Okuma, a Maker of New Japan*

Imuta, Toshimitsu, ed. (1991). *Senjitaiseika no kinyukozo* (Financial structure in the wartime regime)

Inoue, Junnosuke (1931). *Problems of the Japanese Exchange 1914–1926* (trans. by E. H. De Bunsen) (London)

Inoue Junnosuke Ronso Henshuiinkai (1935). *Inoue Junnosuke den* (Biography of Junnosuke Inoue)

Iriye, A. (1972). *Pacific Estrangement: Japanese and American Expansion, 1897–1911* (Cambridge, Mass.)

Ishii, Kanji (1984). *Kindainihon to Igirisu shihon* (Modern Japan and British capital)

Ishii, R. (1937). *Population Pressure and Economic Life in Japan* (London)

Ishii, Takashi (1987). *Bakumatsu kaikoki keizaishikenkyu* (Study of economic history during the period of the last days of the *bakufu* and the opening of the ports) (Yokohama)

Ito Hirobumi Kenkeimonjo Kenkyukai (1973/81). *Ito Hirobumi kankeimonjo* (Hirobumi Ito papers)

Iwanamishoten (1991). *Kindai Nihon sogonenpyo* (Consolidated chronological table of modern Japan), 3rd edn

Iwasaki, Hiroyuki (1972). 'Meijiki niokeru Mitsuike omotokataseido no kozo to sono kino' (Structure and working of the headquarters system of Mitsui in the Meiji era), *Mitsui Bunko ronso*

(1973). 'Mitsuike dozokukai no seiritsukatei' (Making of the managing board of the house of Mitsui), *Mitsui Bunko ronso*

Iwasaki Yataro Denki Hensankai (1967). *Iwasaki Yataro den* (Biography of Yataro Iwasaki), 2 vols.

Iwata, Masakazu (1964). *Okubo Toshimichi, the Bismarck of Japan* (Berkeley)

Jacobsen, H. and A. L. Smith Jr. (1979). *World War II, Policy and Strategy: Selected Documents with Commentary* (Santa Barbara and Oxford)

Jansen M. B. (1989). *The Nineteenth Century*, vol. 5 of *The Cambridge History of Japan* (Cambridge)

Jansen, M. B. and G. Rozman, eds. (1986). *Japan in Transition* (Princeton)

Jao, Y. C. (1974). *Banking and Currency in Hong Kong* (London)

Japan Business History Institute (1976). *The Mitsui Bank: A History of the First 100 Years*

Japan Business History Society (1985). *Keieishigaku no nijunen* (Twenty years of business history)

Japan Statistical Association (1988). *Historical Statistics in Japan*, vol. 3

Johnson, Chalmers (1982). *MITI and the Japanese Miracle*

Jones, F. C. (1949). *Manchuria since 1931* (Oxford)

Jones, Geoffrey, ed. (1990). *Banks as Multinationals* (London and New York)

Kagawa, Takayuki (1974). 'Mitsui ryogaeten no keiei to chikuseki' (Management and funding of the *ryogae* shop of Mitsui), *Mitsui Bunko ronso*

    (1979). 'Bakumatsu Ishinki no okawase Mitsui Ginko' (Mitsui Bank the authorised exchange dealer during the last days of the *bakufu* and the restoration period), *Mitsui Bunko ronso*

Kajinishi, Mitsuhaya, et al., eds. (1965). *Nihonkeizaishi taikei* (Outline of Japan's economic history), vol. 5

Kanagawaken (1971/82). *Kanagawakenshi shiryohen* (Materials on the history of Kanagawa Prefecture), 46 vols.

Kasuya, Makoto (1988). 'Meijizenki niokeru Mitsui kasan no saihenkatei' (Reorganising process of house resources of Mitsui during the early years of Meiji), *Shakai keizai shigaku*

Kato, Toshihiko (1957). *Honpo ginko shiron* (Studies on banking history of our country)

Kato, Toshihiko, ed. (1983). *Nihon kinyuron no shitekikenkyu* (Historical review of studies of Japan's money and banking)

Kato, Toshihiko and Tsutomu Ouchi, eds. (1963). *Kokuritsu ginko no kenyu* (Studies on the national banks)

Katsu, Kaishu (1972/83). *Katsu Kaishu zenshu* (Collected works of Kaishu Katsu), 22 vols.

Kauffman, James Lee (1947). 'A Lawyer's Report', *Newsweek* 1 December 1947

Kawai, T. (1938). *The Goal of Japanese Expansion*

Kennedy, M. D. (1963). *A History of Japan* (London)

    (1969). *The Estrangement of Great Britain and Japan* (London)

Keswick, M., ed. (1982). *The Thistle and the Jade: A Celebration of 150 years of Jardine, Matheson & Co.* (London)

Kindleberger, C. P. (1974). *The Formation of Financial Centers* (Princeton)

King, Frank H. H., ed. (1983). *Eastern Banking* (London)

    (1987/91). *The History of the Hongkong and Shanghai Banking Corporation*, 4 vols. (Cambridge)

    (1990). 'Joint Venture in China: The Experience of the Pekin Syndicate, 1897–1961', *Business and Economic History*

King, W. T. C. (1936). *History of the London Discount Market* (London)

Kinoshita, Yetaro (1902). *The Past and Present of Japanese Commerce* (New York)

Kinyukeizai Kenkyujo (1979). *Kinyukeizai Kenkyujo gojunenshi* (Fifty-year history of the Institute of Financial Studies)

Kinyukenkyukai (1934). *Wagankuni ni okeru ginkogodo no taisei* (Overview of the bank amalgamation movement in our country)

Klein, Laurence and K. Ohkawa, eds. (1968). *Economic Growth: the Japanese Experience since the Meiji era* (Illinois)

Kobayashi, Masaaki (1977). *Nihon no kogyoka to kangyo haraisage* (Japan's industrialisation and privatisation of governmental firms)

Kobayashi, Ushisaburo (1922). *War and Armament Loans of Japan* (New York) (1930). *The Basic Industries and Social History of Japan* (London)

Kobe Ginko (1958). *Kobe Ginkoshi* (History of Kobe Bank)

Kokusai Newsjiten Shuppaniinkai, ed. (1989/90). *Gaikokushinbun nimiru Nihon* (Japan in foreign newspapers), 2 vols.

Koyama, Yukinobu (1991). 'Bakumatsuki Nagasaki shoninkan no kabuido' (Licence transfers among Nagasaki merchants during the last days of the *bakufu*), *Chuo shigaku*

Kume, Kunitake (1878). *Tokumeizenkentaishi Beiou kairan jikki* (True account of the special embassy in America and Europe) (reprinted 1978)

Kuroha, Hyojiro, ed. (1934/1940). *Osaka shogyo shiryo shusei* (Collection of historical materials of commerce in Osaka), 5 vols.

Kyowa Ginko (1969). *Honpo chochiku ginkoshi* (History of savings banking in our country)
(1969a). *Kyowa Ginkoshi* (History of Kyowa Bank)

Lane-Poole, S. and F. V. Dickins (1894). *The Life of Sir Harry Parkes*, 2 vols. (London)

Lanman, C. (1883). *Leading Men of Japan* (Boston)

Large, S. S. (1972). *The Rise of Labor in Japan: The Yuaikai, 1912–1919*

Lazonick, William (1992). *Business Organization and the Myth of the Market Economy* (Cambridge)

Lebra, Joyce C. (1973). *Okuma Shigenobu: Statesman of Meiji Japan* (Cambridge)

Lee, B. A. (1973). *Britain and the Sino-Japanese War, 1937–1939* (Stanford)

Lee, S. Y. and Y. C. Jao (1982). *Financial Structures and Monetary Policies in Southeast Asia* (London)

Lehman, J. P. (1978). *The Image of Japan* (London)
(1982). *The Roots of Modern Japan* (London)

Lippit, Victor D. (1978). 'Economic Development in Meiji Japan and Contemporary China', *Cambridge Journal of Economics*

Lloyd, A. (1909). *Every-day Japan* (London)

Lockwood, William W. (1954). *The Economic Development of Japan* (Princeton)

Lockwood, William W., ed. (1965). *The State and Economic Enterprises in Japan* (Princeton)

Longford, J. H. (1913). *The Evolution of the New Japan* (Cambridge)
(1915). *Japan of the Japanese* (London)

Lowe, P. (1969). *Great Britain and Japan, 1911–15* (London)

Maat, Huucc (1991). 'Financial Development and Industrial Organisation in Japan 1873–1899: The Case of Mitsui', *Japan Forum*

Mackenzie, Compton (1954). *Realms of Silver: One Hundred Years of Banking in the East* (London)

McLaren, W. W. (1916). *A Political History of Japan during the Meiji Era* (London)

Mclean, Robert A. (1903). 'Finance of Japan', *Transactions and Proceedings of the Japan Society* (London)

Macpherson, W. J. (1987). *The Economic Development of Japan 1868–1941* (Basingstoke)

Maeda, Masana (1881). *Chokusetsuboeki iken ippan* (On direct foreign trade)

Management and Coordination Agency (1987/88). *Historical Statistics of Japan*, 5 vols.

Marriner, Sheila (1961). *Rathbones of Liverpool* (Liverpool)

Mason, R. H. P. and J. G. Caiger (1972). *A History of Japan* (Melbourne)

Masuda, Takashi (1908). *Japan, its Commercial Development and Prospects* (London)

Matsukata, Masayoshi (1899). *Report on the Adoption of the Gold Standard*

Matsukata, Mineo, et al., eds. (1979/93). *Matsukata Masayoshi kankei monjo* (Archives of Masayoshi Matsukata), 14 vols.

Matsuyoshi, Sadao (1932). *Nihon ryogae kinyushiron* (History of *ryogae* financing in Japan)

(1937). *Meijiishingo niokeru ryogaeshokinyu* (*Ryogae* financing in the post-Meiji-restoration period)

Mayet, Paul (1893). *Agricultural Insurance in Organic Connection with Savings Banks, Land Credit, and the Commutation of Debts* (London)

Meiji Shiryokenkyurenrakukai, ed. (1957). *Meijiseiken no kakuritsukatei* (Process of the making of Meiji administration)

MF (1880). *Okurasho enkakushi* (History of the Ministry of Finance), MF (1931/36), vols. 2 and 3

(1896/1943). *Ginkosoran* (Survey on banks), 49 vols.

(1900/42). *Kinyujiko sankosho* (Monetary statistics)

(1925/28). *Meiji zaiseishi* (Financial history of Meiji), 15 vols.

(1927). 'Kyugyo oyobi kyugyodoyoginko shirabe' (The examinations of closed and nearly-closed banks), BOJ (1961/74), vol. 25

(1928). 'Zaikaikyokogo ni okeru ginko no seiri oyobi zaikaizengosochi' (Bank liquidation and aftercare for business world in the wake of economic crisis), BOJ (1961/74), vol. 25

(1931/36). *Meijizenki zaiseikeizai shiryoshusei* (Collection of historical materials on finance and economy during the first half of Meiji), 21 vols.

(1936/40). *Meiji Taisho zaiseishi* (Financial history of Meiji and Taisho), 20 vols.

(1952/91). *Ginkokyoku kinyunenpo* (Annual financial bulletin of banking department of MF)

(1954/65). *Showa zaiseishi* (Financial history of Showa), 18 vols.

(1969). *Okurasho hyakunenshi* (One-hundred-year history of MF), 3 vols.

(1970/71). *Nihon zaiseikeizai shiryo* (Documents on Japan's financial and economic history), 10 vols.

(1976/84). *Showa zaiseishi* (Financial history of Showa), 20 vols.

Michie, R. C. (1987). *The London and New York Stock Exchanges 1850–1914* (London)

Mikami, Ryuzo (1987). *Toraisen no shakaishi* (Social history of coins brought from overseas)

(1989). *Yen no shakaishi* (Social history of yen)

(1989a). *Yen no tanjo* (Birth of yen)

Mitsubishi Economic Research Bureau (1936). *Japanese Trade and Industry, Present and Future* (London)

Mitsubishi Economic Research Institute (1955). *Mitsui–Mitsubishi–Sumitomo: Present Status of Former Zaibatsu Enterprises*

Mitsubishi Ginko (1964). *Mitsubishi Ginkoshi* (History of Mitsubishi Bank)

Mitsui, Takasumi (1931). *Edo niokeru ryogaenakama no hensen to sono tokusei* (Chronology and characteristics of the associations of *ryogae* in the Edo era)

(1932/33). *Ryogae nendaiki* (Chronology of *ryogae*), 3 vols.

Mitsui Bank (1926). *A Brief History*

Mitsui Bunko (1971/80). *Mitsui jigyoshi* (Business history of Mitsui), 3 vols. and Materials (4 vols.)

Mitsui Ginko (1895). *Mitsui Ginko annai* (Guidebook of Mitsui Bank)

(1901). *Gomeikaisha Mitsui Ginko Obei shuchoin hokokusho* (Report of Mitsui Bank delegates dispatched to the United States of America and Britain)

(1957). *Mitsui Ginko hachijunenshi* (Eighty-year history of Mitsui Bank)

(1976). *The Mitsui Bank: a history of the first 100 years*

Mitsui Gomeikaisha (1933). *The House of Mitsui: a record of three centuries*

Mitsui Hachiroemon Takamine Den Henshuiinkai (1988). *Mitsui Hachiroemon Takamine den* (Biography of Hachiroemon Mitsui)

Miyake, Setsurei (1950). *Dojidaishi* (Contemporary history), 6 vols.

Miyamoto, Mataji (1958). 'The Merchants of Osaka (I and II)', *Osaka Economic Papers*

(1970). *Ono Gumi no kenkyu* (Study of the house of Ono), 4 vols.

(1988). *Sumitomoke no kakun to kinyushi no kenkyu* (Family precepts of the house of Sumitomo and the study of monetary history)

Miyamoto, Mataji, Yotaro Sakudo and Yasukichi Yasuba (1965). 'Economic Development in Pre-industrial Japan, 1859–1894', *The Journal of Economic History*

Mizunuma, Tomokazu (1958/76). 'Yokohama Shokin Ginko no gaikokugawase boekikinyu no tenkai' (Development of foreign exchange and trade finance of YSB), Yokohamashi (1958/76), vol. 4

Mochikabukaisha Seiriiinkai (1951). *Nihon zaibatsu to sono kaitai* (Japan's *zaibatsu* and their liquidation), 2 vols. (reprinted 1973)

Morgan, E. V. (1943). *The Theory and Practice of Central Banking 1797–1913* (Cambridge)

Morikawa, Hidemasa (1992). *Zaibatsu*

Morley, J. W., ed. (1971). *Dilemmas of Growth in Prewar Japan* (Princeton)

Morris, J. (1906). *Makers of Japan* (London)

Moulton, Harold G. (1931). *Japan: An Economic and Financial Appraisal* (Washington)

Myers, M. G. (1970). *A Financial History of the United States* (New York)

Myers, R. H. and M. R. Peattie, eds. (1984). *The Japanese Colonial Empire, 1895–1945* (Princeton)

Nagai, Michio and M. Urrutia, eds. (1985). *Meiji Ishin* (Meiji Restoration)

Nagasakishi (1990). *Shisei Nagasaki nenpyo* (City of Nagasaki time chronology)

Nakamura, Naomi (1961). *Okuma Shigenobu* (Shigenobu Okuma)

(1968). *Okuma zaisei no kenkyu* (Studies on Okuma's financial policies)

Nakamura, T. (1983). *Economic Growth in Prewar Japan* (trans. by R. A. Feldman) (New Haven)

Neary, I. (1989). *Political Protest and Social Control in Pre-war Japan* (Atlantic Highlands)

Nihon Chokishinyo Ginko (1962). *Nihon Chokishinyo Ginko junenshi* (Ten-year history of Japan Long-term Credit Bank)

Nihon Fudosan Ginko (1967). *Nihon Fudosan Ginko junenshi* (Ten-year history of Japan Realty Bank)

Nihon Kaihatsu Ginko (1963). *Nihon Kaihatsu Ginko junenshi* (Ten-year history of Japan Development Bank)

Nihon Kingendaishi Jiten Henshuiinkai (1978). *Nihon kingendaishi jiten* (Dictionary of Japan's modern and contemporary history)

Nihon Kogyo Ginko (1934). *Nihon Kogyo Ginko saikinjunenshi* (Recent ten-year history of the Industrial Bank of Japan)

 (1982). *Nihon Kogyo Ginko shichijugonenshi* (Seventy-five-year history of the Industrial Bank of Japan) with appendix vol.

Nihon Yushitsunyu Ginko (1963). *Junen no ayumi* (Ten-year history)

Nikko Shoken Kabushikikaisha (1970). *Nikko Shoken Kabushikikaisha gojunenshi* (Fifty-year history of Nikko Securities Co.)

Nimmo, William F., ed. (1990). *The Occupation of Japan: the Impact of the Korean War* (Virginia)

Nish, I. H. (1966). *The Anglo-Japanese Alliance: the Diplomacy of Two Island Empires* (London)

 (1968). *The Story of Japan* (London)

 (1972). *Alliance in Decline* (London)

 (1977). *Japanese Foreign Policy, 1869–1942* (London)

 (1985). *The Origins of the Russo-Japanese War* (London)

 (1988). *Contemporary European Writing on Japan* (Kent)

Nish, I. H. and C. Dunn, eds. (1979). *European Studies on Japan* (Kent)

Nishida, Yoshiaki and Yasuo Kubo, eds. (1991). *Nishiyama Koichi nikki* (Diary of Koichi Nishiyama)

Nishikawa, Shunsaku and Osamu Saito (1985). 'The Economic History of the Restoration period', in Nagai and Urrutia, eds. (1985).

Nomura Shoken Kabushikikaisha (1976). *Nomura Shoken Kabushikikaisha gojunenshi* (Fifty-year history of Nomura Securities Co.)

Norman, Egerton Herbert (1940). *Japanese Emergence as a Modern State: Political Economic Problems of the Meiji Period* (New York)

Obata, Kyogoro (1937). *An Interpretation of the Life of Viscount Shibusawa*

Odaka, Konosuke and Yuzo Yamamoto, eds. (1988). *Bakumatsu Meijiki no Nihonkeizai* (Japan's economy during the last days of the *bakufu* and the Meiji era)

Odate, G. (1922). *Japan's Financial Relations with the United States* (New York)

Ogawa, Gotaro (1930). *Shinginkoho riyu* (Reasoning of the new Bank Act)

Ogino, Nakasaburo (1926). *Sonoda Kokichi den* (Biography of Kokichi Sonoda)

Oguchi, Yujiro (1981). 'Bunkyuki no bakufuzaisei' (*Bakufu* finance during the period of Bunkyu), *Nenpo kindai Nihon kenkyu*

(1988). 'Goyokin to kinsatsu' (Forced loans and gold notes), in Odaka and Yamamoto, eds. (1988).

Okada, Shunpei (1974). 'Allan Shand no kokuritsuginko hihan' (Allan Shand's criticism of the national bank), *Keizai kenkyu* (Seijo University)

Okamoto, S. (1970). *The Japanese Oligarchy and the Russo-Japanese War* (New York)

Okubo, Toshiaki (1957). 'Meiji juyonen no seihen' (Political change of the fourteenth year of Meiji), in Meiji Shiryokenkyurenrakukai (1957)

(1976). *Iwakurashisetsu no kenkyu* (Studies on the Iwakura Mission)

Okuma, Shigenobu, ed. (1910). *Fifty Years of New Japan*, 2 vols. (London)

Ono, G. (1922). *Expenditures of the Sino-Japanese War* (New York)

(1922a). *War and Armament Expenditures of Japan* (New York)

Ono, Kazuichiro (1963). 'Nihon niokeru kinhonisei no seiritsu 1' (Establishment of the gold standard in Japan), *Keizai ronso* (Kyoto University)

Orchard, John E. (1930). *Japan's Economic Position* (New York)

Osakashi (1965). *Osakashishi* (History of the city of Osaka), 8 vols.

Osborn, S. (1859). *A Cruise in Japanese Waters* (Edinburgh)

Ott, D. (1961). 'The Financial Development of Japan, 1878–1959', *Journal of Political Economy*

Ouchi, Hyoe, ed. (1964). *Kinyuronkenkyu* (Studies on money and banking)

Palyi, M. (1972). *The Twilight of Gold* (Chicago)

Patrick, Hugh T. (1967). 'Japan 1864–1914', in Cameron, ed. (1967)

Pollard, S. (1970). *The Gold Standard and Employment Policies between the War* (London)

Pooley, A. M. (1915). *Secret Memoirs of Count Tadasu Hayashi* (London)

Powell, E. T. (1915). *The Evolution of the Money Market* (London)

Prindl, Andreas R. (1981). *Japanese Finance: A Guide to Banking in Japan* (New York)

Ranis, G. (1959). 'The Financing of Japanese Economic Development', *Economic History Review*

Reischauer, Edwin O. (1965). *Japan Past and Present*

(1970). *Japan: The Story of a Nation* (London)

(1986). *My Life between Japan and America* (New York)

(1988). *The Japanese Today* (Cambridge, Mass.)

Reischauer, E. O. and Albert M. Craig (1979). *Japan Tradition and Transformation* (Boston, London and Sydney)

Reischauer, Haru Matsukata (1986). *Samurai and Silk, A Japanese and American Heritage*

Revel, J. (1973). *The British Financial System* (London)

Richardson, B. M. and T. Ueda (1981). *Business and Society in Japan* (New York)

Roberts, John G. (1973). *Mitsui: Three Centuries of Japanese Business* (New York)

Rose, Peter S. (1991). *Japanese Banking and Investment in the United States* (New York)

Rosovsky, H. (1961). *Capital Formation in Japan* (New York)

Royal Commission on Chinese and Japanese Immigration (1902). *Report of the Royal Commission on Chinese and Japanese Immigration* (Ottawa) (reprinted 1978)

Saito, Hisahiko (1988). 'The Formation of Japanese Specie Held Abroad', *City University Business School Discussion Paper Series*

Sakairi, Chotaro (1985). *Nihon zaiseishi* (Financial history of Japan)

Sakatanishishaku Kinenjigyokai, ed. (1951). *Sakatani Yoshio den* (Biography of Yoshio Sakatani)

Sakudo, Yotaro (1969). 'Ryogaesho kinyukenkyu no genjo to mondaiten' (Present stage and problems in studies of *ryogae* merchant financing), *Nihon rekishi*

Sansom, G. B. (1951). *The Western World and Japan* (London)

Sanwa Ginko (1983). *Sanwa no ayumi* (History of Sanwa)

Sawada, Akira, ed. (1921). *Segaiko jireki* (Career of Segaiko) (reprinted 1978)

Sayers, R. S. (1967). *Modern Banking* (Oxford)

(1976). *The Bank of England*, 3 vols. (Cambridge)

Scalapino, R. A. (1975). *Democracy and the Party Movement in Prewar Japan* (Berkeley)

Scammell, W. M. (1968). *The London Discount Market* (New York)

Schumpeter, E. B., ed. (1940). *The Industrialization of Japan and Manchukuo* (New York)

Schwank, F. and Frank R. Ryder, eds. (1986). *Banks Abroad* (London)

Segawa, Minoru (1986). *Watashino shoken Showashi* (My career in securities business in Showa)

Sheldon, C. D. (1958). *The Rise of the Merchant Class in Tokugawa Japan, 1600–1868* (New York)

Shimazaki, Kyuya (1989). *Yen no shinryakushi* (History of yen's invasion)

Shinbo, Hiroshi (1968). *Nihon kindai shinyoseido seiritsushiron* (Studies on the making of Japan's modern credit system)

(1978). *Kinsei no bukka to keizaihatten* (Prices and economic fluctuations in the modern age)

Shinjo, Hiroshi (1962). *History of the Yen*

Shinnichibei Shinbunsha, ed. (1961). *Beikoku Nikkeijin hyakunenshi* (One-hundred-year history of Japanese Americans)

Shirai, Kikuwaka (1939). *Nihon no kinyukikan* (Financial institutions of Japan)

Shoda, K. and Y. Sakudo (1978). *Gaisetsu nihon keizaishi* (An introduction to Japanese economic history)

Silberman, Bernard and H. D. Harootunian, eds. (1974). *Japan in Crisis* (Princeton)

Sinha, S. (1968). *Aspects of Japan* (London)

Skully, M. T. (1980). *Merchant Banking in the Far East* (London)

(1987). *Financial Institutions and Markets in the South Pacific* (London)

Skully, M. T. and G. J. Viksnins (1987). *Financing East Asia's Success* (London)

Smethhurst, R. J. (1974). *A Social Basis for Prewar Japanese Militarism* (Berkeley)

Smith, T. C. (1955). *Political Change and Industrial Development in Japan: Government Enterprise, 1868–1880* (Stanford)

(1959). *The Agrarian Origins of Modern Japan* (Stanford)

Soda, Osamu (1973). *Maeda Masana* (Masana Maeda)

Sorifu Tokeikyoku (1949–). *Nihon tokeinenkan* (Japan statistical yearbook)

Soyeda, Juichi (1898). *The Adoption of Gold Monometallism by Japan* (Boston)

Stead, A. (1904). *Japan by the Japanese*, 2 vols. (London)

Stevens, Charles R. and Owen D. Nee (1986). 'Japan', in Schwank and Ryder, eds. (1986)

Storry, G. R. (1960). *A History of Modern Japan* (Harmondsworth)

Sugiyama, Chuhei and Hiroshi Mizuta, eds. (1988). *Enlightenment and Beyond: Political Economy Comes to Japan*

Sugiyama, Shinya (1988). *Japan's Industrialization in the World Economy 1859–1899* (London)

Sumitomo Ginko (1979). *Sumitomo Ginko hachijunenshi* (Eighty-year history of Sumitomo Bank) (Osaka)

Sumiya, M. and K. Taira (1979). *An Outline of Japanese Economic History 1603–1940*

Suzuki, Gengo (1990). 'The Impact of the Korean War on the Occupation of Japan: an Overview' in Nimmo, ed. (1990)

Suzuki, Toshio (1991). 'Foreign Loan Issues on the London Capital Market 1879–1913, with special reference to Japan' (unpublished PhD thesis, University of London)

Suzuki, Yoshio (trans. by John G. Greenwood) (1980). *Money and Banking in Contemporary Japan* (New Haven and London)

(1987). *The Japanese Financial System* (Oxford)

Sykes, J. (1926). *The Amalgamation Movement in English Banking 1825–1924* (London)

Taiwan Ginko (1919). *Taiwan Ginko nijunenshi* (Twenty-year history of the Bank of Taiwan) (Taipei)

(1939). *Taiwan Ginko yonjunenshi* (Forty-year history of the Bank of Taiwan)

Takahashi, Korekiyo (1976). *Jiden* (Autobiography), 2 vols. (reprint)

Takaki, M. (1903). *The History of Japanese Paper Currency* (Baltimore)

Takeuchi, Kazuo (1972). *Edojidai no ryogaesho* (*Ryogae* merchants in the Edo era)

Takezawa, Masatake (1968). *Nihon kinyu hyakunenshi* (One hundred years of Japan's money and banking)

Takizawa, Matsuyo (1927). *The Penetration of Money Economy in Japan* (New York)

Takizawa, Naoshichi (1912). *Kohon Nihon kinyushiron* (Studies on the history of Japan's money and banking) (reprinted 1968)

Tamaki, Norio (1988). 'Economists in Parliament', in Sugiyama and Mizuta, eds. (1988).

Tamura, Toshio (1963). *Shibusawa Eiichi to Takuzenkai* (Eiichi Shibusawa and Selection Society)

Tanabe, Taichi (1966). *Bakumatsu gaikodan* (Anecdotes of diplomacy during the last days of the *bakufu*), 2 vols.

Tanaka, Ikuo (1964). 'Meiji yonen no ginkoronso' (Bank controversy of the fourth year of Meiji), in Ouchi, ed. (1964)

Tanshikyokai (1966). *Tanshishijo shichijunenshi* (Seventy-year history of call-loan market)

Tatewaki, Kazuo (1987). *Zainichi gaikokuginkoshi* (History of foreign banks in Japan)

(1991). *Banking and Finance in Japan* (London and New York)

(1992). 'The Role of Foreign Banks in Japan during the Ansei Tragedy Period 1859–1899', *The Waseda Business and Economic Studies*

Teranishi, Juro (1982). *Nihon no keizaihatten to kinyu* (Japan's economic development and finance)

(1983). 'Matsukatadefle no macrokeizaigakuteki bunseki' (Macro-economic analyses of Matsukata deflation), in Umemura and Nakamura, eds. (1983)

Teraoka, Juichi (1978). *Meijishoki no zairyugaijin jinmeiroku* (Japan directory of foreigners in early Meiji)

Teruoka, Shuzo (1963). 'Daishi Kokuritsu Ginko' (Fourth National Bank), in Kato and Ouchi, eds. (1963)

Timberlake, R. H. (1978). *The Origins of Central Banking in the United States* (Cambridge, Mass.)

Tokai Ginko (1961). *Tokai Ginkoshi* (History of Tokai Bank) (Nagoya)

Tokeiin (1882/1941). *Nihonteikoku tokeinenkan* (Statistical yearbook of the Empire of Japan)

Tokutomi, Iichiro (1935). *Koshaku Matsukata Masayoshi den* (Biography of Marquis Masayoshi Matsukata), 2 vols.

Tokyo Ginko (1980/84). *Yokohama Shokin Ginko zenshi* (Whole history of YSB), 6 vols.

Tokyo Kabushiki Torihikijo (1928). *Tokyo Kabushiki Torihikijo gojuenshi* (Fifty-year history of the Tokyo Stock Exchange)

Tokyo Metropolitan Government (1972). *Financial History of Tokyo: A Century of Growth Amid Change*

Totman, C. (1980). *The Collapse of the Tokugawa Bakufu* (Honolulu)

(1983). *Japan Before Perry* (Berkeley)

Toyo Keizai Shinposha (1911). *Meiji zaisei shiko* (Abstract history of Meiji finance)

(1926). *Meiji Taisho zaisei shoran* (Financial statistics of Meiji and Taisho) (reprinted 1975)

(1927). *Meiji Taisho kokuseisoran* (Census of Meiji and Taisho) (reprinted 1975)

(1980). *Showa kokuseisoran* (Census of Showa), 2 vols.

Trescott, P. B. (1963). *Financing American Enterprise* (New York)

Tsuchiya, Takao (1936). *An Economic History of Japan*

(1956/61). 'Ginkobokiseiho kaidai' (Introduction to *Detailed Accounts of Bank Bookkeeping*), BOJ (1956/61), vol. 5

(1969). 'Kinyukyoko kankeishiryo kaidai' (Introduction to materials of financial crisis), BOJ (1961/74), vol. 24

(1976). 'Alexander Allan Shand no jireki to ningenzo nitsuite' (Career and character of Alexander Allen Shand), *Transactions of Japan Academy*

Tsuchiya, Takao, ed. (1961). *Chihoginko shoshi* (Short history of local banking)

Tsurumi, E. P. (1977). *Japanese Colonial Education in Taiwan 1898–1945* (Cambridge, Mass.)

Tsutsui, W. M. (1988). *Banking Policy in Japan* (London)

Tyson, G. (1963). *100 Years of Banking in Asia and Africa* (London)

Uchida, Kusuo and Michiho Shimono, eds. (1989). *Bakumatsu Ishin Kyoto chonin nikki* (The diary of a Kyoto merchant during the last days of the *bakufu* and the Restoration period) (Osaka)

Umemura, Mataji and Takafusa Nakamura, eds. (1983). *Matsukata zaisei to Shokusankogyo seisaku* (Matsukata's financial policies and 'increasing-production and founding-industry' policies)

Umemura, Mataji and Takafusa Nakamura et al., eds. (1988/90). *Nihon keizaishi* (Economic history of Japan), 8 vols.

University of Tokyo (1937/43). *Ishin shiryo koyo* (Abstract of historical materials of the Restoration), 10 vols. (reprinted 1983/84)

Wakatsuki, Reijiro (1983). *Meiji Taisho Showa seikaihishi* (Secret history of political world in Meiji, Taisho and Showa)

Ward, R. E. and F. J. Shulman (1974). *The Allied Occupation of Japan, 1945–1952* (Chicago)

Warner, Fred (1991). *Anglo-Japanese Financial Relations* (Oxford)

Waseda University (1952). *Okuma monjo* (Okuma archives)

Waswo, A. (1977). *Japanese Land Lords: Decline of a Rural Elite* (Berkeley)

Watanabe, Sahei and Dokan Kitahara, eds. (1966). *Ginko* (Bank)

Whale, P. Barrett (1930). *Joint Stock Banking in Germany* (London)

Whittlesey, C. R. and J. S. G. Wilson, eds. (1968). *Essays in Money and Banking* (Oxford)

Wiley, Peter B. (1990). *Yankees in the Land of the Gold: Commodore Perry and the Opening of Japan* (New York)

Wilkins, Mira (1989). *The History of Foreign Investment in the United States to 1914* (Cambridge, Mass.)

Wray, H. and H. Conory, eds. (1983). *Japan Examined: Perspectives on Modern Japanese History* (Honolulu)

Wray, W. D. (1984). *Mitsubishi and the N. Y. K. 1870–1914* (Cambridge, Mass.)

Yakura, Shintaro and Yoshiro Ikushima, eds. (1986). *Shuyo kigyo no keifuzu* (Genealogy of major firms)

Yamagata, Akeshichi (1924). *Zaisei junen* (Ten years of finance)

Yamaguchi, Kazuo (1976). *Nihonkeizaishi* (Japan's economic history)

Yamaguchi, Kazuo, ed. (1966). *Nihon sangyokinyushi kenkyu: seishikinyu hen* (Studies on the history of industrial finance in Japan: finance for silk reeling)

(1970). *Nihon sangyokinyushi kenkyu: bosekikinyu hen* (Studies on the history of industrial finance in Japan: finance for spinning)

(1974). *Nihon sangyokinyushi kenkyu: orimonokinyu hen* (Studies on the history of industrial finance: finance for the textile industry)

Yamaichi Shoken Kabushikikaisha (1958). *Yamaichi Shokenshi* (History of Yamaichi securities)

Yamamoto, Yuzo (1988/90). 'Meijiishinki no zaisei to tsuka' (Finance and currency during the Meiji restoration period), in Umemura and Nakamura, eds. (1988/90) vol. 3

Yamamura, Kozo (1967). 'The Role of the Samurai in the Development of Modern Banking in Japan', *Journal of Economic History*

(1967a). 'The Founding of Mitsubishi: A Case Study in Japanese Business History', *Business History Review*

(1968). 'A Re-examination of Entrepreneurship in Meiji Japan, 1868–1912', *Economic History Review*

(1972). 'Then Came the Great Depression: Japan's Interwar Years', in Der Wee, ed. (1972)

(1972a). 'Japan 1868–1930: A Revisited View', in Cameron, ed. (1972)

(1974). *A Study of Samurai Income and Entrepreneurship* (Cambridge, Mass.)

Yamawaki, Teijiro (1964). *Nagasaki no tojinboeki* (The Chinese trades in Nagasaki)

Yano, Fumio (1925). *Yasuda Zenjiro den* (Biography of Zenjiro Yasuda)

Yasuda, Zenjiro (1911). *Tomi no ishizue* (Basis of wealth)

Yasuoka, Shigeaki (1961). 'Ryogaeshobekke no keiei nitsuite' (Management of branch houses of *ryogae*), *The Doshisha shogaku* (Doshisha University)

Yokohamashi (1958/76). *Yokohamashishi* (History of the city of Yokohama), 5 vols.

Yonekawa, S. (1985). 'Recent Writing on Japanese Economic and Social History', *Economic History Review*

Yoshida, Shigeru (1961). *The Yoshida Memoirs* (Connecticut)

(1967). *Japan's Decisive Century, 1867–1967* (New York)

Yoshino, M. Y. (1968). *Japan's Managerial System* (Cambridge, Mass.)

Yoshino, Toshihiko (1974). *Wasurerareta moto Nichiginsosai – Tomita Tetsunosuke den* (A forgotten ex-governor of the Bank of Japan – A biography of Tetsunosuke Tomita)

(1975/79). *Nihon Ginko shi* (History of BOJ), 5 vols.

Young, A. M. (1928). *Japan under Taisho Tenno 1912–1926* (London)

(1938). *Imperial Japan, 1926–1938* (London)

YSB (1920). *Yokohama Shokin Ginkoshi* (YSB history), with Appendices (4 vols.) and Materials (4 vols.) (reprinted 1976)

Yui, Tsuneshiko, ed. (1966/81). *Eigyohokokusho shusei* (Collection of business reports) microfilm

Zengage, T. R. and T. Ratcliffe (1988). *The Japanese Century* (London)

Zenkoku Ginkokyokai Rengokai (1979). *Ginkokyokai sanjunenshi* (Thirty-year history of the bank association)

Index

DATE DUE

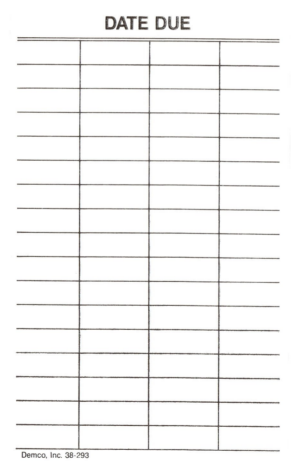